Globalism and Local Democracy

Globalism and Local Democracy

Challenge and Change in Europe and North America

Edited by

Robin Hambleton

Hank V. Savitch

and

Murray Stewart

palgrave
macmillan

First published in hardcover 2002

First published in paperback 2003 by
PALGRAVE MACMILLAN
Houndmills, Basingstoke, Hampshire RG21 6XS and
175 Fifth Avenue, New York, N. Y. 10010
Companies and representatives throughout the world

PALGRAVE MACMILLAN is the global academic imprint of the Palgrave Macmillan division of St. Martin's Press, LLC and of Palgrave Macmillan Ltd. Macmillan® is a registered trademark in the United States, United Kingdom and other countries. Palgrave is a registered trademark in the European Union and other countries.

ISBN 0–333–77225–3 hardback
ISBN 0–333–99373–X paperback

This book is printed on paper suitable for recycling and made from fully managed and sustained forest sources.

A catalogue record for this book is available from the British Library.

Library of Congress Cataloging-in-Publication Data

Globalism and local democracy : challenge and change in Europe and North America / edited by Robin Hambleton, Hank V. Savitch, and Murray Stewart.
p. cm.
    Includes bibliographical references and index.
    ISBN 0–333–99373–X
    1. Local government--Europe, Western. 2. Local government--North America. 3. Globalization. 4. Democracy. I. Hambleton, Robin. II. Savitch, H. V. III. Stewart, Murray

JS3000. G58 2003
320.8'094--dc21

2003049810

10   9   8   7   6   5   4   3   2   1
12   11   10   09   08   07   06   05   04   03

Printed and bound in Great Britain by
Antony Rowe Ltd, Chippenham and Eastbourne

Contents

List of Figures

List of Tables

Acknowledgements

This book was inspired by conversations and discussions at an international conference 'Shaping the Urban Future' we co-organised in Bristol, England, in 1994. The conference, which brought together 60 academics from Europe and North America, led to the creation of a new international association – the European Urban Research Association (EURA). This association has, in turn, fostered a growth in transatlantic academic exchange between European urban scholars and their counterparts in the North American Urban Affairs Association (UAA). Our first thanks, then, go to colleagues in the UAA and EURA who have stimulated our thinking, challenged our ideas and encouraged us to produce this volume.

As editors we would like to thank all the 13 authors who have contributed so much to this book. We were delighted that all the authors we approached readily accepted. We thank them for responding to editorial comments and suggestions and we hope they feel the outcome is worthwhile.

On behalf of all the authors we thank the support staff who make an academic enterprise like this possible. Librarians and secretaries in the UK, the USA, France and the Netherlands deserve thanks.

As editors our greatest debt is to Brigitte Tod of the Faculty of the Built Environment, University of the West of England, Bristol. She single-handedly transformed the 12 diverse chapters – all written by individuals with their own foibles and preferences – into a first-class manuscript for submission to the publishers. This, in itself, was a significant international achievement. We thank Brigitte for her professional skill, hard work and, surprising under the circumstances, her good sense of humour.

Lastly our thanks go to Heather Gibson and Kate Schofield at Palgrave, and to Philip Tye, our excellent copy-editor.

We have enjoyed collaborating on this book and we hope you enjoy reading it. Its limitations are ours.

ROBIN HAMBLETON
HANK V. SAVITCH
MURRAY STEWART
Bristol, England and Louisville, USA

Notes on the Contributors

François Ascher is Professor at the French Institute of Urban Affairs, University of Paris, and at the University of Genève. He published a book on what he calls 'the third modernity, its new urban revolution, and the reflexive urbanism' – *Ces événements nous dépassent, feignons d'en être les organisateurs. Essai sur la société contemporaine* (2001).

Scott Bollens is Professor and Chair, Department of Urban and Regional Planning, University of California, Irvine. He studies ethnicity and urban planning, intergovernmental planning, and regional governance. He is author of *On Narrow Ground: Urban Policy and Ethnic Conflict in Jerusalem and Belfast* (2000) and *Urban Peace-Building in Divided Societies: Belfast and Johannesburg* (1999).

Dennis Broeders is a member of the scientific staff of the Scientific Council for Government Policy (WRR) in The Hague. The WRR is an independent advisory body within the Dutch Prime Minister's department that directly advises the government on long-term strategic issues.

Andrew Church is Professor of Human Geography at the University of Brighton. He is Honorary Secretary for research at the Royal Geographical Society – the Institute of British Geographers.

Terry Nichols Clark is Professor of Sociology at the University of Chicago. He has taught at Columbia, Harvard, the Sorbonne, University of Florence and UCLA. His most recent book is *The New Political Culture*, edited with Vincent Hoffman-Martinot (1998). He is Co-ordinator of the Fiscal Austerity and Urban Innovation Project.

Susan E. Clarke is Professor of Political Science at the University of Colorado at Boulder and Associate Dean of the Graduate School. She is the Editor (with Mike Pagano and Gary Gaile) of the *Urban Affairs Review* and she serves on the Executive Council of the American Political Science Association. Her most recent book is (with Gary Gaile) *The Work of Cities* (1998).

Chris Collinge is Senior Lecturer in the Centre for Urban and Regional Studies at the University of Birmingham. His research interests mostly concern the interaction of economic and political change at different spatial scales.

Robin Hambleton is Dean of the College of Urban Planning and Public Affairs at the University of Illinois at Chicago. He was previously Professor of City Management and Associate Dean in the Faculty of the Built Environment, University of the West of England, Bristol. He is Chair of the European Urban Research Association and a member of the Governing Board of the Urban Affairs Association. He has written or edited eight books on urban governance and numerous articles.

Bernard Jouve is Researcher at Ecole Nationale des Travaux Publics de l'Etat, Lyons. He is also Associate Professor at the Political Science Institute in Lyons. He is carrying out research on territorial policies in Europe and is the co-author (with Christian Lefèvre) of *Local Power, Territory and Institutions in European Metropolitan Regions* (2002).

Robert C. Kloosterman is Professor of Economic Geography and Planning in the Department of Geography and Planning, and a member of the Amsterdam Study Centre for the Metropolitan Environment (AME), University of Amsterdam.

Christian Lefèvre is Professor of Urban Government and Planning in the French Institute of Urban Affairs, University of Paris. He has written extensively on urban governance and has been a consultant on this topic for various French and international bodies including the United Nations and the OECD. He is the co-author (with Bernard Jouve) of *Local Power, Territory and Institutions in European Metropolitan Regions* (2002).

Margaret F. Reid is Associate Professor of Political Science and Director of the Master of Public Administration Programme at the University of Arkansas, Fayetteville. She is a member of the Centre for the Study of Representation and her research centres on transformation of urban areas in the USA and in international settings.

Peter Reid is a Senior Lecturer in Geography at the University of Greenwich. He is a member of the Institute of Management.

Hank V. Savitch is the Brown and Williamson Distinguished Research Professor at the University of Louisville. He is a former Fulbright Scholar, a co-editor of the *Journal of Urban Affairs*, and has served as a research scholar at the Woodrow Wilson Centre and the National Centre for Scientific Research, Bordeaux, France. Professor Savitch has written or edited eight books on urban affairs and numerous journal articles.

Alan Srbljanin completed his doctoral thesis on models of partnership working at the Centre for Urban and Regional Studies at the University of Birmingham. He has carried out research on social housing and the impacts of information and communications technology (ICT) on regional economies. He is now ICT Business Growth Manager for the East Midlands Regional Development Agency.

Murray Stewart is Professor of Urban and Regional Governance, and Director of the Cities Research Centre in the Faculty of the Built Environment at the University of the West of England, Bristol. Previously working at the Universities of Glasgow, Kent and Bristol, he has numerous research publications focusing on contemporary urban policy and governance.

Preface

All too often the stories that hit the headlines about global events bring bad news. The terrorist attacks on the World Trade Center in New York City and the Pentagon in Washington, DC provide the most shocking example. They have jolted our understanding and feelings about globalisation into a new era. One thing is clear – the crimes which took place on 11 September 2001 could not have been conceived, let alone executed, in the pre-global era. Like global cities, global terror has found a place in a 'borderless world'. While global cities are increasingly free-floating and de-linked from their national economies, so too has terrorist warfare transcended national locations (Lever 1997). Further, as globalisation evolves, and cities attain a strategic niche in a fluid, market-driven world economy, so too has terror been able to find its place in a new type of inchoate, formless warfare (Savitch and Ardashev 2001).

It is not just the growth in international terrorism that is challenging the status quo, but also popular opposition to the underside of globalisation. By the turn of the last century, meetings of the World Trade Organisation (WTO) were met by massive demonstrations. In Quebec anti-riot police were called out to suppress violent protesters. In Seattle demonstrators threatened to disrupt WTO proceedings, and police used tear gas and rubber bullets. In Genoa mass demonstrations rose to a deadly crescendo. In 2001, that city was gripped by chaos when the worst-ever anti-globalisation riots saw one young protester shot dead by police and others seriously injured.

A more optimistic interpretation of current trends suggests that global awareness is growing rapidly in the population at large. Well-organised and peaceful protest movements are, for example, bringing together people from different backgrounds and cultures to contest the imperatives of global capitalism. Transnational migrants are refreshing the culture and politics of many countries. Globalisation is not, on this analysis, simply a political and economic phenomenon – it has major social and cultural dimensions. These aspects offer prospects for enhancing understanding and tolerance as diverse communities come to understand each other and work out ways of living together.

This book examines the local democracy dimension of globalism. It does not offer a global analysis – rather, it examines the globalisation process as it affects North America and Europe. By bringing together authors from different continents, the book aims to enrich understanding about how globalisation processes work and how they impact on particular localities. More than that, it explores the key tensions now facing city leaders, local politicians and urban managers, and outlines some of the more significant innovations now taking place in urban governance.

Our hope is that the book enhances international understanding and provokes fresh thinking. It may not be easy but policies and practices can be improved. In our view, cities and citizens are not helpless in a global flow of events. The negative aspects of globalisation may dominate the headlines but they tell only part of the story. If the book encourages local people to take action on behalf of their communities we will be more than satisfied.

ROBIN HAMBLETON
HANK V. SAVITCH
MURRAY STEWART
Bristol, England and Louisville, USA

1
Globalism and Local Democracy

Robin Hambleton, Hank V. Savitch and Murray Stewart

For those who lead and manage cities, the transition to an internationalised world has not been easy. Nor is it likely to become easier. Promises of free trade, open borders, industrial restructuring, mobility of labour, technology transfer and electronic communication all create remarkable opportunities, but they also pose major challenges. On the economic side, many Western democracies now have a dual, segmented labour market with increased unemployment and growing inequality. Industry may succeed by, for example, redeploying operations offshore to take advantage of low labour costs in far-off countries, but the consequences of disinvestment can be traumatic for specific cities and for particular areas within cities.

The social reverberations are no less important – the marginalisation of vulnerable groups within the labour market, and the resultant exclusion, is not merely from the world of work, but also from access to housing, public services and even the rights of citizen participation. Throughout the world, those at the margins of society are either spatially trapped and unable to seize opportunities for a better life, or are forced to move – to another town, city or country – in order to eke out a living.

The increased mobility of the disadvantaged is visible not simply in the movement of individuals seeking work, but also in movement of those whose motivation lies in the search for protection and ultimately survival. Refugees, outcasts, asylum seekers, fugitives are often indistinguishable from the flow of job seekers moving across national and continental boundaries. This ebb and flow of social, political and economic migrants, followed in many cases by the subsequent movement of their families, has created a world in flux, with confusion of economic status compounded by crises of identity and culture. While

1

the impact of global forces varies widely from nation to nation, from region to region and from city to city, there is a generalised manifestation common to these times of transition. State sovereignty is being challenged, as is the very concept of nation-based citizenship (Sassen 1996). Major questions are raised for politics, governance and accountability when the institutional pillars on which they rest are being unsettled if not transformed.

But these are not the only features. Hutton and Giddens (2000) suggest that globalisation involves four overlapping trends: a worldwide communications revolution which has in recent years been boosted by the extraordinary growth of the internet; the arrival of the 'weightless' or knowledge-based economy with financial markets at the leading edge; the fall of Soviet communism and the creation of a 'post-1989' world; and transformations at the level of everyday life with changes in family life, the roles of men and women and lifestyles in general. Few would dispute this account, but there are differences of view about the significance of the changes being brought on by globalisation. Some see significant continuities and parallels with the past. Others take the view that we are experiencing a profound transition in human history. The truth is probably in between. The essential point, however, is that globalisation is a process which cannot be ignored.

The political responses to globalisation

Globalisation has engendered a range of responses. Many national governments occupy a position from which macroeconomic policies and management seek to maintain the competitiveness of industry and services, where welfare provision is rethought, restructured and re-financed, and where governments strive to maintain their position in the global league tables by forging alliances and enlarging markets. The philosophy is that efficiency and equity can be simultaneously pursued, that there is a middle or 'third way' which can transcend both old-style social democracy and neoliberalism (Giddens 1998).

Away from the middle ground, however, sharper responses emerge. From the left there remains a strong complaint from socialist and marxist groups about the fickle nature of capital, about the loss of traditional higher-paid manufacturing jobs, about rampant economic insecurity, about widening gaps between rich and poor, and about the diminishing level and quality of welfare provision. There is a growing body of literature which suggests that many people experience globalisation as threatening their jobs and communities, diminishing democracy and stimulating social disintegration, while devouring the last remnants of resources and wilderness (Mander and Goldsmith 1996). The political demands from the left are in part for greater regulation of capital and in part for a commitment to greater redistribution of wealth but also of the social wage – of benefits and public services.

To judge by media coverage the reaction on the fringe right has been more extensive, provocative and couched in populism. Typically, this right-wing populism embraces blue-collar workers, whose factories have closed and whose families are forced into low-paying jobs. On this theme, the populist right evokes images of class antagonism and sounds remarkably like the marxist left. Consider, for example, arch anti-communist Patrick Buchanan's lament about what globalism has done to US workers:

> On the one side is the new class, Third Wave Americans – the bankers, lawyers, diplomats, investors, lobbyists, academics, journalists, executives, professionals, high-tech entrepreneurs – prospering beyond their dreams. Buoyant and optimistic, these Americans are full of anticipation about their prospects in the Global Economy. . . . On the other side of the national divide is the Second Wave America, the forgotten Americans left behind. White collar and blue collar, they work for someone else, many with hands, tools and machines in factories soon to be hoisted onto the chopping block of some corporate downsizer in some distant city or foreign country.
>
> (Buchanan 1998, pp. 6–7)

Right-wing populism also rails against the influx of immigrants, the erosion of national sovereignty and the capture of national pride by faceless markets or international capital. In America, Buchanan points to threats posed by non-Western people against a white, Christian belief system and warns of a 'culture war'. On the European side, Buchanan is joined by a similar array of populist right-wing nationalists. For example, in France Jean Marie Le Pen led the charge against immigrants from Africa and the Islamic East. Le Pen's National Front claimed immigrants had taken jobs, heightened crime and would destroy the French character of the nation. In Italy Gianfranco Fini led a nationalist, semi-fascist movement and endorsed similar claims. Italy's Lombardy League, situated in the north, also took up the cudgels against immigrants and threats to national culture. Right-wing populists have developed a following in east Germany and more recently in Bavaria. The Netherlands and Flemish-speaking provinces in Belgium have also experienced a nationalist reaction to globalism. Even some nations with vibrant economies, relatively few immigrants and scant crime, have veered rightward. Austria's Freedom Party and Switzerland's People's Party have, for example, won votes on the immigration/culture issue. In Britain the issue of asylum seekers has generated political friction and become a major electoral issue at local level.

Within the academic field of urban studies there is a lively ongoing debate about globalisation and urban development. Some writers, notably Harvey (1985, 1996), argue that cities are key sites within a systemic 'urban process' which is a reflection of the larger evolution of capitalism on a global scale. Harvey, in parallel with Sassen (1991) and others, puts the emphasis on economic and technological explanations for global city development at the expense of political, social and cultural factors. Other academics, notably Cox (1997) and Smith (2001), argue that the 'global cities discourse' has underplayed the national and local constraints on capital mobility which limit the global reach of multinational companies. Smith (2001), for example, argues that cities and urbanisation processes are social constructs and that it is more helpful for analysis to focus on the growth in the rich patterns of transnational urbanism than on the so-called economic dominance of 'global cities'. In his view transnational migrants, refugees, ethnic networks, entrepreneurs, political activists and so on should be viewed as creative actors able to influence and shape local events. Approaches to globalisation have, in his opinion, attributed too much power to capital.

It is certainly the case that transnational networks opposed to rampant capitalism are now on the increase. Take, for example, the protests and riots aimed at world leaders in Seattle and Nice in 2000 and in Genoa in 2001. International summits, which used to be seen as dull events in far-off places, have emerged as the destination of choice for a disaffected generation. Interestingly the diverse groups, and also people not involved in groups, communicate using the most visible symbols of the globalisation process they so vehemently oppose: e-mail and mobile phones.

Globalism, then, is far more than a socio-economic phenomenon. It has far-reaching consequences for local culture and local politics and how urban governments manage a range of political, economic, social and environmental issues. In particular, it has major implications for the conduct of local democracy. The political questions are daunting. Given the radical restructuring of local economies (from industrial to post-industrial uses), what is likely to be the effect on neighbourhoods, on the attitudes of old and new social classes, on relationships between different national groups, and on the delivery of municipal services? How is local government affected by increasingly competitive economies? Who, if anyone, is likely to hold control of local decisions? Not the least, what is the effect on the vital issues of governance – citizenship, voting, community group activity and the distribution of power between public and private interests?

Implications for cities and urban research

These are immensely important questions, and they touch on the very structure and institutions of the new local governance. This is *not* a book about global cities – the New Yorks, Sydneys, Londons and São Paulos of the twenty-first century (Savitch 1988; Sassen 1991; Knox and Taylor 1995). It is rather about how globalism may affect cities, and in particular about how questions of local autonomy and democracy can be addressed within the global context. Today, many local governments *are* being taken apart, reassembled, modernised and reinvented in innumerable ways. In the USA, regionalism and metropolitan government have regained adherents. In France, decentralisation has taken hold and localities have gained greater control over spending and policy priorities. Scotland and Wales have moved towards devolved governments, while in England localities are facing choices about whether to adopt strong mayor systems, cabinet government or city manager systems. Throughout Eastern Europe new political regimes struggle to attain the institutional foundations to stabilise their markets while attempting to shed the legacy of top-down, planned economies.

In this environment of flux and change, cities are called upon to develop new strategies that are capable of dealing with uncertain political and economic environments. But can this be done while holding an eye towards ensuring that citizens can fully participate and feel they are an integral part of local decision making? Whether such citizenship is compromised by increasingly competitive and autonomous local economies is an empirical question that can only be answered in the long run. One thing is apparent, that localities are resilient and are constantly reinventing themselves with new institutional arrangements, such as public–private partnerships and intergovernmental linkages.

Although widely acknowledged for some years, this discovery became apparent to the editors of this collection when, in 1994, they organised a major cross-national conference in Bristol, England. The conference, which focused on the theme 'Shaping the Urban Future', drew together 60 academics from a dozen or so countries. Those present felt that, at a time when global forces were strengthening and localism was struggling to reassert itself, it was timely to strengthen cross-national comparative study of the place which cities are taking in the emerging social and economic order. Further consultation with colleagues across Europe and further afield led, in 1997, to the launch of the *European Urban Research Association* (EURA) at an international conference in Brussels.

The aims of EURA are threefold: to provide a European forum for people from different disciplines and policy backgrounds to exchange information about and findings from research on towns and cities as the basis for closer cooperation; to encourage interdisciplinary and cross-national approaches to research in and education for urban and regional studies as a professional and academic field; and to bridge the gaps between academic, professional and policy interests, inform public debate and improve the quality of urban policy.[1]

This edited volume contains reworked versions of papers given at various EURA conferences. It is the first book to stem directly from the activities of EURA and is, in part, a celebration of the emergence of a new international association. EURA is quite distinct in terms of its name, its philosophy, its constitution and its activities from the well-established Urban Affairs Association (UAA) based in North America. But EURA has strong links with the UAA, and this particular volume draws together leading urban researchers from both sides of the Atlantic. As editors we are delighted that all the authors we approached agreed to collaborate in this enterprise.

A cross-national approach

There has been growth in cross-national urban research in the last decade or so. Useful texts have appeared which offer a comparative approach to urban politics and local governance (Keating 1991; Wolman and Goldsmith 1992; Clark and Hoffmann-Martinot 1998; Pierre 1998; Beauregard and Body-Gendrot 1999), whilst other studies have built an analysis of urban issues by drawing on case studies of particular cities (Judd and Parkinson 1990; Body-Gendrot 2000). In addition, international organisations, like the OECD, have carried out thematic studies of urban issues by drawing on the experience of cities in their member states (OECD 1995, 1998). This growth in comparative

urban research is valuable because it does more than juxtapose different cities from across the world. Similarities between cities, and similarities in the circumstances of neighbourhoods within them, are of
course interesting and have often stimulated policy makers to borrow
potential solutions from other countries. Indeed one benefit of comparative research is what has been termed its 'shock value' (Duncan
et al. 1985). This provokes re-examination of received ideas, stimulation
of new questions and the challenge to what is taken for granted. In one
country urban governance can address socio-economic problems in
ways that in other countries are – or at least have been – unthinkable.

But too often governments have simply borrowed ideas from other
countries without considering issues of transferability and application.
In the 1980s programmes such as Enterprise Zones and Urban Development Grants passed each other in opposite directions across the
Atlantic as UK and US governments sought to innovate in urban policy
(Hambleton 1995). Again it took many years for English urban policy
makers to understand that the multiple landlord system in France
underpinning *habitations à loyer modéré* (HLMs) could not be trans-
ferred in a simplistic way to dilute local authority monopoly land-
lordism in the UK. On the other hand, there are important lessons to
be learned from the similarities which cities of certain types display
regardless of national affiliation – port cities, for example – or cities
dominated by and dependent upon particular industrial sectors – steel,
defence, the automobile industry. Cities fulfilling specific administrative functions also have much in common. There are also those cities
which cannot be attributed solely to the country in which they are formally located. Gateway and border cities fulfil a cross-national function which defies simple political and administrative geography.

Nevertheless much of this strand of thinking relies on descriptive
comparison. The best comparative research involves rather the application of theoretical concepts across national boundaries with the objective of exploring both the differences and the similarities, in this case
between cities, in order to draw out and distinguish between those
understandings which transfer transnationally and those which are
particular to one nation, region or even urban area. This is a gradual
process requiring sympathetic cross-cultural understanding and famili-
arity with both national and local social and political structures, as
well as rigorous analysis of the extent to which theoretical constructs
are embedded in national rather than international paradigms.

A helpful illustration of this approach is provided by regime analysis
which has been applied in an essentially incremental and reflective

way to the European urban scene. Originally emergent from the North American literature of community power (Elkin 1987; Stone 1989), there has been both a gradual theoretical exploration of the relevance of the concept to Europe (Harding 1994; Stoker and Mossberger 1994; Lauria 1997), as well as empirical investigation of its applicability in European cities (Haughton and While 1999, for example). For the Bristol-based editors of this volume the longitudinal research of DiGaetano and Klemanski (1999) in over a decade of research in Bristol (and Birmingham, Boston and Detroit) has both stimulated our own work (Stewart 1996b) and framed a new interpretation of regime theory. In short there is much to be learned from comparative urban research and this volume makes a small contribution to this debate.

Globalism and local democracy

This book examines the links between globalism and local democracy and falls into three parts. The first discusses the globalisation process and its implications for cities. The second addresses in a more specific frame, a number of the socio-economic challenges which globalism sets for urban governments, and in particular looks at these challenges in turn through political, cultural, spatial and policy lenses. Part 3 is concerned with innovation in urban governance – it considers how local authorities and other agencies are responding to the new challenges. The logic of the edited volume is that it is essential to recognise the nature of global forces in order to identify the challenges which cities face and thence in turn design policies and practice which provide the scope for responding to global pressures in a manner which respects local democracy. In one way or another all the authors see democracy at risk. Economic pressures can force cities into a competitive mode within which economic goals dominate social goals and locally expressed aspirations succumb to wider forces; fiscal constraints inhibit the capacity of local administrations to respond to social needs; spatial fragmentation prevents the establishment of robust city–regional strategies and compounds territorial jealousies; and minority cultures feel unrepresented and exploited in formal political processes. Equally, however, all our authors see at least some possibilities for cities and local community action to mediate and adapt to global forces. Globalisation does not mean local democracy must be worse off. Indeed, every change presents challenges that can spur a progressive response. The sheer challenge of globalisation could also strengthen local democracy. Thus, the onset of industrialisation brought about the dissolution of a rural *Gemeinschaft*, which was replaced by different conceptions of democracy rooted in collective participation (trade unions, mass organisations).

In much the same way globalisation could bring about increased democratic fervour. Better communications, rising prosperity and a widening of the middle class may very well introduce democracy to heretofore closed, authoritarian societies. For example, satellite dishes in Iraq, Iran and other parts of the Middle East transmit news from around the world, stirring expectations of more citizen participation and greater accountability. The overthrow of Indonesia's dictatorship has been attributed to the availability of the internet across that archipelago. We should also add that the movement of people across national boundaries has a profoundly liberalising effect. Concerns about social exclusion and diversity can gain momentum when societies are made more heterogeneous.

Summing up globalisation presents its challenges, but we need not suffer from technological determinism. Societies are capable of adapting, producing all kinds of innovations, and making life better. It is for this reason that we are able to link three parts to this volume, dealing with the globalisation process, its risks and opportunities and, above all, its innovative potential.

The chapters in *Part 1* – by Savitch, Clarke, Ascher and Clark – highlight the challenges faced by localities in their struggle to maintain local identity in the face of external pressures. The dilution of the 'local' base – whether this be neighbourhood, city-wide, metropolitan or regional – and the increasing disconnection of local economic and social networks from their local anchor points, emphasise the threat to local democratic institutions. Local democracy represents the capacity of the locality to influence, interpret, mediate or ultimately counter the forces of globalisation in pursuit of the democratically expressed wishes of the local population. Savitch and Ascher both point to the delocalisation of the locus of decision making in private and public spheres, but both also point to the opportunities for the coexistence of global and local strategies – the 'glocalisation' referred to by Ascher, for example. Ascher and Clark, indeed, point to the fact that globalisation of some aspects of economic and social life provide an incentive and opportunity for the enhancement of other more localised aspects. Not all elements of the urban economy are affected by the global market; in many, if not all, cities there remains a locally and regionally generated sector of small-scale manufacturing, or of consumption services. While tourism and the heritage industry are certainly globalised in some senses, the capacity of small and medium-sized towns to find their own niche is not inconsiderable.

It is quite wrong, therefore, to assume that the impacts of globalisation have similar impacts within and across countries. While the homogenisation of urban life in the face of global influences is a common theme in the debate, Ascher argues strongly that the variety – and especially the variety of the European city – creates a diversity of experience which allows for, indeed demands, a response which is locally generated and is owned by the local population.

Nevertheless the thrust of much of Part 1 is that there is a struggle to maintain local autonomy and urban self-determination in the face of the need to remain competitive in world markets. To an extent this is a shared experience. Savitch talks of the mutuality of interest which stems from the unifying characteristics of globalism; all cities are in the same boat so to speak. This mutuality can create recognition of interdependence and lead to the consolidation of city region authorities into larger units, to cross-boundary and increasingly cross-national networks, and to systems of fiscal equalisation. Nevertheless there is a sense of inter-city competition with urban assets – of infrastructure, amenities, knowledge – the key to survival and wealth creation, and wealth creation in turn the key to redistribution. However, redistributive policies and programmes appear to be politically hazardous. Clarke talks of the prospects of more contentious politics – in part because the scope for local action is hedged around by national policies and controls, but also because the new entrepreneurial leaders tend, as both Clarke and Clark point out, to be more strongly oriented to economic than social goals.

Part 2 of this volume takes the debate to a more specific and focused level. In three different ways it illustrates the tensions faced at the urban level by changes brought about by global movements. Reid addresses the nature of local democracy from a political perspective in the light of the changes in Eastern Europe from communist regimes to more democratic and market-oriented forms of governance. Her arguments are that the transformations in Eastern Europe have had ambiguous impacts. On the one hand, the institutions and powers of local governance have been reintroduced and reinforced as disenchantment with centralised government is given constitutional meaning. At the same time it has become apparent in reforming countries that the new localism has insufficient power (or resources) to address the challenges of transformation. The consequences are that the local investments in housing, health, education, environmental improvement and social welfare necessary to sustain local well-being are beyond the reach of the new municipalities to provide. The evidence is of an emergent polarisation as some Eastern European cities (or parts of these cities) experience public and private investment in infrastructure and growth in jobs and wealth, while other parts remain unable to exercise the capacity to compete.

Bollens approaches the urban crisis from a different perspective, although one which also addresses the problems of social polarisation. His focus is on ethnicity and on the impact which ethnic division has upon urban living. His analysis of the issue moves from the global to the local in that his starting point is in the fluidity and movement of beliefs and people. He points to the way in which, thanks to the globalisation of communications media, the interests of minority ethnic groups can now be articulated and expressed worldwide. But not just ideologies and beliefs travel the world; so do people, and the increased geographical movement of ethnic minority people and groups places new burdens on urban governance. What has hitherto been seen as a significant but relatively modest accommodation of one or more minority ethnic interests within any individual city has reached a more complex and complicating level than hithcrto, with the economic, cultural, political and social needs of ethnic groupings competing and often conflicting with the interests of more established communities.

Kloosterman and Broeders in turn look to the neighbourhood as the focus for the challenges posed by globalisation. In a chapter which provides perhaps the most concentrated case example of the themes of this volume, they describe and discuss the changing circumstances of The Hague Southwest, a neighbourhood where successive interventions have attempted to protect the local communities from the ravages of globalisation. The study illustrates both the essential ingredients of a specific neighbourhood approach and re-examines the nature both of the traditional *Gemeinschaft* and of the contemporary community. Their chapter bridges the divide between neighbourhood policy and city-wide strategy and argues strongly that resident involvement at the small area level must be reinforced with strong national labour market, welfare and educational systems.

All of these chapters point to the vulnerability of cities to social and political tension. Their lessons are that the democratic processes of urban governance must necessarily be sufficiently flexible to respect the variety of ethnic, religious, cultural and micro-political interests which are present in communities of place and interest, but must also be sufficiently robust to impose order into the democratic process. If

competitiveness and cohesion are to coexist it is important that local
political processes are respected and collectively owned by local populations however disparate their interests. This applies as much to the
role of women, as Reid emphasises, as to the role of ethnic minorities,
as Bollens argues. It applies to the forgotten blocks of the peripheral
estates as much as to the pressured quarters of the inner city. It suggests that the extremes of right and left to which we referred earlier
must find common ground in recognition of a city which recognises
the importance of people.

Inherent in this analysis is the management of uncertainty. The
capacity to respond to the needs of local citizens is reliant on the
capacity of city governance to reduce its dependency on external
influences and to exercise some control over its own future. It is on
this reduction of dependency that the final sections of our volume
concentrate.

There remains confusion over the terms 'government' and 'governance'. The former – *government* – is the activity of the formal governmental system which takes place within specific administrative
boundaries, involves the exercise of particular powers and duties by
formally elected or appointed bodies, and uses public resources in a
financially accountable way. Government is perhaps best seen as the
formal presence and representation of the state in the locality. The
business of government is conducted under clear procedural rules,
involving statutory relationships between politicians, professionals and
the public. *Governance* is a much looser process of steering localities
(*gubernator* – the rudder), which often involves issues transcending geographical or administrative boundaries, which is multi-sectoral, and in
which networks, alliances and coalitions play an important part. Such
networks are informal (although they may become formalised into
structural arrangements such as partnerships) and are often ambiguous
in their memberships, activities, relationships and accountabilities.
Governance is the process of multi-stakeholder involvement, of multiple interest resolution, of compromise rather than confrontation, of
negotiation rather than administrative fiat.

Part 3 is concerned with this shift from government to governance
and with innovations in urban management that accompany it.
Hambleton explores the way political leaders and city managers are
modernising their approaches to policy making and decision making.
His chapter examines two significant shifts – the change from local
government to local governance and the shift from public administration to 'new public management'. He argues that changes in society are

spurring the development of the 'new city management'. This involves more than the introduction of 'new public management' techniques to local government – it requires a rethink of the triangular relationships between politicians, officers and citizens. In many Western democracies local politicians and public service managers are bringing about significant shifts in the role of local government – from a perspective which emphasises the delivery of important public services to a new emphasis on community leadership and citizen participation. This has implications for institutional arrangements and procedures – for example, directly elected mayors, cabinets, city managers, the representative roles of councillors, public consultation – as well as for styles of leadership. A more outgoing approach is needed to win public support as well as influence other agencies.

Collinge and Srbljanin examine the theme of inter-agency networking in some detail. Their analysis of developments in the economic governance of the West Midlands, England and in the German state of Bavaria lead them to conclude that claims about a new 'network paradigm' in urban governance have been overstated. Economic development initiatives have certainly expanded markedly. But they argue that the growth of networking does not amount to the emergence of a new order, rather the scale and level of networking have shifted up a few gears.

Debates about the reform of metropolitan governance are discussed by Jouve and Lefèvre. They note that there is a tension between enhancing the power and expanding the geographical boundaries of city authorities to create units capable of withstanding international economic competition, and the importance of ensuring that these same authorities can be held to account by citizens and local communities. Their analysis suggests that the institutional context, particularly at the regional level, is a key factor in explaining whether or not metropolitan governance can succeed.

In the final chapter Church and Reid consider the internationalisation of local governance. For many urban authorities in the European Union, collaboration with local authorities and other organisations in other member states has become a significant part of their activities. Their analysis of international cooperation between authorities in the south of England, Belgium and France suggests that new cross-border spaces are being created. There are tensions between competition and cooperation within these new spaces. It is too early to draw firm conclusions about the future of these transnational arrangements but, in the European context at least, it is likely that they will grow in importance.

Towards a strategy for local democracy

What, then, do the contributions to this volume suggest are the key pressures on local democracy resulting from forces of globalisation? Three main tendencies appear. On the one hand, globalisation brings in its wake fragmentation of national and regional boundaries, not simply in terms of economic functions but also in the much wider sense of fragmented cultures, identities, language and communication. There is a mobility of ideas as well as of capital and labour, and the role of cities in both fuelling and dampening the struggle between competing ideologies and values, hopes and fears, makes cities exciting and challenging but also turbulent and conflictual. Consensus is less easy to reach; 'contentious politics' emerge. In this sense the democratic environment is a pluralist one in which competing claims struggle one against the other. Not all demands will be met; protest, complaint, grievance will be rife. In the face of potential unrest, and with evidence of increased potential for urban violence, the risk is that the democratic process will be perceived as restricted and exclusive.

The possibilities, on the other hand, are for an inclusive democracy which respects variety, which seeks to give voice to all those who wish to speak, and which offers empowerment to the disempowered. This is likely to be a more *participative democracy* which provides some feeling of control to those who resent the forces – global, national, regional, city – which they perceive to oppress and exploit them. There is recognition of this in the espousal of community and neighbourhood-based democracy which in its best forms allows some power – over budgets, services, territory – to the disenfranchised. Our authors suggest, from their analysis of North American and from Eastern and Western European experience, that a more community-oriented democracy of place and interest is now needed in the face of advancing globalism.

A second unifying strand of the chapters, however, lies in the identification by several authors of the tendency towards the reduction of risk and dependency. Metropolitan enlargement and consolidation, regional network building, cross-national alliances all form part of the risk management repertoire of a number of urban authorities. This interdependent behaviour reflects recognition of the risks of globalisation and realisation of the need for mutuality, coalition building and partnership working. The fiscal base needs to be enlarged, bargaining power expanded, resources shared. Even if some authors play down the force of networks, there is no doubt that the new governance – involving multiple stakeholders in cross-sectoral collaboration – has become the name of the game for many urban leaders.

But a price is paid in terms of reduced transparency and accountability since many of the priorities of collaborative working are established outside formal democratic structures. There is often a lack of communication between the high-level strategic partnerships of metropolitan governance and the communities of place and interest which need democratic involvement in order to engage with and be engaged by the wider urban structures of power and influence. Again the implications are of a threat to the democratic process, but once more there are possibilities for an enhanced *representative democracy*. This has hitherto been largely understood as the outcome of local voting, with an emphasis in the UK on local councillors, in the USA on the elected mayor, and in continental Europe on mixed systems of mayoral and councillor representation. There is a clear need to enhance the representational role and function of those who hold positions within the emergent structures of the new governance. If globalism is forcing local institutions into new alliances as many of our authors suggest, how best can representative democracy be not simply legitimised but rather enhanced? How can the people operating in these increasingly important multi-agency arrangements be held to account?

Thirdly, the analysis suggests a hollowing out, not of the state (the more usual basis for the hollowing out debate), but of the local authority. The analogies with the 'state hollowing' model are close. In many countries powers are being taken upwards to regional, subregional or metropolitan levels. There are attempts (admittedly fewer in number and undertaken with less conviction) to devolve responsibilities downwards to communities and/or third sector organisations which may take some of the responsibility and cost of welfare provision off municipal budgets. Efforts to increase 'community-owned' government are on the increase. In those countries in which the state – central, regional and local – has delivered services there are shifts to arm's length provision or privatisation. The new management of local government, therefore, is seeking a new role – orchestrator, facilitator, catalyst – a role where influence rather than power matters and where what gets done matters rather more than who does it.

There are echoes here of Clarence Stone's (1989) distinction between power 'over' and power 'to', but picking up again the reference to regime theory earlier in this introduction we would want to argue that this exercise of power be done less behind closed doors. Local government must exercise these *community leadership* functions in an open and transparent manner responsive to the needs and aspirations of its citizens, even if it has also to mediate these needs and aspirations in the wider negotiations of governance. As we argued earlier, the essence of government is its formality, but it is essential that these formal processes are informed by a more open, responsive and interactive style of government.

The conclusion, then, is that the forces of globalisation *can*, indeed, pose a threat to localism and local democracy. Responding to global pressures, however, does not necessarily suggest the abandonment of democratic principles, and our authors imply the need for sophisticated and responsive innovations in both participative and representative democracy.

Note

1. In the period since it was launched in Brussels the European Urban Research Association (EURA) has held several international conferences and workshops – in Venice, Oslo, Paris, Dublin, Copenhagen, Prague and Turin – to further the aims of the association. A EURA newsletter provides up-to-date news and comment on urban research and urban policy developments in Europe, and the association now has a growing number of institutional and individual members in more than 20 countries. The EURA website address is: http://www.eura.org

Part 1
The Globalisation Process

2
The Globalisation Process

Hank V. Savitch

Exploring globalisation

Despite its use as a coherent idea, globalisation is actually a slippery and uncertain term. Globalisation can convey a set of conditions, a current state of being or a decisive outcome. Rather than any of these perspectives, we approach globalisation as a continuing process of flux, transition and even disorder. The process operates through international networks, whose participants engage in communications, economic trade, sociocultural and political activities. Much like a vast market, the globalising process has no central controls and no cohesive group of managers. At best, it is self-adjusting and at worst it is in a precarious state of imbalance. Results are often tentative, outcomes are unpredictable, and the course of events is determined by the interaction of multiple, free-flowing forces.

Globalisation encompasses an enormous range of activities and is propelled by a revolution in transportation and communication. That revolution has not only shrunk time and contracted space, but has also made transmissions across national boundaries breathtakingly cheap. In 1930 a three-minute phone call from New York to London cost $300 and a trip across the Atlantic amounted to several thousands of dollars (adjusted in current terms for inflation). Today the same call costs less than $3 and one can travel from New York to Paris for as little as $250. Globalisation has also made it infinitely easier to penetrate vastly different kinds of social orders – from fundamentalist Islamic brotherhoods to tribal villages. Electronic messages now reach everywhere with everything from cellular phones to CNN newscasts and the internet.

There is more. The process of globalisation also involves the integration of national economies. This universality is shown in an increasing reliance upon common global standards, whether for electronic components or patent regulations. Increasingly, goods and services are produced by a web of activities that span nations. Nowadays, it is difficult to identify a single origin for the production of a complex piece of machinery. A typical automobile may have its chassis built in Mexico, its electrical equipment made in Germany and its steel manufactured in Brazil.

Next, globalisation is a political process and connotes an intense interaction between states, localities and societies across the world (Held 1991). Its residue can be seen in the rise of multilateral organisations, regional pacts and talk of a borderless world. States, localities, non-governmental organisations and labour have obliterated old boundaries, and are driven by the seemingly contradictory stimuli of cooperation and competition. Common trade practices, monetary standards or interest rates undergird this process. The most prominent of these pacts are between nation states. These include the European Union (for West Europe), NAFTA (for the United States, Canada and Mexico), ASEAN (for South-east Asia) and Mancusor (for Brazil, Argentina, Paraguay and Uruguay). These associations are in varying stages of development and the European Union is the most advanced.

Finally, globalisation contains a sociocultural element, which conveys the idea of an open, multipolar and multicultural society (Knight and Gappert 1989). Immigrant and ethnic cultures are now said to thrive in 'transnational space' in which language, habit and tradition continue regardless of geography. Still another aspect of this sociocultural revolution is the rise of new social classes – popularly dubbed as 'yuppies' and sometimes called a 'post materialist' class by academics (Inglehart 1990). Terry Clark has investigated this phenomenon under the rubric of the New Political Culture, and finds it to be widespread in cities of Europe and North America. Clark has been among the early pioneers in highlighting the political character of this new social class and its consequences for local democracy – see Chapter 5.

A general idea unifying all aspects of global flux is the mutual vulnerability it fosters between nations, localities and organisations. These entities now depend upon one another in ways thought inconceivable a century ago. In a matter of minutes, a crisis in a single great bank can upset finance at the other end of the world. Disease travels as swiftly as airline flights and has acquired an international character. Vulnerability also has an opposite side which can be found in cross-national synergy. This kind of complementary interdependence has brought about joint ventures in space exploration, multinational research collaboration and the rise of multinational corporations. Trade, currency exchange and financial transactions are at the core of the globalisation process, and can be used to demonstrate the changing nature of economic relationships. Table 2.1 provides an indication of the economic side of global flux. It shows the movement of goods and currency throughout the world and begins with an already sub-stantial base in 1972. The world has changed a good deal – even over the last two decades – and the numbers are revealing.

We can appreciate the magnitude of change by considering the nations involved. All told, each of the 16 nations in the list either exceeded $40 billion in exports or experienced at least a tenfold increase over the last quarter-century. The average industrial nation increased its exports more than 1200 per cent in just 26 years. Among OECD members, Germany and France increased exports more than ten times, while Spain's exports exploded more than 25 times. Together the USA and Japan had more than a trillion dollars of exports. Pastoral nations such as Ireland and Portugal joined the ranks of exporters with 17 and 34-fold increases respectively.

Table 2.1 Exports from OECD member countries, 1972–98 (adjusted for inflation in US dollars)

	1972	1998	% Increase	Average annual % increase
Australia	7.28	55.80	666	26
Austria	4.29	63.19	1374	53
Canada	23.88	212.20	789	30
France	29.83	302.00	912	35
Germany	52.68	544.70	934	36
Ireland	1.81	61.14	3276	126
Italy	20.97	238.20	1036	40
Japan	32.22	380.90	1082	42
Netherlands	21.60	170.00	687	26
Norway	3.61	41.00	1036	40
Portugal	1.46	25.00	1609	62
Spain	4.30	110.50	2469	95
Sweden	9.88	95.60	867	33
Switzerland	7.74	76.40	887	34
UK	27.04	274.40	915	35
United States	55.20	689.18	1148	44

Notes
1. 1998 data estimated.
2. 1998 figures for Italy, UK and United States are 1997 data.
Sources
1. Department of State Country Reports on Economic Policy and Trade Practices.
   http://www.state.gov/www/issues/economic/trade_reports/index.html
2. Government information sharing project.
   Oregon State University – Information Services.
   US Imports/Exports History: 1993–97.

Cities and uneven development

How do cities fit into this picture? As globalisation progresses and markets open, so too do opportunities. The agglomerative features of cities make them natural centres for coordination and direction. In effect cities have become the strategic nodes through which the new economy could be planned and facilitated (Bell 1973; Savitch 1988; Sassen 1991). They provide the critical spaces needed to organise a dizzying array of functions; they hold the infrastructure needed to support millions of white-collar workers; and they furnish the conduits for rapid transfer of goods, money and information.

Currency has always played an important role in urban life, but it is now the fuel which drives all else. The ability to process capital through 'trade centres' and 'smart buildings', the availability of financial and business services, access to capital markets and proximity to sources of information and investment are the stuff of today's world cities. Whether a city can make use of and exploit these assets has a great deal to do with how it will fare in the decades ahead.

Control over land and possession of capital is a key to urban prosperity. One indication of this wealth is the number of banks and major deposits held within a city. Tokyo, Paris, Frankfurt, London, New York, Brussels, Amsterdam, Zurich and Milan have traditionally been at the forefront of the banking industry (*American Banker* 1993). Many of the newcomers, however, are lodging themselves in East Asia (Beijing, Hong Kong) or the South Pacific (Sydney, Melbourne). The axis of financial power appears to stretch from north-western Europe across to North America, veering sharply into the South Pacific and up into East Asia.

Indeed, this trend in banking and finance matches global exports shown in Table 2.1. Much of the existing and growing trade encompasses West Europe, North America, the South Pacific and the eastern corners of Asia. Several points should guide our understanding of how globalisation has changed relationships. At the outset, the increased competition and numbers have caused cities to adopt new development strategies. Many cities now actively seek clientele by promoting demand for their products or by supplying investors with lavish incentives (Eisinger 1988). In varying ways a substantial portion of cities behave like profit-seeking enterprises seeking additional sources of capital (Peterson 1981). Clarke and Gaile (1998) show us how, in the wake of globalisation, cities have adopted different strategies. Some stress new communications technologies, while others promote themselves as tourist centres, and still others stress investments in human resources and training.

The new global environment may be perfectly natural for cities. After all, cities are 'corporations'. From the time of the ancient market place to the Italian and Hanseatic trading ports up through modern office complexes, cities have specialised in promoting enterprise. By nature, cities are small, flexible collections of economic activity and quite capable of flourishing in this environment. Give or take modifications in national habits, localities are striving to compete under conditions of global flux. They supply entrepreneurs with staffing, infrastructure and strategic space. When cities have been unable to incubate their own industry, they have welcomed new ones from abroad.

But most significantly, globalisation produces differential impacts between cities, and not all cities share the same fate. The new era has sharpened urban differences between cities in the democratic West. Some cities, like New York, London or Frankfurt, have come through the process with massive amounts of wealth and increased property values. Other cities, like Detroit, Liverpool and Essen, have been hit with devastating losses in jobs, trade and population. The differences can be palpable and told in the built environments of cities. A booming central business district, sleek office towers and chic hotels arise in one city, only to be contrasted with boarded up storefronts and vacant factories in another city.

Additionally, globalisation produces differential impacts within cities. Rich, professional and business classes may gentrify former working-class neighbourhoods, but still live blocks apart from a new underclass. Even the most prosperous cities have their underside and are blighted by unemployment, substandard housing and an underclass. There are more than a few instances where whole neighbourhoods are ridden in abject poverty and where generation after generation subsists on public assistance. This picture is particularly true for the USA, but distressed urban neighbourhoods can be found in cities across Europe.

Prosperous and distressed cities

Since the 1960s, scholars have talked about the demise of central cities and the predictions continue (Fishman 1990; Garreau 1991). Central cities are seen as vestiges of an era when proximity was crucial and when limitations of transportation and communication placed a premium on highly concentrated space. Why maintain congested cities, when business transactions can be consummated within the time span of an electronic message and executives can move across continents on Concorde jets? Indeed, some might argue that cities impede economic progress and clog development (Webber 1963; Bruegmann 1995).

Table 2.2   Gross domestic product for selected cities in West Europe and North America, 1970–1990s (billions of dollars)

	GDP (city) 1970	1990s	% change 1970–1990s	Year
Amsterdam		17.94		1996
Glasgow	12.85	9.93	–23	1990
Hamburg	20.42	38.57	189	1990
Liverpool	9.46	6.62	–30	1990
London	10.75	112.39	1045	1990
Paris	39.22	48.32	123	1990
Barcelona	0.74	36.65	4953	1990
Milan	22.28	23.48	105	1990
Marseilles	10.87	14.41	133	1990
Frankfurt	9.67	60.85	629	1990
Naples	10.03	11.34	113	1990
Chicago	19.33	67.41	349	1996
New York	9.82	171.98	1751	1996
San Francisco	4.47	21.05	471	1996
Cleveland	3.98	10.79	271	1996
Los Angeles	16.46	92.73	563	1996
Houston	6.68	51.14	766	1996
Toronto	11.67	13.31	114	1996
Montreal	6.02	16.92	'281	1996
Vancouver		10.25		1996

Sources of 1970 data
Labour force American cities – *County and City Data Book: a Statistical Abstract Supplement*, 1972.; Labour force for others – *Cities of the World*, Vol. I–V, 1988, UN; Labour force and GDP for each country – *Statistical Yearbook Annual Statistique*, 1981.
Sources of 1990 data
Labour force for each city – *The World Factbook*, 1994; Labour force and GDP for each country – *The World Factbook*, 1994.
Sources of 1996 data
Labour force for American cities – *County and City Extra, 1998;* Labour force for Canadian cities – *Statistics Canada* http://www.statcan.ca/; Labour force for Amsterdam – http://www.onderzoek-en-statistiek.amsterdam.nl/eng/beroepsbevolking.php3; Labour force and GDP for each country – Department of State Country Reports on Economic Policy and Trade Practices http://www.state.gov/www/issues/economic/trade_reports/index.html
Sources of data for Glasgow, Liverpool, Paris, Marseilles, Milan and Naples
Glasgow, Liverpool – 'Census 1971: England and Wales: Report for the County of Merseyside', Her Majesty's Stationery Office, London, 1975; General Register Office, Edinburgh, 'Census 1971: Scotland: County Report Glasgow City', Her Majesty's Stationery Office, Edinburgh, 1975; British Office of Population Censuses and Surveys, 'Census 1981: County Report: Merseyside: Parts 1 and 2', Her Majesty's Stationery Office, London 1983; 'Census 1991: County Report: Merseyside: Parts 1 and 2, Her Majesty's Stationery Office, London, 1993; General Register Office for Scotland, '1991 Census: Strathclyde Region: Part 1 (volume 2 of 2) and Part 2', HMSO, Edinburgh, 1993; Institut d'Estudis Metropolitais de Barcelona, *Cities of The World*, 1988.

Table 2.2   (*continued*)

Paris, Marseilles – Direction de l'Urbanisme et des actions de l'Etat, Sous-Directions des Affaires Economiques, Bureau de l'Action Economique, Préfecture de Paris, *Paris: Chiffres*, Edition 1993, donnés au 31 décembre 1991; Ville de Marseille et Agence d'Urbanisme de l'Agglomération Marseillaise, *Marseille en Chiffres*, Edition 1995; Institut d'Estudis Metropolitais de Barcelona, *Cities of the World*, 1988.
Milan, Naples – Istat, Censimento generale della popolazione, 1991, 'Popolazione in condizione professionale per ramo di attivita economica'; Istat Censimento generale della popolazione,1971. 'Popolazione in condizione professionale per ramo di attivita economica'; Istat, Censimento generale della popolzione, 1971, 1981, 1991.
*Labour force data for Liverpool, Glasgow, Milan, Naples – 1971, 1981, 1991; Marseilles – 1968, 1982, 1990; data for Liverpool 1990 is based on 10% sample.

The truth is, cities are extraordinarily efficient and are bound to grow as globalisation proceeds. François Ascher shows us how changes in technology and demographics enable cities to increase their strategic presence – how, in effect, they can become repositories and incubators for both global and local innovation (Ascher 1995). Cities optimise the use of human and mechanical energy, they allow for fast, cheap transportation, and they provide flexible, highly productive labour markets (Newman 1994; Prud'homme 1994). In addition, cities facilitate a diffusion of products, ideas and human resources between urban, suburban, exurban and rural spaces. We can appreciate how cities optimise their work by examining their economic performance over a period of time.

Table 2.2 presents data on gross domestic product for 20 cities between 1970 and the 1990s.[1] The year of last available data is listed together with amounts in dollars and the percentage change. Urban centres have always led in the creation of national wealth, and many now occupy a special place in the global era. Cities are the international growth machines of the new economy, and their pace has accelerated. The figures and proportional increases are impressive. With the exception of Liverpool and Glasgow, none of the listed cities decreased in GDP. The proportional increases vary a good deal and Barcelona registered nearly a 5000 per cent increase. Big cities did especially well, with London and New York increasing by over 1000 per cent. We should realise that most of these cities have mature economies and the gains for the 1990s occurred on an already substantial base.

Much of this productivity has poured back into the city. The most prosperous cities now profit from new skylines, converted waterfronts and rejuvenated neighbourhoods. A new urban middle class, trained in high technology, now blankets great cities and earns a livelihood which would be the envy of their medieval trading forebears.

Central cities have grown in all directions – not only inwardly but outwardly towards suburbs and exurbs, and they nurture people who have moved into the hinterlands. Cities and their surrounding regions are connected by transportation, business and fiscal networks. Over 2 million commuters pour into Manhattan each day, and acquire more than half the income earned in the city. Washington DC's commuter population exceeds its inhabitants, and they too collect more than half the earnings made in that city (Savitch and Vogel 1996; Bureau of Economic Analysis 1991). Much the same story can be told for Paris, Frankfurt and Tokyo. Even medium-sized cities (Pittsburgh, Strasbourg, Cologne) are closely linked with and sustain outlying areas.

Successful cities find ways to pick up the slack in their economic base, nurture mixed land use, and promote synergies between traditional manufacture, high technology and research and information. Economic diversity is a sure asset, and it is important to modernise and retain traditional industry. While experience with economic conversion may differ, the most successful cities follow a pattern of diversity and incorporate features of the new social paradigm. In North America, Pittsburgh is an example of a single-industry town (steel) which managed a successful conversion to post-industrial activity. The city enlisted business (Allegheny Conference), diversified its economic base and coupled high technology and information services to an export strategy. In West Europe, Hamburg stands out as a port city which managed a successful conversion. A combination of moderate politics and the city's merchant tradition helped bridge class differences. This allowed business and labour to rationalise port facilities, diversify the economy and take the lead in robotics and media services. Today, Hamburg is one of Europe's most aggressively competitive cities (Dangschat and Ossenbrugge 1990).

There is, too, another side to urban productivity, and that is the relentless pace of competition, its acceleration in the late 1990s and the disparities which ensue. Like most races there are winners and losers, and developed economies have no lack of losers. Many of these are former sites of heavy manufacture or have ports which are no longer in use. Often characterised as 'rust belts', they appear to have been left in a time warp. Their signals are obvious – underutilised or closed factories, dilapidated docks, scarce capital, and long lines of people seeking work. Some distressed cities tried to recuperate by appealing to tourist trade. After the automobile factories closed, Flint (Michigan) converted its historic remains into an automobile museum, and heralded a first-class hotel. Both establishments are now closed.

Distressed cities in the developed world include Detroit, Liverpool, Belfast, Naples and Valenciennes (Darden et al. 1987; Bianchini 1991; Cheshire et al. 1986). These cities are characterised by shrinking private resources and lack the political capacity to mobilise investment. This puts them at odds with powerful paradigmatic and international currents. Still another aspect of this distress is the rise of social polarisation and exclusion within cities. Usually, class polarisation is reinforced by ethnic antagonisms. Industrial Belfast immediately comes to mind as an afflicted city, but so too is sunny, white-collar Los Angeles. The new social strife can be traced to the de-industrialising impacts and migratory effects of globalisation. Both Belfast and Los Angeles exemplify how old and new urban centres can be struck. The distress is simultaneously drawn from the same source – capital moving out of urban centres in search of cheap labour and poor labourers moving into urban centres in search of capital-created jobs.

Global challenges and the delocalised city

As globalisation melts national borders and intensifies competition, cities assume new roles. They become progressively delocalised, and drift from their national moorings, becoming a geographic nexus of global interaction. More precisely put, the economies and social structure of delocalised cities become a function of broader international currents.

Delocalised cities are profoundly affected by global changes in economics, technology and culture. Their central business districts are tied together by a net of multinational corporations, financial and brokerage houses. Their waterfronts receive tourists from other places and their neighbourhoods house foreign executives, guest workers, migrants and transients. Although delocalised cities refract national habits and mores, their reference points are international and compete for capital and prestige. William Lever refers to this as 'delinking' and provides empirical evidence which shows how some types of cities economically deviate from national norms (Lever 1997).

Delocalised cities seek their own business, and in doing so are apt to recruit internationally and carry a broad portfolio of activities. In the 1980s and 1990s cities have begun to adopt their own 'foreign policies', establishing representation across the world. Cities have even begun to conduct their own foreign policies by declaring themselves to be nuclear-free zones, by disinvesting in certain nations, and by offering sanctuary to refugees (Hobbs 1994). Currently 42 states and over 1000 American localities participate in some kind of 'micro diplomacy', and many have created offices to manage international affairs (Stempel 1991). Cities in advanced industrial nations use their delocalisation to forge alliances with similarly situated localities within the same general region. This often makes for interesting cross-border collaboration over similar functions. Genoa, Marseilles and Barcelona have identified common issues and forged links on questions of research, technology and development. Frankfurt, Paris and London have found common issues relating to banking, finance and trade. Portland, Seattle and Vancouver have joined together in establishing themselves as North America's link to the Pacific rim (Clarke and Gaile 1998). With the passage of time, these links seem to be stretching further, and so-called 'sister city' relationships across continents may be the harbinger for a more formal international association.

New challenges confront delocalised cities. First, some cities may be able to modernise factories and upgrade blue-collar workers, but most will have to build a new economy based on information, finance and services. This will require a massive effort to attract capital, train local populations and rebuild the urban infrastructure. In effect, older cities will need to renew their built environments and create social environments that can incubate new technology and talent. In most cities of West Europe the process has already begun, but is hardly complete and not without its pain. As Reid explains in Chapter 6, East Europe is still coping with the initial repercussions of globalisation. While some nations and cities are more successful than others, the learning curve is steep for all.

Second, cities face an inherent tension between the economic need to develop and the political demand to redistribute income. They must attract private capital and development while also providing amenities and public assistance for their populations. Urban populations want job growth, a healthy tax base and a thriving central area. At the same time they complain about congestion, air pollution and neighbourhood displacement. Politicians must deal with the contradictory aspects of these claims, and find the fiscal means to support these claims, ideally without raising local taxes. It seems obvious that without large-scale assistance from national or regional governments, cities will find it difficult to sustain coherent policies. Yet national governments also want to lower fiscal burdens and trim budgets (Clarke 1989: Clark 1994a, b).

Third, cities must create common policy solutions from increasingly disparate populations. It is one matter for West Europeans and North Americans to deal with poorer immigrants from southern or eastern Europe or Mexico. But quite another matter when poverty is compounded by profoundly different traditions. Immigrants and 'guest workers' from North Africa, the Middle East and Asia and Africa present altogether different styles of life and religious practices. The role of women, type of dress, observance of holidays, and use of public facilities are just a few differences bound to flabbergast local administrators. Forging a policy consensus on housing, schools and public order poses substantial difficulties.

Finally, if cities are going to meet these challenges they will have to adopt new practices and do things differently. As Hambleton argues in Chapter 9, cities have experimented with various techniques and tried to 'reinvent' themselves by adopting new ways of raising revenue, reforming bureaucracies and introducing market pressures. The tourist industry is one way of tapping outsiders, stimulating employment and infusing cities with new revenue. This is one of the reasons why so many cities have rebuilt their waterfronts, constructed pedestrian walkways and converted old buildings into historic sites (Judd and Fainstein 1999). People seek what they have lost and being 'quaint' is a natural commodity for older cities.

Privatisation is an attempt to bring market accountability to bear on city services, and make them more efficient. Its threat may be a tactic designed to make public employees compete with private enterprise or at least make them work harder. Some cities have sought to introduce citizen accountability by surveying residents or establishing oversight committees. Administrative decentralisation and neighbourhood government have also been employed to put large cities on a more human scale and sensitise municipal services to diverse needs. Paris, Amsterdam and Milan have been at the forefront in breaking down large government into more manageable units.

It is ironic that declocalised cities would have a strong local component. And it is curious that globalisation would emphasise the value of cities, point up the importance of localism and underline the utility of small-scale organisation. The process has developed a logic of its own. Complements create synergies and globalisation scales can only be offset by their opposite. Like smaller organisms that survive during great periods of upheaval, cities have the capacity to innovate and create unexpected niches within a larger process of disorder.

Note

1. City GDP is calculated as labour force (city)/labour force (national) × GDP (national) = city GDP.

3
Globalism and Cities: a North American Perspective

Susan E. Clarke

Introduction

As a heuristic, globalisation sometimes seems an intellectual Rashomon[1] in which each sees just what they wish. Most see monetary flows becoming globalised, the international division of labour accelerating wage competition and pressuring national and local wage rates, and the nature of competition transforming as human capital becomes more salient. But less consensus is evident when considering the relationship of globalisation and cities. This chapter considers globalisation processes and global–local links as – in part – socially and historically constructed concepts. It approaches global–local linkages in North America 'from the bottom up' – by identifying aspects of globalisation processes that appear especially salient for local policy making in North American cities and by sketching the evidence of diverse local responses to globalisation trends.[2] This emphasis on intentionality and constructivism allows us to anticipate and analyse the continuing struggles and negotiations over global–local links at different scales (Smith 1998).

The focus on a North American perspective on globalism and cities rather than on 'the North American city' is more than a matter of semantics. For many years, the uncritical assumption that Canadian and US cities shared a relatively homogeneous, if lagged, urbanisation experience forestalled scholarly analysis of 'the Canadian city' as a distinctive entity (Ley and Bourne 1993, p. 12). Goldberg and Mercer's (1986) challenge to these 'continentalist' views emphasised the cultural values, regulatory state roles, interest in collective action, and public service and social welfare commitments distinguishing Canadian society from US arrangements. To them, distinctive constitutional regimes and political cultures undermine any notion or 'myth of the North American city'. With greater attention to 'the Canadian city', the significant regional variations in poverty rates, ethnic and racial diversity, central city well-being and economic health among Canadian cities became more apparent.

Now, globalisation trends are reintroducing the prospect of converging urban futures and forcing us once again to reconsider the 'myth of the North American city' (Garber and Imbroscio 1996). As the impacts of globalisation unfold, differences among cities on both sides of the 49th parallel seem starker and dissimilarities between the Canadian and US experiences pale. Globalisation processes featuring economic integration at different political scales, transborder mobility of capital, labour, products, services and ideas, and consequent governance issues and sociocultural changes stemming from these new dimensions are experienced in both Canadian and US localities. Most accounts of the impact of such trends on cities in the USA agree on the significance of growing income inequality despite economic growth, city–suburb disparities, technological changes, racial polarisation, spatial isolation of poor and minority groups, and high immigration rates (Rondinelli et al. 1998; Stegman and Turner 1996; Wyly et al. 1998). Impacts in Canadian cities are remarkably similar, with the exception of the lesser degree of racial polarisation and spatial isolation of minority groups. As Rothblatt (1994, p. 516) points out, these converging trends, impacts and, increasingly, policy responses do not signal the 'Americanisation' of Canadian cities and urban policy nor the 'Canadianisation' of US practices. Rather they present a template of North American experiences of globalisation and government responses.

Hence an empirically grounded North American perspective on global–local linkages rather than an uncritical continentalism presuming an imaginary North American city seems appropriate. This chapter briefly considers two common metaphors used by Canadian and US scholars and policy makers to represent or 'script' globalisation trends and impacts. It then analyses a series of policy responses being adopted in many North American cities. The most familiar global–local metaphors bundle together several features such as the shift to post-'Fordist' economic networks and the 'hollowing out' of the state. In many North American cities, these metaphors elicit responses involving new local roles and more diverse local policy agendas – including the pursuit of entertainment and tourism dollars, local efforts to construct global links through trade and telecommunications, regional initiatives and crafting local social programmes.

Metaphors of globalisation and localism

By viewing global–local links as the social and political construction of a new scale of political interaction (Delaney and Leitner 1997), we see places as linked, not necessarily in a hierarchical structure mirroring their status in a world system or federal structure, but through the interests and influence of actors at different scales – that is, through political processes (Beauregard 1995, p. 239). Delineating global–local metaphors reminds us that local policies are not inevitable responses to broad globalisation processes nor are they merely 'mediating' global forces. They are intentional strategies emerging from local struggles and negotiations over how to define and deal with the issues emerging in a global era.

The post-Fordist metaphor: trends towards new economic networks

Many metaphors attempt to interpret the economic consequences of globalisation for cities. One influential argument posits that flexible specialisation processes are superseding the 'Fordist' modes of production (Scott 1993; Jessop 1992). Jessop, for example, emphasises the changing nature of competition: he contends that globalisation entails shifts from the familiar Fordist factor-driven competition which leads to homogenisation at each scale of production to the Schumpeterian notion of innovation and investment-driven competition. To others, transaction costs are at the heart of these new processes. Scott (1992) argues that flexible accumulation means the sources of profitability shift from internal economies of the firm, gained through more efficient use of the factors of production, to economies gained from minimising transaction and linkage costs among firms, suppliers, innovators and so on.

Local industrial districts are often portrayed as critical sites for these new economic networks (Piore and Sabel 1984). These new spatial forms feature small firms embedded in regional networks of producers, suppliers and distributors and engaged in specialised production tailored to quickly changing consumer demands and market needs. The labour market is local and flexible, tied to the district rather than particular firms; capital is also often local and patient, relying on trust and long-standing ties to counter investment risks (Markusen et al. 1999). It appears that these features are more widespread and more variable than assumed; they are also amenable to deliberate state intervention aimed at creating these conditions in diverse locales. In particular, second-tier cities – fast-growing medium-sized cities – with distinctive internal structures are now alternative sites for new industrial organisations (Markusen et al. 1999).

Along with Michael Porter and others, Robert Reich (1991) focuses on the effects of the global diffusion, by the 1970s, of methods of high volume production of standardised goods. This diffusion shifts attention to the role of human capital investment as a critical element in value-added production processes. The key change in production processes in Reich's formulation is the shift from high *volume* to high *value* production. Human capital, the analytic and information skills critical to the capacity to innovate, becomes the key elements of profitability and wealth creation. In Reich's perspective, wealth and the potential for gain, are no longer best measured by fixed assets, stock (e.g. plant and equipment), but by accumulated knowledge and experience – human capital. By shifting the focus from product to process, this creates a new geography of human capital that centres on determining when, where and by whom value is added.

The post-Fordist charge to North American local officials centres on three tasks: to sustain a local climate in which firms' transaction costs are minimised and premature closure on policy choices is avoided (Scott 1992), to pursue strategies differentiating locales and supporting clusters of economic activity, and to foster human capital development. Whereas the factor-driven Fordist competition encouraged the 'smoke-stack chasing' and 'arms race' economic development policies characterising many localities' agendas, innovation and investment-driven competition in a post-Fordist era requires policies that accentuate differences among localities, or as Hanson (1993) puts it, greater product differentiation. And to the extent that these new production systems and forms of competition place a premium on the continued capacity for innovation, local policy makers are compelled to consider how to enhance their human capital stocks, particularly marginalised racial and ethnic minorities. But given the federal context and the mobility of human capital, local interests may have few economic incentives to invest in human capital at the local scale. To the extent that devolution shifts human capital responsibilities to the state, provincial and local levels – as is increasingly the case in Canada and the USA – this may prove to be a profound weakness for North American cities.

The 'hollowing out of the state' metaphor: trends towards state restructuring

The political consequences of globalisation for cities are captured by metaphors of political restructuring. Jessop (1993) argues that changes in economy and technology are contributing to a 'hollowing out' of the state. The expectation is that economic and political power are shifting *upward* to supranational institutions, *outward* to transnational networks of cities and *downward* to urban and regional scales (Jessop 1997). Not that the nation state withers away – indeed, there is a compelling argument that national frameworks significantly affect local capacities to deal with globalisation pressures. But, in contrast to the nation state orientation of the Fordist era, important economic and political functions shift to other scales due to the inability of the central state to pursue sufficiently differentiated and sensitive programmes needed by investors.

This metaphor anticipates more interventionist local governments, taking on new economic development roles and abetting the reorganisation of local institutional arrangements to allow greater flexibility and collaboration with private sector interests. Although not inevitable, the state discourse of planning is often displaced by a rhetoric of entrepreneurial agendas across policy arenas. In particular, in what Jessop (1993) labels the 'Schumpeterian workfare state' version of this prospective role, social policy orientations are framed in terms of labour flexibility, competitiveness and business needs.

To many observers, these trends appear to be unfolding in North American cities. In the 1980s, many American and Canadian politicians voiced support for workfare provisions and began to devolve significant social responsibilities to the states, provinces and localities. As Lemon (1993, p. 276) argues, the 'less centralised' Canadian federal system limited the wholesale dismantling of the Canadian social welfare system; urban voters continue to dominate many provinces and can articulate demands through less fragmented local and metropolitan governments. But in the USA, the devolution of welfare responsibilities seems to fit the 'hollowing out' metaphor. While Clinton eventually carried out his campaign promise to 'end welfare as we know it' by signing the Personal Responsibility and Work Opportunity Reconciliation Act of 1996 (PRWORA), devolution of welfare roles actually began under the Reagan and Bush administrations. Most significantly, 1981 legislation allowed states to apply for waivers exempting them from federal guidelines if they agreed to monitor the results of their alternative programmes. With the passage of the Family

Security Act in 1988, workfare elements were incorporated into welfare programmes through the required state-level JOBS programme mandating work and training for Aid for Families with Dependent Children (AFDC) recipients.

These state experiments prompted a new political consensus on defining welfare problems in terms of family responsibility and long-term dependency and solving them with workfare requirements (Weaver 1995). Budgetary legislation emphasising revenue-neutral policy design and the political impetus to eliminate budget deficits further enhanced support for devolving welfare responsibilities to the states. These factors shifted the focus from poverty to dependency (Blank 1997): they softened up passage of the 1996 legislation emphasising workfare initiatives and replacing national welfare entitlement programmes with state block grants for Temporary Assistance to Needy Families (TANF).

TANF rolls are shrinking, but many localities will be unwilling or unable to provide the support services necessary to make workfare work when the economy slows and states and localities must deal with the remaining, most disadvantaged, recipients using their own funds. Wisconsin's vaunted workfare programme, generously supported by state revenues, is over 1.5 times as expensive ($15,000 per person) as the yearly costs (roughly $9000) under the former national programme (Wills 1998). And, as Blank (1997) points out, jobs are not enough: the changing employment structure and the long-term decline in wages at entry levels make it difficult to earn your way out of poverty. Since 1993, the job base in US central cities has been increasing and unemployment has been declining. But most new jobs continue to be created in the suburbs and half of all welfare recipients live in cities (US Department of Housing and Urban Development 1999). The ratio of welfare recipients to jobs, however, varies dramatically by community, from 1 per cent in Indianapolis in 1996, for example, to 9 per cent in New York City (McMurrer et al. 1997). While there is some renewed effort to make work pay, as Blank (1997) puts it, through increased minimum wage levels and enhanced Earned Income Tax Credit provisions, localities will bear the burden of increasing concentrations of unemployed and working poor created by globalisation restructuring trends.

In the USA, these political restructuring processes are accelerated by state and local use of initiative and referendum procedures (where allowed by state legislatures) to initiate new programmes or eliminate existing ones. These popular initiatives stem from 10th Amendment provisions that powers not specifically assigned to national government are reserved to the states; in 24 states, the state legislature has passed enabling legislation allowing citizens to place initiatives and referenda items on state and local ballots. The results of these 'direct democracy' provisions thus vary by state and locality, but have ranged from charter schools and voucher programmes, reinstatement of capital punishment, tax caps and expenditure limits, to gay rights ordinances as well as bans on homosexual marriage, and assisted suicide provisions (Wills 1998; Bowler et al. 1998). The use of these provisions is increasing dramatically, particularly on cultural issues such as gay rights and abortion (Sharp 1999), fiscal prerogatives and environmental issues.

The new localism in North America

These metaphors of the economic and political aspects of global–local linkages contributed to the 'rediscovery' of the city as an arena for globalisation and economic dynamism (Amin and Graham 1997; Clarke and Gaile 1998). Amin and Graham highlight the diverse economic, social, cultural and institutional assets cities provide in a global era. The multiplex city they describe provides more scope for local initiatives bringing together social and economic concerns than anticipated in early globalism models. While a hollowed-out state may be 'flatter and more permeable' (p. 424), they argue it can still address governance issues by relying on multiple networks, actors and institutions.

The local politics of globalisation

The prospects for the multiplex city and the new localism in North American cities are both enhanced and constrained by their institutional context. While there are few national controls over provincial, state or local government other than through purse strings and the courts, local governments only have powers and authorities granted by state and provincial governments. So provinces and states determine which functions localities are responsible for, with tremendous variations by state in the USA in fundamental policy areas such as education. In the USA, people's everyday lives are more directly influenced by the 50 state governments and the more than 83,000 local governments – counties, cities, special districts – than by national government. Local governments are perceived by US citizens as more effective than federal and state government: in a 1997 poll, 74 per cent of the respondents agreed that 'Government should run only those things that can't be run at the local level' and 53 per cent agreed that 'The federal government is interfering too much in state and local matters' (Carney 1998: pp. 800–1). Thus state and local governments shoulder primary responsibilities for social, educational, land use, health and now, welfare, programmes in the USA. These historical and constitutional conditions are now reinforced by political realignments giving Republicans control of the majority of state governments in 1998. The traditional Republican support for states' rights (as articulated in the 10th Amendment), minimal government and local control amplifies the trends and historical conditions encouraging a new localism in American politics.

One of the most urbanised countries in the world, Canada is characterised as 'an urban nation without the benefit of a national urban policy' (Artibise 1988, p. 260). In Canada, the federal system historically tied local concerns to provincial oversight; direct national ties to local governments are modest and provinces have much more extensive controls over cities than do American states. These provincial roles vary, but most provinces are responsible for health care, housing and welfare while sharing police, roads and education responsibilities with cities (Frisken 1994). Local government expenditures are dominated by transportation and communication, environmental, social services and safety issues. Land use planning is a provincial responsibility, but developmental planning often involves joint federal–provincial efforts. Since the 1970s, more direct federal–local ties – often mediated by development corporations (Leo and Fenton 1990) – are evident in specific redevelopment projects such as the False Creek and Granville Island areas in Vancouver BC and Toronto's Harbourfront. Although Canadian cities do not have the constitutional 'home rule' provisions enjoyed by some US cities, nevertheless there is considerable variation in province–city relations and growing evidence of local activism and inter-city competition (Reese and Fasenfast 1996). To the extent that provinces follow the lead of British Columbia's Municipal Reform Act (1998) devolving significant policy responsibilities to municipalities and regional districts removing provincial oversights, the 'hollowing out' metaphor will be increasingly apt for Canadian cities.

City limits

Fiscal constraints further limit local policies: the most elastic and buoyant taxes in the USA are captured by the national government; the elasticity of the income tax provides increased national revenues without tax rate increases while non-buoyant and regressive taxes predominate at the state and local level. Canadian cities face a similar dilemma: in the 1930s and 1940s, provincial authorities in Canada eliminated local income taxes and personal property taxes while also reducing or eliminating local shares of other provincially collected taxes (Taylor 1986, p. 278). Nowadays, property tax, sales taxes and special purpose transfers from provincial governments provide the lion's share of Canadian local revenues.

In contrast to most European nations, North American cities rely on local property tax and increasingly, in the USA, sales tax for revenues; in the USA, cities set their own rates and assessments so there are no uniform rates. This creates tremendous incentives to compete with other communities and to cater to business since more local investment means increased tax revenue for the community treasury. With each community in competition with other communities, there is the anticipated threat that both residents and firms can exit from the community whenever they perceive the benefit/tax ratio is no longer favourable (Peterson 1981). The local imperative to maximise the tax revenue base is traditionally a key distinction of American cities, although it may be less so in the future with the decline of central grant equalisation strategies in Europe and Canada. Canadian cities are also reliant on property taxes and tax at higher rates than US cities. Canadian cities count on fees, fines and non-tax revenues but receive even less intergovernmental aid from the national government than do American cities. As a consequence, Canadian cities also face limits in the initiatives they can undertake.

Changing features of city initiatives in the 1990s

Local economic development activism in US and Canadian cities is surging even in the absence of significant national initiatives. A growing body of research indicates that US, and increasingly, Canadian cities are responding to global competition and national retrenchment with more diverse, rather than more limited, policy agendas. These empirical studies also reveal evolving local activism, hollowing out processes, greater risk-taking by local officials, and a reliance on public–private partnerships. This expansive pattern is shaped by fiscal concerns and political constituencies pressuring for new approaches.

Evolving local activism

Recent national surveys of local economic development report an increase in such initiatives, even in the absence of federal funds supporting such initiatives.[3] In these surveys, cities report an evolutionary pattern of policy activism reflecting changes in their goals and their roles in the development process. Clarke and Gaile (1998) describe waves of policy adoptions in which cities move towards roles of risk takers and development partners, similar to the roles Jessop and others deductively theorise. The first wave of policy adoptions – those reported as first used before 1980 by at least 30 per cent of the cities responding – rely heavily on cities' ability to regulate and facilitate development through land use controls, public services and provision of infrastructure. There are only limited, traditional financial tools entailing debt or cheap loans and scant evidence of higher risk strategies.

The second and third waves of strategies adopted since 1980 are characterised by a stronger investment and entrepreneurial approach. Cities show a clear interest in market-oriented strategies, including business incubators, carving up the local tax base, and adopting a more business-oriented approach towards use of local assets and public capital. Many of these entrepreneurial strategies are capital-oriented and investment-related strategies; many cities may be hampered from using these tools because of the absence of state enabling legislation or more risk-aversive stances when their own funds are at stake.

Hollowing out processes

Most US local officials (88 per cent) reported they were more active in economic development in the 1990s. Clarke and Gaile (1998) find some evidence of 'hollowing out' processes: when asked whether important decisions on economic development issues were moving up to regional and state decision levels or down to the local level, a majority (59 per cent) reported the devolution of these issues while 23 per cent saw such issues shifting to higher levels. In response to these shifts, 71 per cent reported a stronger economic development capacity in the 1990s, 14 per cent reported weaker capacity and 14 per cent estimated their capacity had not changed.

Greater local risk-taking

These findings correspond to other empirical evidence that American and Canadian cities are adopting more entrepreneurial policy orientations.[4] As Reese and Fasenfast (1996) put it, the differences between American and Canadian cities tend to be of scale and timing, not substance. Although an 'entrepreneurial' local government may seem an oxymoron to some, it reflects a range of programmatic policy options emphasising demand-side strategies that foster new market and growth opportunities in contrast to traditional locational incentive strategies that subsidise firms (Eisinger 1982; Clarke and Gaile 1992, 1998).

These do not necessarily replace locational incentives but are over-laid with these historical orientations. Indeed, both Goetz and Reese find that cities with more entrepreneurial policies are more active across the board – they are doing more of everything. Furthermore, Reese (1997) finds that Canadian cities are less likely to rely on financial incentives and more likely to link development incentives to provisions for directing the benefits of development to designated targets. In both Canadian and American cities, it is possible that there is a periodicity to adoption of entrepreneurial strategies as well; some studies show cyclical adoption of more entrepreneurial approaches during economic downturns and backing away from these interventionist strategies during economic prosperity.

Reliance on partnerships

These efforts increasingly centre on public–private partnerships rather than public bureaucracies or elected officials.[5] As state restructuring and devolution occur in response to the changing nature of competition in a global economy, such partnerships are increasingly familiar governance strategies in local governments (Clarke 1998; Savitch 1998). In 1996 89 per cent of American city officials claimed that public–private partnerships were more important in the 1990s than in the past (Clarke and Gaile 1998; Clarke 1998).

But these community-based partnerships differ in important ways from those encouraged by federal programmes. In contrast to the commercial development featured in the Urban Development Action Grant (UDAG) programme partnerships of the 1970s and 1980s, officials place greater emphasis on using partnerships to support manufacturing and job creation. Non-profit organisations are cited as more important in contemporary partnerships; in part, this may stem from housing legislation in the late 1980s and early 1990s encouraging incorporation of non-profit organisations in public–private partnerships. But it also signifies the coming of age of the non-profit sector in the late 1980s, especially community development corporations (CDCs) and intermediary organisations (Vidal 1992).

Why local activism?

The increase in activism and use of more entrepreneurial approaches in American, and to some extent Canadian, cities appears to be shaped by fiscal concerns. US cities with weak fiscal health are significantly more likely to be active in economic development adoption (Clarke and Gaile 1998). This activism of needy cities corresponds to Rubin and Rubin's (1987) findings of greater activism in poor cities, as well as Goetz's analyses (1990, 1993) and Reese's (1997) findings on Canadian cities. Goetz (1993, p. 184; 1994, p. 100) notes that wealth and poverty measures now mask complex realities: income polarisation – the existence of high levels of both wealth and poverty (Massey and Denton 1993) – is an important condition prompting policy innovations. And, in contrast to the earlier federal period, when well-off cities were more entrepreneurial in using federal funds – that is, more likely to establish complex financing arrangements, to become equity partners, to establish special conditions on development deals (see Clarke and Gaile 1998) – it is now the poorer cities that are more entrepreneurial in the absence of federal funds.

Local political conditions are also salient. In *The Work of Cities*, the presence of African-American mayors and city council members supported more entrepreneurial efforts. Reese's (1998) analyses support these findings. She finds that economically distressed US cities with strong mayoral leadership and, often, with well-organised African-American constituencies and coherent business leadership, were more likely to adopt strategies that directly targeted benefits of economic development policies.

More recently, the 1993 Empowerment Zone (EZ) legislation provides some national resources to selected US cities. It is characterised by some (Gittell et al. 1998), as bringing together the orientations of the 1960s anti-poverty programmes with the neighbourhood strategies and organisations of the 1980s. Others (Goozner 1998), however, see it as a weak, vestigial urban development strategy. The Clinton programme emphasised the importance of community partnerships and empowerment by mandating the participation of community-based organisations in the strategic planning processes designing city EZ proposals and boundaries and in public–private partnerships. Initial analyses, however, suggest cities tend to favour the more entrepreneurial, non-advocacy, CDCs as community representatives and to promote traditional business development approaches in the EZ areas (Gittell et al. 1998, p. 554).

More diverse local policy agendas

A further wave of policy initiatives emerged in the 1990s featuring new policy targets. Five development policy initiatives not easily traced in national surveys and aggregate analyses are discussed here. Initiatives centred on trade, regionalism, telecommunications, tourism and social policy provide growing evidence that many cities are constructing more diverse policy agendas than anticipated by the limited localism model.

Cities and trade

In many accounts (e.g. Clarke and Gaile 1998; NLC 1997), American city officials are remarkably sanguine about globalisation trends: a majority usually report seeing globalisation as bringing benefits to the community rather than costs. Many see social and cultural contacts with foreign cities as part of this positive impact, with most characterising foreign tourism and foreign direct investment as positive economic impacts. For many cities (89 per cent of the large cities in the 1997 NLC survey), export promotion is a major new initiative. But as Noponen et al. (1997) point out, cities are differentially positioned to take advantage of global markets; the comparative advantages of cities within the same state may vary markedly. Thanks to containerisation, even port cities do not necessarily enjoy an advantage over inland cities in global trade. And as they point out, some cities are heavily trade affected, while other city economies are shaped by import competition and exports to competitive domestic markets. Since these features suggest different policy responses, they argue for city-specific policies for international business rather than state or national strategies. Rondinelli and Vastag (1997) underscore the importance of government roles and cooperation with the private sector in human capital development and infrastructure development in creating local settings with competitive international profiles.

Cities and regionalism

Metropolitan and regional planning are historic features of Canadian urban development, generally in response to provincial regulations. In Canada, these traditional structures are now more subject to local controls and less governed by rational planning protocols – in short, they are becoming more politicised (Reese and Fasenfast 1996). In the USA, these are more infrequent arrangements but political pressures are now promoting more regional and metropolitan cooperation. Strategically, by highlighting the interdependence of US cities and suburbs, 'the regional agenda is the first attempt in years to bring cities out of their embattled crouch and into majority coalitions, pushing for genuine, systemic change' (Katz 1999).

This interdependence is often portrayed as an issue of sustainable development in the USA, with curbs on sprawl and congestion possible only through cooperative efforts. But two persuasive economic rationales also bolster the new regionalism argument: concerns about the spillover effects of concentrated poverty and de-industrialisation in the inner city and older working-class suburbs, and a broader argument portraying cities as engines of growth and cultural centres of critical importance for regional growth and prosperity. These arguments are gaining some political currency. In May 1999, 97 per cent of the local officials surveyed by the US Conference of Mayors and the National Association of Counties agreed that 'the most important challenges facing their communities are regional challenges' (US Department of Housing and Urban Development 1999).

Do these and more modest regional initiatives in Charlotte, NC, San Jose, Calif., Baltimore, Md, Allegheny Country, Pa and other cities and states (Broder 1998; Savitch and Vogel 1996) herald the era of 'citi-states' in North America, one where healthy cities power the national economy and contribute to international competitiveness? (Peirce et al. 1993). As Barnes and Ledebur point out, this is about 'federalism, not feudalism' (1998, p. 177). Using the metaphor of a 'US Common Market', they argue for a paradigm shift that recognises local economic regions as the basic, functional economic units of a spatially differentiated national economy (Swanstrom 1996).

Despite the intellectual appeal of the regionalism metaphor, however, there are relatively few institutional mechanisms for collective action at the regional and local levels in the USA. National policies on regional cooperation in the USA are notoriously episodic and ambivalent. One notable exception is embedded in the 1990 ISTEA (Intermodal Surface Transportation Efficiency Act) legislation requiring formation of metropolitan-wide, multi-jurisdictional planning organisations (MPOs) as a precondition for receiving federal transportation funds. More recently, the Clinton Administration requested $50 million in fiscal year 2000 for a Regional Empowerment Zone Initiative to award competitive grants to existing zones for projects linking their strategies with broader regional markets (US Department of Housing and Urban Development (HUD) 1999). Similarly, HUD's Regional Connections Initiative would fund local partnerships for 'smart growth' strategies linking inter-jurisdictional areas and workforces.

Local efforts at cross-border regional cooperation in North America are also emerging. Although the North American Free Trade Area (NAFTA) is an obvious explanation for the recent upsurge in trans-border agreements, there is a remarkable pre-NAFTA legacy of cross-border agreements, particularly on environmental and water resource issues, between state, provincial and local governments in the United States, Canada and Mexico. In the Pacific north-west, for example, the ecological concept of a Cascadia region encompassing the Georgia Basin–Puget Sound bioregion is spurring new institutional structures to protect the quality of life (Artibise 1995, 1998; Kaplan 1998; Scherer and Blatter 1994). But Cascadia is also promoted as the tenth largest economic centre in the world – a giant high-tech trading bloc, with major bulk-shipping ports in Portland and Vancouver and container-shipping ports in the Seattle–Tacoma area (Kaplan 1998). As some regional leaders put it, it is necessary to 'cooperate regionally in order to compete globally' (Agnew and Pascall 1997). To foster this, a wide range of binational alliances and multi-party groups and forums is in place: for example the Pacific Northwest Economic Region (PNWER) group formed (1989) by 60 British Columbia and North American legislators; the Pacific Corridor Enterprise established (1990) by over 200 British Columbia, Alberta and North American business leaders; and the Cascadia Planning Group of planners and policy makers.

Similar cross-border mobilisation is evident along the Interstate 35 'NAFTA corridor' linking Mexico City, Monterrey and the US Midwest (Garza 1999), promoted by the efforts of organisations such as North America's Superhighway Coalition (NASCO). NASCO is a multi-governmental, public–private lobbying group formed in 1994 to mobilise state and local officials and businesses along international trade corridors, particularly in the Midwest, and to campaign for improving transportation and border facilities. In reauthorising national transportation legislation in 1998, Congressional representatives and such 'border and corridor' coalitions pushed for inclusion of fiscal incentives for trans-border cooperation on transportation corridors. US states and Canadian provinces agreeing to plan and implement cross-border transportation projects now will share in Transportation Equity Act of 1998 (TEA-21) funds. Even in the absence of European Union-style regional incentives, these trans-border issues elicit similar responses in North America and Europe: establishing decision-making structures and civic organisations to deal with the structural tensions of relations between transnational, national, state and local governments.[6]

Cities and telecommunications

Not all cities see themselves as global trading partners, but nearly all see telecommunications as an alternative means of linking up with the global world wide web. In the 1996 *The Work of Cities* survey, over two-thirds of the communities recognised this as a new element in their economic development agenda. Nearly every community reported having or creating a home page on the web; over 50 per cent reported that some or all city hall offices were linked by e-mail and most provided job and education information through publicly accessible terminals in libraries and at kiosks. To establish this information infrastructure, cities are striking up partnerships bringing together city, county and state officials as well as public school districts, higher education institutions, local utilities and private telecommunications corporations. Where cities are limited in planning for 'the virtual city' by state laws and prohibitive costs, many are adopting new organisational structures such as municipal telecommunications commissions (for example, Milpitas, Calif., 1995) and non-profit corporations to operate a telecommunications network.

Despite this hubris, Graham (1997) challenges five myths about the telecommunications and the future of the cities: the myth of technological determinism and direct urban impacts, the myth of urban dissolution in the face of new communications technologies, the myth of universal access and greater equality, the myth of substituting telecommunications for transport, and the myth of local powerlessness. Although there are ongoing debates centred on each of these myths, more immediate and mundane local problems are created by these technological advances. In the American context, the inability to tax internet sales creates fiscal dilemmas for cities. Since state and local governments increasingly rely on sales and excise taxes for up to 50 per cent of their revenues (rather than the historical reliance on property tax), the opportunity to buy tax-free goods on the internet is seen as a growing threat to the state and local tax base. In 1998, states and localities were pitted against the major telecommunications corporations who advocated an Internet Tax Freedom Act to protect themselves from new state and local taxes. Given Congress's failure to resolve this issue, it promises to be a continuing source of tension between national and subnational officials.

Cities and tourism

As Judd and Fainstein (1999) put it, creating 'places to play' is an increasingly important element in local economies and inter-city competition.[7] For North American cities, sports stadiums are prime examples of such entertainment and tourism ventures. While some US sports stadiums are privately financed (e.g. the San Francisco Giants'

Pacific Bell Park, Denver's Pepsi Center or the Boston Celtics' Fleet Center), most rely on substantial public subsidies. In the 1980s, US cities spent $750 million on sports arena financing; since 1992, over $1 billion in public funds has been spent on sports arenas, with another $7 billion earmarked for future construction (Barringer 1997). By continually threatening to leave if cities do not meet their demands for new stadiums, sports teams create their own version of the arms race described above. In what the city attorney described as 'the worst sports deal in history' (Mathesian 1998), St Louis and the state of Missouri paid the full costs (estimated at $300 million) of the new TransWorld Dome football stadium in St Louis to attract the Rams from Los Angeles, throwing in a new practice facility and a $29 million relocation fee to sweeten the deal.

Team owners and players clearly gain from the subsidised stadiums but the state and local benefits are less obvious. The usual taxpayer share in stadium construction is 80–100 per cent, mostly for construction, but governments often pay for land and street improvements (Barringer 1997). Local residents may be unable to pay the ticket prices at the new stadium, and many will never see a game but will have to pay increased taxes to raise public funds for the stadium. In a sense, such arrangements transfer dollars from people who pay sales taxes – especially middle- and lower-class citizens – to owners and players who spend it elsewhere. While most citizens enjoy sports, polls, referenda and elections consistently show few are willing to pay for sports stadiums with public funds. They see little reason to do so since most economic assessments fail to show increases in per capita income, wages or even net employment associated with stadium development (Rosentraub et al. 1994; Baade and Dye 1988). When sports venues or teams lose favour relative to other tourism options, as in Toronto's SkyDome, local taxpayers are left holding the bill (Euchner 1999).

Cities and social initiatives

Counter to the assumptions of the *City Limits* model, some US and Canadian cities are responding to these trends by crafting local social initiatives. O'Regan and Conway (1993, p. vi) distinguish recent initiatives in US cities from past local efforts by their emphasis on empowerment, on linking poverty alleviation directly to broader economic development goals, on pursuing market-based strategies that are often sector-specific, and on seeking to become sustainable elements of the local economy rather than third-party assistance entities. These are seen as new paradigms – new, local development systems for the unemployed and the poor rather than merely different programmes. Albany, New York, for example, created Kid Improvement Districts in 1996 to bring together sports, job creation, crime and drug prevention, skills training and urban land reclamation programmes to target low-income youth. These programmes, and similar efforts in other US cities, tend to be more comprehensive and holistic than the national anti-poverty programmes of the 1960s; they are also more family oriented and attempt to integrate, as in Albany, people and place-oriented programmes at the neighbourhood level (Rich 1993).

In Toronto and British Columbia, social planning bodies are shifting to local policy designs linking economic and social policy. In the late 1980s, Portland, Oregon, began to link new and expanding businesses with local labour pools. The city garnered commitments from firms gaining city assistance to give the city an initial monopoly on information about upcoming jobs and the opportunity to supply job candidates to the firm. Armed with these promises, the city created a job-training delivery system linking city agencies, neighbourhood organisations and community colleges in an effort to find and train appropriate candidates for these emergent jobs. The value-added processes centred on the creation and supply of an appropriate internal labour force in selected sectors; by relying on neighbourhood organisations to identify potential workers, the city brought new workers outside conventional information loops into the workforce.

These local initiatives often reframe local poverty issues in terms of underutilised assets rather than social needs and pathologies. Many are influenced by Michael Porter's (1997) efforts to identify the competitive advantages of inner cities. Porter faults past models for treating the central city as an island isolated from the city and focusing on public subsidies rather than creation of wealth via private investment. Porter advocates building on the competitive advantage of the central city by identifying the *clusters* of activities that would gain from central city location, respond to local demand (such as specialty foods, financial services), link with other regional clusters, and export goods and services to broader markets. While it could be argued that disinvestment by these private institutions created much of the difficulties facing these areas, Porter relegates government to a supportive role to business leadership.

Critics blast Porter's model as a return to notions of 'ghetto bootstrap capitalism' that understate the realities of racism, crime and poor schools (Goozner 1998). Many prefer Kretzmann and McKnight's (1993) model of asset-based community organising and its role for strong public and civic leadership. Kretzmann and McKnight also reject past policy designs, characterising them as 'needs-driven' deficiency models creating client neighbourhoods and ensuring only survival. In their alternative view, poor people – not their inner-city location – are the underutilised assets. Kretzmann and McKnight argue explicitly for rediscovering local assets as the means to development solutions. Among their many examples are Community Development Credit Union Loans to low-income residents for financing the purchase and repair of used cars in Chicago to enable residents to get to jobs.

Globalisation and local democratic practice in North American cities

While the institutional designs and ideologies shaping the choices described here are distinctively North American, the trends of global-isation and localism are evident elsewhere (Cochrane 1993; King 1990; Reese 1997), as are similar patterns of uneven economic changes, increases in social polarisation, and growing demands to reduce public expenditures, especially place-based aid, in the face of international competition. As described by Hambleton in Chapter 9, many European local governments, for example, are undergoing transformations from mainly welfare service delivery systems based on local elected govern-ments to more complex and *fragmented* systems of 'local governance' involving a wider range of elected and non-elected agencies and mix of public, private and voluntary sector interests (Harding 1993; John and Cole 1998). We are far from understanding the changing contours of local governance in North American cities, particularly, as the Canadian case suggests, the importance of historical, political and cul-tural features in mediating the effects of these trends (Reese 1997; Levine 1995).

Nevertheless, the parallels make questions of local democratic prac-tice in the face of globalisation particularly salient. This new political space raises three significant issues for democratic practice: interests and representation in local governance, the prospects for more contentious politics as local governments cope with the impacts of globalisation, and new democratic practices accommodating these governance concerns.

Interests and representation

Both the changing institutional and interest group context highlight representation and citizenship issues. American cities already seem relatively unrepresentative from a Canadian and European perspective because of the weak party structures, small councils and lack of proportional representation that might allow minority and disadvantaged groups more voice. In addition, the local institutional landscape is no longer dominated by bureaucratic agencies and officials concerned with re-election and tax-based budgets as presumed in public choice models. Instead, a complex terrain of public–private organisations (Vidal 1992; Ferman 1996; Leo and Fenton 1990), non-elected non-profit actors (Horan 1991; Savitch 1998) and national and local private foundations is emerging in service delivery, housing and economic development arenas in both Canadian and US cities. Whether these new arenas provide opportunities to reconnect citizens and government is problematic.

Contentious politics

A significant share of future local political agendas is likely to be devoted to managing and minimising the domestic repercussions of globalism processes. Polarisation and increases in inequalities may serve as a potential ground for social movements at the neighbourhood level – when citizens link spatial and social concerns around, for example, housing issues (Goetz 1993). Uneven development within cities, in particular, appears to create a charged political context in which alternative policy options may be pursued if viable demand mechanisms are in place (Goetz 1994, p. 103). This could create a political logic – a focus on distributive policies and their effects on local re-election chances, the logic of dispersion or spreading benefits to construct local coalitions, politicians' need to recognise and respect past obligations as well as future needs – supporting a broader range of policy options than anticipated, including more 'progressive' policies than expected from local political dynamics (DeLeon 1992; Goetz 1994).

Nevertheless, this optimistic prospect of more popular demands and more democratic governance must be balanced: local governments may also respond to this discontent with repressive measures aimed at increasing the costs of collective action. This is especially likely when localised conflicts over social and cultural values threaten city images and economic development prospects (Sharp 1999). Similarly, the local costs and tensions stemming from immigration create both symbolic and substantive conflicts in Canadian and US cities.[8] For these and other reasons, governance issues are likely to become more contentious. These prospects for collection action and protest remain relatively unexplored.

New democratic practices

For North American cities, globalisation brings more diverse local actors seeking cooperation in the face of greater complexity, the emergence of a third sector of non-profit organisations, and the reconstruction of the local institutional infrastructure to accommodate different bargaining and negotiating processes. This exacerbates the dilemma of generating 'enough cooperation' to get things done (Stone 1989). Bringing the necessary actors to the table and then moderating differences and negotiating cooperation is now a new local government responsibility, demanding a new leadership style (Amin and Graham 1997). As a result, we see a variety of new bargaining systems and institutions as local officials seek arrangements with sufficient scope, responsiveness and flexibility to accommodate these competing ideas and interests.

Often, however, these operate outside formal government structures; thus, these new state roles and diverse actors all raise the prospect of weakening the autonomy of local political institutions and the transparency of public decision making (Clarke 1998; Hansen 1989; Jessop 1993; Peck and Tickell 1994a). Sustaining the flexibility and scope necessary for adapting to complex new environments may challenge the dialogic processes necessary to enhance local democratic practice. For citizens of North American cities, this will be the critical dilemma as they negotiate their links with a globalising world.

Notes

1. Akira Kurosawa's (1950) classic drama centres on four different viewpoints of a crime in ancient Japan, each revealing more detail but each raising questions about the nature of truth.
2. Policy responses in Canadian and Mexican cities will be referred to as part of the North American context but many of the examples are cities in the USA. For more extensive discussions of local Canadian responses to globalisation, see Reese (1997), Reese and Fasenfast (1996), Garber and Imbroscio (1996) and Kresl and Gappert (1995); for recent analyses of responses in Mexican cities, see Garza (1999) and Kresl and Gappert (1995).
3. *The Work of Cities* (Clarke and Gaile 1998) reports on two national surveys conducted in 1989 and 1996 of local development officials in cities with populations of 100,000 or more in 1975. See Wolman and Spitzley (1996) and Fisher and Peters (1998) for overviews of strategies in American cities; see Reese and Fasenfast (1996) and Reese (1997) for overviews of local Canadian strategies.
4. See Clarke and Gaile (1998), Goetz (1990, 1994), Miranda and Rosdil (1995) and Elkins (1995). Imbroscio (1993) and Wolman and Spitzley (1996) discuss

particular local strategies; see Reese (1997) and Reese and Fasenfast (1996) for review of similar trends in Canadian cities.

5. This discussion draws on Clarke (1998).

6. Similar to their European counterparts, these North American trans-border networks also take coherent positions and lobby on national legislation in Canada and the USA: the PNWER group lobbied the Canadian government on the impacts of aspects of the proposed Canadian Citizenship and Immigration Act on tourism and trade; it similarly lobbied the United States government opposing border crossing fees proposed in the extension of ISTEA legislation.

7. Hiernaux-Nicolas (1999) describes the consequences of the Mexican government's tourism development strategy for Cancun and its subsequent withdrawal leaving Cancun development to market forces.

8. Canada receives more immigrants (on a per capita basis) than any other country in the world, with twice the rate of foreign born in the population as in the USA.

4

Urban Homogenisation and Diversification in West Europe

François Ascher

The concept of West Europe remains ill-defined. To begin with, which are the countries of West Europe? Clearly, the question is only partially a geographical one. Implicitly included under this umbrella are the Nordic nations, as well as the Mediterranean countries and even Austria, which lies predominantly in the eastern half of Europe. In my view, the question is a legacy of the political division of Europe. It is, therefore, a very recent phenomenon, especially with regard to urban history, and its relevance will probably continue to diminish fairly quickly. Indeed, this political rupture has mainly left its mark on East Europe; so much so that its impact cannot be disregarded. This is due to a variety of factors: urban growth which is generally slower than in the West, a lack of large-scale modernisation and renovation, a huge stock of public housing, fewer cars, restricted provision for businesses and office buildings, etc. Certainly several 'Western' countries have had one or more of these characteristics in common, but never, it would seem, all of them together. The conjunction of these factors means that there are many characteristics that are specific to Eastern European cities, and that it is primarily these specificities which, through differentiation, make up the common characteristics of Western cities. These specificities do not seem destined to last. Indeed, will the face of East European cities be very different from that of Western cities, once they have experienced 20 years of accelerated urban growth, the development of large-scale commercial distribution, a huge increase in private car and home ownership, etc.? We must hope so, because theoretically they should be able to take advantage of Western cities' experience so as not to repeat the mistakes. Moreover, East European cities will encounter simultaneously, rather than succes- sively, the motor car, environmental demands, the internet, positive interest rates, the development of private housing, integrated shopping centres, high-speed trains, etc. These factors will have a different role from the one they played in the countries of the West.

Once we have established that all cities in Europe have a common geography, it is difficult to dwell further on their very great diversity. And indeed, if we consider the recent period, it would also seem that globalisation, even if it is in some ways a powerful homogenising factor, has also had diversified effects. The ways in which West European cities have entered and become embedded in this global dynamic have varied considerably.

The diversity of European cities

The cities of Europe present multiple differences whether in terms of their urban structure and networks, the spatial structures of built-up areas, the social and functional differences between districts, modes of political administration, architecture, and the relationship between public and private space. The explanatory factors are numerous.

Some countries, such as Western Germany, the Netherlands and Britain in particular, have been extensively urbanised since the beginning of the last century. France, on the other hand, was still about 50 per cent rural just after the Second World War. As for Spain, Portugal and Greece, their urbanisation is even more recent. More fundamentally still, urban histories and cultures differ profoundly. Some countries have long been centralised (generally the old monarchies), while others have a more fragmented urban history (imperial and federative). For this reason urban systems cannot easily be compared.

The ways in which countries and their cultures have 'negotiated' the city–nature relationship are also very different. Nature as a value is perceived very differently in Germany, where it imposes a profound historical respect, in France where it has been incessantly urbanised, and in England where the uses made of the countryside by city-dwellers represent a kind of pragmatic compromise. Urban density and the varying proportions of private and public housing are also differentiating factors in the long term. The same goes for institutions: in some countries, such as France, where municipalities have always been very numerous, but until very recently they had little power. In Switzerland things are evidently very different, and direct democracy has remained a significant factor in territorial evolution. In Germany, a very hierarchical system has not only divided up responsibilities, but amenities as well, profoundly influencing urban structures. Indeed, the majority of countries carried out reforms of their territorial institutions after the Second World War and, with just a few exceptions, decentralisation marked this period.

Metropolisation – the emergence of new forms of urbanisation

Although the cities of West Europe differ in geographical, historical, cultural, political and social terms, there are nevertheless a number of common features in their evolution, of which the most important is undoubtedly the process of metropolisation, or 'metapolisation' (Ascher 1995). In fact, metropolisation is a process which is inextricably linked to globalisation, both being ways of increasing the technical, social and spatial division of work.

'Metropolisation' has in recent years become a key concept when describing the territorial evolution of economically advanced countries. The precise definitions vary from one author to another, but all are agreed that Western societies concentrate more and more of their human and material wealth in big cities.

This is in fact the contemporary form of a well-established process of urban concentration which has been taking place in Europe for hundreds of years. It began with the depopulation of rural areas and country towns; for several decades now the relative importance of small and medium-sized towns has been eroded. And just as the rate of urbanisation has varied from country to country, so metropolisation is today present to a greater or lesser degree in the various regions of West Europe. Some countries are still at an almost primitive stage in the development of their big cities, Finland for example; others are only just entering the phase of suburbanisation, which is generally one of the first stages of metropolisation: southern Italy, Portugal, Ireland, Greece, Sweden. On the other hand, northern Italy, Austria, Spain and France passed this stage some time ago and are witnessing the development of phenomena which are already familiar to countries that underwent urbanisation at an earlier stage (the UK, Belgium, Germany and the Netherlands). This entails the decline of certain large industrial cities, the depopulation of city centres, large-scale urban reconstruction, the formation of vast urban regions, and the new growth of certain large conurbations due to the globalisation of their economy.

Spread, fragmentation and reconstruction

If the form of metropolisation varies from one country to another according to its history, a common factor is its tendency to form larger and more densely populated areas. Those who inhabit these urban zones actually live and function not so much on the scale of a district or town, but rather that of a vast area within which they travel. The urban areas which are being formed vary in terms of population, density and polarisation. However, they present some identical characteristics:

- the metropolised areas extend the old conurbations and stretch for tens of kilometres outwards from the big cities
- overall urban densities are diminishing, but periurban zones are becoming denser
- the urban fabric is no longer continuous but fragmented
- the built-up areas are more scattered, sometimes interspersed with rural sections
- the distinctions between the city and the countryside are becoming less marked, and
- new peripheral polarisations are being formed, which diminish the importance of the radioconcentric system which characterised old European cities

Indeed, in the most densely populated countries huge multi-centred conurbations are being formed.

Metropolisation, then, is not simply a phenomenon of the growth of big cities. It is a process which brings towns and villages from ever further afield into the daily sphere of activity of these large conurbations, thus engendering new types of urban morphology (Leresche et al. 1994). The metropolises are in fact undergoing double growth: 'internal' by the extension of normal urbanisation; 'external' by the absorption of increasingly distant outlying areas, thanks notably to increasingly efficient transport systems and telecommunications (May 1998).

The 'central towns' of these metropolitan zones tend to lose inhabitants and jobs, but in most countries, they have a concentration of increasingly highly qualified workers, an increasingly wealthy population (middle class and upper middle class, students, graduates, those with older children, retired executives, young professionals) (Martens and Vervaeke 1997). In France, 'executives and middle-ranking professionals' are increasingly concentrated in central towns. They account for more than 50 per cent of the active population of the city of Paris, and nearly 45 per cent in Lyon, Grenoble, Toulouse, Nantes, Bordeaux and Rennes. This gentrification (*City-Druck* in German, *embourgeoisement* in French), sometimes goes hand in hand with the 'encystment' of very poor populations in some central areas. However, this phenomenon does not generally reach the same proportions of North American cities, which have become 'restructured' by the ghettos of various minorities. Indeed, in Europe, city centres have generally retained a strong functional value, as well as a symbolic one, even in relatively small cities.

As for the inner suburbs of big cities, they are experiencing slow growth in terms of population and employment. But they are also in the process of being transformed. It is here principally that the city is turning in upon itself. The urban fabric is getting denser: property developers are finding new interest in derelict sites and waste ground, which may cost less to develop and which seem to meet an affordable new demand; employment is concentrated along bypasses, ring roads and urban motorways. It is in or around these areas, too, that the polarisation of new businesses and services is taking place. In some countries, these zones also have a concentration of council housing for the large numbers of long-term unemployed.

The outer suburbs, the outlying towns and villages now integrated into the metropolitan process, are showing steady growth for the most part. These zones attract, in varying proportions, the lower and intermediate sectors in terms of employment and qualifications. Urban sprawl is to be found everywhere, linked to an increase in car ownership and more general improvements in transport and communications, and is controlled to a greater or lesser extent by the public authorities (Dubois-Taine and Chalas 1997).

New kinds of specialised places of activity are also coming into existence on a metropolitan scale, punctuating and polarising the urban landscape (Veltz 1996). These include: technology parks; logistical platforms based on the interconnection of various modes of transport; trade corridors, which make use of the rapid connecting routes between urban centres; 'air towns', situated near airports; theme parks which provide large-scale leisure facilities; and integrated commercial centres of shops and services.

Metropolisation – the connection to globalisation

Many authors have examined the causes of metropolisation (Veltz 1996; Sassen 1991). Inasmuch as it is the pursuit of the general process of urbanisation, its determining factors are not essentially new, and economic factors play a dominant role. The continued accumulation of capital, the broadening of markets and the technical and social division of work necessitate ever larger urban groupings. Thus, it is in the metropolitan zones that firms find the increasingly diversified employment markets that they need, the companies that provide specialised services, the subcontractors whose proximity is made ever more indispensable by the demands of contemporary industrial organisation, and the contacts with the various professionals and groups needed to keep up with market knowledge and innovation.

It is true that new methods of organisation, rapid transport and telecommunications allow firms to delocalise some of their operations, but that only applies to the least qualified, most repetitive tasks. On the other hand, the process of internationalisation means that the presence of major transport and telecommunication infrastructures, which only the biggest cities can have access to, are of the utmost importance for urban economic development. There is evidently a correlation between this economic dynamic and the concentration of the most highly qualified social strata in large urban centres. It is also in big cities that these social groups find the public and private educational, cultural, commercial and sporting facilities, which meet their needs as consumers and allow them to pursue and advance their social activities. Thus the economic and social dynamic go hand in hand, supporting one another in a process of metropolisation driven by the dominant socio-economic groups. Only a part of metropolitan activity is directly globalised. The other part, that which provides services to consumers, is sometimes indirectly linked to the international economy, but is nonetheless increasingly dependent on it. Some analysts have deduced that this structuring of employment could bring about a duality of society (Sassen 1991). This theory is, however, largely unfounded, because a vast conglomerate of the middle classes occupies a growing place in the employed population (Martens and Vervaeke 1997; Bagnasco and Le Gales 1997). All the same, the metropolises have a high concentration of social groups which are marginalised or excluded by contemporary technical and economic changes and developments. These populations are often housed in huge districts on the outskirts of cities or in older central areas. Their concentration in such places adds to individual difficulties and increases social hardship.

Territorial dualism

Metropolisation does not only affect the big cities but the towns and villages which are absorbed into their zones of operation. It is a process that transforms the entire landscape of advanced countries, modifying the relationships between cities, between cities and rural areas, and between one rural area and another.

To begin with, the territorial and social divisions between cities and rural areas are becoming less marked. The physical frontiers between metropolitan and rural zones are becoming blurred, with built-up areas alternating with open spaces. People's ways of life are becoming similar: country folk, now often in a minority even in rural areas, are living increasingly like city-dwellers, following similar work patterns, and even eating the same products bought in the same supermarket chains. The relatively hierarchical urban framework of old is progressively giving way to a dualised territorial system, made up on the one hand of vast metropolitan areas integrating small and medium-sized towns into their functional zones, and on the other hand, of small and medium-sized towns having no direct links with the flow of international trade. The urban system is thus tending to restructure itself on the basis of a distinction or rather an opposition between metropolised urban zones or those in the process of metropolisation, and non-metropolised or non-metropolisible urban zones.

Rural and agricultural areas are experiencing the same type of restructuring as are urban areas. A proportion of them form part of the globalised economy and need to have good access to the metropolitan zones, their infrastructures and facilities; the rest are gradually emerging from the market tradition of agricultural production, despite efforts to streamline the distribution of local products.

This triple metropolitan dynamic distends and dislocates pre-existing territorial relationships. The regions are losing their hinterland function, upon which the big cities used to draw for a significant part of their resources and activities. At the very most they now constitute expansion zones and recreation areas for the metropolises. But the majority of the latter are tending to have closer economic relations with distant cities than with the non-metropolised (non-'metapolised') part of their surrounding region. The distinction between cities and rural areas is thus becoming less pertinent than the division between zones under metropolitan influence and zones outside this influence. The countryside is now seen less as an area of agricultural production. Village life, once rejected for its narrowness and its constraints, is now often perceived by city-dwellers as having the values of comfort and freedom that were formerly attributed to city life. A part of this countryside, that which has been least transformed by large-scale agricultural production, is becoming valued as a public resource, a national treasure to be preserved.

From territorial displacement to double embeddedness

Metropolisation also constitutes a profound modification of the ways in which the economy is territorialised. The insertion of businesses into increasingly internationalised systems and networks in effect modifies their relationships with the local area. Of course, this is still where they look for employment markets, infrastructures and amenities, etc., but their performance also depends increasingly on the quality of the 'extralocal' systems and networks to which they belong. The inelegant term 'glocalisation' is sometimes used to express this double movement, which means that companies and, in part, those who work for them, belong at the same time to a global network and to their local area. The issue of the embeddedness of the economy in local areas and society has gained prominence since the works of Karl Polanyi and Mark Granovetter (Polanyi 1944; Granovetter 1985). The English sociologist Anthony Giddens speaks of delocalisation to express the extraction of social relationships from local contexts of interaction, and putting them into a new spatio-temporal structure (Giddens 1990).

Most analysts stress that local influence is not really disappearing, that globalisation in some ways gives even greater prominence to the singularities of regions and their societies. But its relative importance is diminishing and the resources required by the economy are changing. Companies are no longer attracted by the proximity of natural resources but by that of markets, by the presence of transport infrastructures and the existence of a qualified workforce. These factors, which are to be found to a greater or lesser extent in all large urban areas, mean that a company no longer needs to put down firm roots, but at the very most needs a temporary 'mooring'. Unfortunately for the cities, it is becoming increasingly easy for firms to weigh anchor and move to where conditions seem more favourable at the time. In fact, it is still the relative immobility of qualified workers which tends to reduce the mobility of capital.

Therefore, while local influence cannot be disregarded, it is becoming more superficial. We are witnessing a paradoxical metropolitan development, in which the city plays a growing role through its population, its forms and infrastructures, and in which, at the same time, economic areas are becoming increasingly free from the permanency of urban structures. It is the displacement of the economy, but not the loss of a local support which remains indispensable. There is a kind of disjunction between the economic dynamic, which comes within the scope of globalised territories and networks, and the metropolitan dynamic, which is developing ever more vast, complex and well-equipped local areas (Godard 1997).

Of course, all of this just describes tendencies, and applies first and foremost to new enterprise. The extension of existing activity is less directly implicated. What is more, pre-existing territories and socio-economic relationships do not simply disappear as such. Indeed, one of the characteristics of cities, especially European cities, is their great resilience and their tendency to protect their heritage. Old urban structures are preserved, and new urban forms are superimposed upon them rather than replace them. Our presentation of metropolisation is for this reason rather schematic. And what ultimately characterises the new relationship between the economy and the metropolis is rather what we could call a double embeddedness. To be efficient, the global must be embedded in the local, in a given locality with its neighbourhood networks, their specific traditions and cultures, their particular social configurations, and their different laws. But the local is also embedded in the global and is used by the multinational firms as a means of differentiation and competitiveness (Borja and Castells 1997). One could even speak of creolisation or hybridation about this double embeddedness, which means a multiplicity of specific mixtures and adaptations of local and global, of 'dominated' and of 'dominant', of tradition and of modernity.

The impact of new communication technologies

Some observers have put forward the hypothesis that the development of new communication technologies could put an end to, or slow down, metropolisation. The reasoning is as follows: we live in a society in which information plays an increasing role; telecommunications erase distances; therefore telecommunications are going to diminish the socio-economic importance of physical proximity, and in so doing weaken one of the key factors of urbanisation. Thus, telework and tele-services will allow small and medium-sizes towns, and even rural areas, to become competitive once again for the inhabitant-consumer as well as for the producer.

These analyses are largely erroneous. For one thing, they ignore any historical perspective and the fact that the development of material and informational communications have always gone hand in hand. New technologies, from the railway to the radio, through telegraphy, the telephone, the electric tram and the private car have, contrary to the above hypothesis, accompanied and 'served' urban concentration. In the course of its development industrial society has used science and technology to concentrate production and consumption within cities, whose growth had until then been held up by the limited range of pedestrian and horse-drawn transport. The telephone, the tramcar, the lift and the motor car have been the instruments of urbanisation and have, since the turn of the last century in the United States, given rise to suburbs and skyscrapers alike. In order to convince people of the positive correlation between urbanisation and the development of systems of communication, one could cite as evidence the history of modes of transport and the stocking of goods, of people and of information systems.

New technologies of information and communication (NTICs) have transformed industrial cities into post-industrial cities. Those analysts who presume that the NTICs must have a 'de-urbanising effect', also choose to overlook two facts which are obvious. It is in the biggest and fastest growing cities where NTICs have taken root; and it is also urban social groups who travel the most and make the greatest use of these tools. Many studies have shown that telecommunications do not take the place of travel (Ascher 1995; Castells 1996; Graham and Marvin 1996). On the contrary, they are utilised by firms and individuals to organise themselves in the context of expanding territorial activity. Thanks to telecommunications, companies can organise themselves differently, separating their various functions in new ways, by de-localising some of them, even at a great distance, and concentrating others locally. The NTICs thus play a part in increasing the division of work, and in the economic concentration or expansion of big cities. They accompany the development of mobility and metropolisation, and in the end create more journeys than they replace. In fact companies are spending more on transport in real terms than on telecommunications.

Telecommunications thus play a part in the evolution of daily life in large cities: they replace some journeys, but create a need for others. Some socio-professional groups who make intensive use of telecommunications are beginning to adopt patterns of residential location which are increasingly independent of their place of work. However, very few are truly able to leave the city areas in which they work, because the 'real city' remains necessary to their family life and their domestic, recreational and professional needs. Those who nevertheless do choose to live far from their place of work, tend to reside close to the main infrastructures of rapid inter-city transport, because they have to replace short daily journeys with less frequent, but much longer ones (Ascher 1998).

The NTICs are therefore not inert; they play a part in the transformation of cities, but not exactly as prophesied by Melvin Webber (1964). Certainly Webber was correct when he pointed out that cities were essentially a bundle of social interactions, and that rapid transportation and telecommunications will dissipate the importance of physical propinquity. But Webber's notion of 'community without propinquity' and his vision of central city obsolescence is faulty. In fact, modern telecommunications has changed the nature of journeys rather than replaced them. NTICs actually help produce new places, new centres, new urban spaces. Sometimes they even have a paradoxical effect. By becoming indispensable, they lose their power to discriminate because everyone must have access to them. In this way, they lose part of their economic, social and symbolic value. Conversely, they confer a new value on everything that is not telecommunicable. The fact that telecommunications are now commonplace makes the concept of the 'teleport' largely obsolete, but reinforces on the other hand the competitive advantage of firms that can be located at the heart of a city such as Paris or at the junctions and interchanges of transport systems. Despite the perfecting of telecommunications in all their forms (notably tele- and video-conferencing), there have never been so many meetings, seminars, conferences, conventions, trade fairs and exhibitions within central cities.

For the individual, too, the real value of a social exchange will increasingly be that of the face-to-face encounter, real life rather than something from the world of multimedia. The development of sporting, cultural and culinary pastimes, and the success of live sporting and other events are evidence of the value people are putting on real life, rather than 'mediated' experiences, and a rediscovery of the importance of taste, touch and smell. Commercial organisations have understood this because, alongside the development of electronic trade and the fantastic modernisation of selling by mail order, they are also relying increasingly on showrooms, replacing sales staff by advisors whose function is to inform and 'educate' customers, who are in turn able to see and handle the products.

Could the concept of quality, indeed of luxury, lie in the ability to dispense with the 'mediation' and not be obliged to rely on telecommunications? Is this precisely what constitutes the prime quality of a city and does this represent a comparative advantage for the cities of West Europe?

This brings us back to our original question: has globalisation–metropolisation retained, and will it continue to retain, particular characteristics in West Europe? The description we have given of West European cities highlights certain specificities of the post-war period, in relation both to Eastern Europe and also the cities of other continents, notably North America. Are these characteristics durable? Will other distinguishing features emerge in the years to come? Will local, regional, national and European public authorities have the will and the power to act to preserve these specifics? This is one of the major issues of the present time. Another question is the future of those European cities and regions which are at the very heart of the Western European dynamic. Is globalisation likely to homogenise European cities, especially with the political support of the European Union and the implementation of the single currency?

Is there an Americanisation of West European cities?

For more than a century now, North America has been a major benchmark for European societies, embodying both the positive and negative values of modernity and of capitalism. Reciprocally, old Europe is a reference point for the Americans, having a certain resistance to modernity, to the primacy of the functional and to the all-powerful economy. The question of the Americanisation of Europe is therefore more than ever on the agenda of globalisation. For, even though the multinationals might take account of local characteristics, even relying on them in order to organise themselves on a global scale, it is clear that they also impose a number of identical operational methods and concrete forms. Thus European cities will probably be increasingly affected by a uniformity of practice in production, as well as in service and distribution. The McDonaldisation of Europe is certainly on the agenda. But McDonaldisation is not a simple process. For not only are McDonald's – the ubiquitous fast food chain – bound more and more to take account of the cultural characteristics of countries, even of regions, both in the organisation of their production and in order to adapt to consumers' tastes, but they also have an increasing need to exploit the particular characteristics of each country so as to innovate and broaden their range of products and their clientele. Furthermore, by promoting fast food, McDonald's were the originators of a creativity in European countries, with a wide variety of fast food concepts: 'brocheries' and 'baguette-renouveau', 'paninis', 'doner kebabs', 'Greek sandwiches', even Chinese and Japanese fast food shops, etc. (unfortunately, some might say, in view of the quality of cooking in fast food restaurants and the reduction in the time devoted to meals in Europe).

But McDonaldisation comes up against a major difficulty: the cities of West Europe are changing more slowly nowadays; 80 per cent of the urban buildings of the 2020s probably already exist. McDonald's can only very marginally impose its architecture, its totem poles and its little pink sloping roofs on the cities of West Europe; they are obliged to 'make do with' existing cities and to fit in with their constraints. In other words, McDonald's ends up participating in the urban sedimentation which is one of the major characteristics of European cities. We might even say that they are participating in the preservation of heritage, a sort of joint accumulation of economic and symbolic values.

The general characteristics of metropolisation–globalisation will of necessity take differing concrete forms in West Europe as compared to North America. Space is more limited and, helped by ecological pressure, urban sprawl will progressively be brought under control. Existing densities will maintain public transport at an appreciably higher level than is the norm in North American cities. The centres of big cities will become much more gentrified and some of them will even become 'museumised'. One can also imagine that public authorities, local ones in particular, will remain strong and will help limit the process of socio-spatial segregation, although it is unlikely that they can prevent it altogether. The numbers of motor cars will probably not reach the levels of the USA, especially as new approaches by the public services allow for different ways of managing individual mobility (in particular, thanks to semi-public transport-on-request, or 'paratransit', integrating electronic routeing and the locating of vehicles by satellite).

On the other hand, it is likely that a certain number of urban forms will become generalised, whether they be distribution systems, out-of-town shopping centres, multiplex cinemas, etc. In so far as these changes began earlier in the USA, it can be said that metropolisation–globalisation may be a form of Americanisation of West European cities (Zijderveld 1998).

But a certain Europeanisation of North American cities is also likely. Admittedly, few American cities will actually be able to reclaim their city centres, and we should probably not be misled by the regeneration of some big cities such as New York or Boston. But from the now ubiquitous expresso bars to the pedestrianised streets (for instance

Santa Monica's Third Street, which looks like a copy of a European street), many examples show the mixture which also characterises North American cities and the exploitation of the smallest historic trace. American cities, especially those on the Pacific coast, have also been strongly influenced by Asian cultures and ways of life.

A single West European model of globalised cities?

One of the major players in European globalisation is of course the European Union, which, with the creation of the single market and by its policies of 'structural funds' over several decades, has striven to make its contribution. More recently, the EU has been keen to bring about a policy of the liberalisation of markets, and the disengagement of national governments in favour of competition and privatisation. The EU is now engaged in the setting up of a single currency and in a new policy of structural funds, which could be concentrated on urban issues.

It is certain that the single currency will have an effect on urban affairs, if only by its impact on the localisation of various activities. When the euro has replaced national currencies, the choice of a country or a region by an investor will no longer be dictated by the conditions specific to that zone, or by the characteristics of an economy or a currency. Paradoxically almost, the single currency will homogenise certain economic conditions, and will give greater strength to other differentiating factors. In a way, the European currency will give new significance to local characteristics. This serves to illustrate the double dimension of the phenomenon of globalisation, which is at once homogenisation and differentiation, globalisation and hyperlocalisation. It is one of the reasons why the term 'glocalisation' is actually a very pertinent one, even if it is yet another rather inelegant neologism.

But the politicians of the EU, at least of the 'commissions', which constitute a kind of neo-governmental machine, also have other unifying ideas. For example, they have seized upon the problem of 'sustainable development', in the name of attempting to promote certain conceptions of the city (Commission Européenne 1996a, b, 1997; Union Européenne 1997). Thus, there could be a tendency to pay too little attention to the role of the city in economic development, in the struggle against social inequality, in the right to urban mobility, and such utopian concepts as the 'short-distance city', or the 'compact city'. Granted, the environment is an issue of great importance for the health of humanity and the future of the planet; but there is a danger that a vision of the European city which corresponds primarily to the cities of Nordic countries, which are often rich, dense and long-since urbanised, could be too readily and uncritically adopted by the European authorities. We must therefore hope that globalisation, metropolisation and Europeanisation, that triple dynamic which marks the evolution of West European cities, preserve their intracontinental as well as their intercontinental characteristics.

5
Globalisation and Transformations in Political Cultures

Terry Nichols Clark

How are globalising forces changing local democracy? This is a central theme of the Fiscal Austerity and Urban Innovation (or FAUI) Project. This chapter draws on work done by myself and project colleagues to show how several core urban concepts and findings fill in the causal link between globalisation and local democracy, and introduces this by elaborating on some assumptions. The core paradigms that guided much urban research in the past are losing their power – for example, land value, growth machines and urban economic development. Globalisation is undermining them. This chapter will argue that a new paradigm is emerging – the New Political Culture. Yet it emerges from past paradigms in ways that one can understand by examining them more closely. Some of the major paradigms for urban thinking are considered first. I then suggest how elements of these past paradigms are in turn synthesised in a new set of rules of the game, the New Political Culture.

Core concepts re-examined

Land use and land value

A density gradient is the core idea in much of urban economics, geography and the Chicago ecology tradition in sociology. Central city land value is highest due to severe competition at the centre for multiple uses; value declines as one moves out from the centre in concentric zones. To this idea were added new twists like distance to public transit and expressways (e.g. by Hoyt). Two critical assumptions underpin this analysis: personal contact is essential for many business decisions, and transit and communication are slow and costly. Both assumptions have been undermined in recent decades. Several leading proponents thus abandoned their paradigm. For example, the urban geographer Brian J.L. Berry wrote that these models were outdated because they left out politics and planning (Berry 1973). Berry did not do this casually, but saw results for instance from tables summarising determinants of land value in Chicago from 1836 to 1960 (Berry and Horton 1970, pp. 300–1). These results showed a continuous decline in the explained variance from 80 to 18. Thus, a powerful and well-established theory was weakened.

The 'growth machine'

This model of urban development, with business dominance at its core, comes from Molotch (1976) and Stone (1989), building on Hunter (1953). It inspired much work for two decades, which Logan et al. (1997) comprehensively reviewed to assess the adequacy of growth machine ideas. They found some support for distinctive business/civic leadership patterns, but far less for business impact on pro-growth policies or actual growth. In particular, the theory falls flat when slower or managed growth emerges. A proper theory should include both growth and anti-growth patterns. With ecology a burgeoning issue, new conceptualising is needed to provide integration. Growth machines surely existed in some locations in the past; but the paradigm is less useful today.

Class and race

In a simpler past, the rich and the white were on top, and black and poor on the bottom. This 'stratification map' was widely used to explain voting behaviour, group membership, political participation and quality of service delivery by city governments. These areas remain hotly contested, but that is the point: they are now contested. A decade or two back, by contrast, class and race seemed largely unquestioned as central explanations of basic social and political phenomena. The decline of orthodox Marxism is clearest. A leading urban Marxist, Manuel Castells, moved to a multi-causal perspective in the 1980s. Committed Marxist theorists are practically all gone, and their paradigm shift supports my general point. What of broader neo-Weberian conceptions of class and race? These too have lost power. Consider as indicators of paradigm questioning the titles of books and papers like: *Are Social Classes Dying?* (Clark and Lipset 1991, 2001) and *The Declining Significance of Race* (Wilson 1978). Besides these broad conceptual debates are such street-like questions as: how do we explain the election of Republican mayors by traditionally Democratic cities like New York or Los Angeles as well as the election of white mayors in heavily African-American cities like Gary (Indiana) and Oakland (California)? What has changed? Class and race are obviously still present, but far more than class and race drive these political processes. The great strength of urban research is that it can identify locations where class and race do, and do not, explain things (Bobo and Gillian 1990). Cross-national variations are huge.

Clientelism

Clientelism is declining the world over. There never was much open clientelism in many American 'reform' towns. The squeaky-clean city manager was and is an icon of local government in many locations (even if most are too boring to interest social scientists to study them). But clientelism was the main rule of the game for decades in places like Chicago or many towns in the US South. In many countries of the world, this was probably even more true. In the last decade or so, attacking clientelism has become one of the most salient political issues in locations from Italy to Argentina to Japan.

Globalisation

Globalisation remains more a phenomenon to be understood than a research paradigm, but it is critical to introduce it here since the challenge globalisation poses to past theories is so huge. The last decade has witnessed more drastic shifts towards globalisation, and interrelated market-like tendencies, than was felt in many previous decades. We have scarcely begun to build globalisation into urban theories, or assess how it shifts past processes, despite provocative first efforts such as Sassen (1991) and Clarke and Gaile (1998). Globalisation thus remains too often a vague label more than a theory of how specific processes operate. But ignoring it is perilous. Globalisation and its associated market and communication processes are a major factor undermining the earlier paradigms just discussed. But rather than discard past theory, the better solution I suggest is to consider more consciously, and very specifically, those points where global processes shift the operation of other national and local factors, suppressing many, increasing others. Below I suggest some steps in this direction.

Globalisation transforms urban contexts

The themes that are shaping the New Political Culture are shown in Figure 5.1. Fiscal stress increased during the 1970s as governments grew more than their socio-economic bases. Innovations emerged in

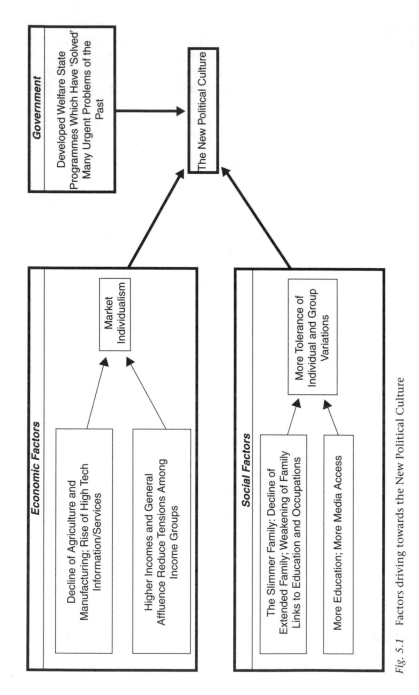

Fig. 5.1 Factors driving towards the New Political Culture

management and service delivery through the 1980s, often moving towards market models. Markets also brought problems. For instance, many local governments sought to spur private local economic development, but their economic incentives lost impact as competing localities offered the same incentives. What is it that we can do? New, amenity-oriented strategies are one alternative. Associated with these policy shifts over time are new forms of political leadership and citizen activity. A New Political Culture has emerged, defining new rules of the game, including a redefinition of democratic practices and responsive government. Smaller, responsive governments are preferred by citizens to broader regional entities.

Fiscal stress

Two global shocks set the scene: Paris in May 1968 and the Arab oil embargo in 1973. The 1968 Paris events reverberated round the world. The attacks on authority and demonstrations for more direct democracy brought profound transformations over the next decade in the rules of the game for national and local governments in many countries. Strong hierarchical leaders with programmes that in retrospect we call traditional, declined. Some were voted out quietly; others left only after a crisis, often a fiscal one. The 1970s suffered the Arab oil boycott, rampant inflation, and thus the end of an era of economic growth which had lasted since 1945. But many governments themselves kept growing. This generated fiscal strain which one can measure by a ratio of government revenues divided by the tax base; fiscal 'slack' is the opposite of strain. Thus strain rises with increased government spending against a stable or declining economic base.

In 1975 the city of New York showed that even that centre of Western finance could experience a huge fiscal crisis; only afterwards did its spending slow as a new mayor came to office with a new agenda. The crisis was so publicised and its details so shocking that it transformed the rules of the game for local officials across the USA, and later much of the world. Many new candidates for mayor emerged. They competed for elected and appointed office less in terms of how to *spend*, and more in terms of how to *cut* spending. Austerity became real. These new leaders and the national climate changed the coefficients of many models, due to changes in system characteristics.

At the time of the New York fiscal crisis, no one in the USA developed any serious measures of fiscal strain for cities, despite an urgent need for national policy. How specifically should the federal government help New York? The mayor of New York and many of his advisors argued that

New York was not unique, and especially not mismanaged. Rather it justified national support since it suffered problems caused by general processes shared with many other cities: a population and job loss like other older central cities with ageing infrastructure, and growing poor populations. This implied general national polices for massive problems in many cities. This interpretation was misleading.

New York was shown to be unique, and national policy should target it alone. Its fiscal problems were minimally caused by the more general socio-economic factors, which were shared with many other cities that did not have fiscal strain problems. To reach this conclusion, we generated the first fiscal strain indicators for a national sample of US cities, and analysed their sources in a report entitled *City Money* (Clark and Ferguson 1983). These techniques were further developed in *Monitoring Local Governments* (Clark 1990), which outlines a system of indicators for monitoring local fiscal stress.

Later studies compare fiscal stress internationally. Strong national differences emerged in urban fiscal stress or its converse, fiscal slack, in Mouritzen (1992). France was less stressed than any of ten countries, except Norway and Finland, from 1978 to 1986. France was one of five countries whose cities still enjoyed more fiscal slack in these years. Fiscal slack was clearly lower in five other countries, with British and US cities the most stressed. US and British cities underwent drastic policy changes, and incurred major political conflicts in the 1970s and 1980s – their rules changed. Even more stressed were Belgian cities; nearly half defaulted on loans in the 1970s, bringing about major changes. By contrast, in the early 1980s, our Scandinavian colleagues would ask rather curiously what fiscal stress was like, as they saw so little. But a decade later, when they finally confronted austerity, they helped their local officials learn from international experiences.

Specific fiscal management strategies

Does austerity lead to innovation? To confront such policy questions, one needs more precise data. To map shifts in policy by localities as they grow, cut or adapt to austerity, we developed a survey method providing more specifics than standard fiscal data. Surveys of most European countries in roughly the mid-1980s showed that a few had interest in new market-related strategies, like user charges instead of taxes, or contracting out for services with private firms. Cities in the USA and Japan scored high on contracting out and user fees. Sweden scored lowest of any on contracting initially (Table 5.1).

Table 5.1 The 33 austerity strategies, indices of importance and the mean across countries

Var. No.	Strategies	Denmark	Norway	Sweden	Finland	England	Holland	France	Canada	Japan	USA	Mean
253	Improve productivity through better management		42	58	67	54	42	66	45	39	54	53
232	Lower surplus	71	39	16	49	69		46	40	56	44	51
231	Increase user fees	51	60			45	40		56	65	58	49
254	Improve productivity by labour-saving technology	72	45	40	64	47	37	31	30	63	45	46
230	Increase taxes		27	14	29	63		67	63	35	47	45
256	Reduce capital expenditures	81	27	21		42	47	65	56	19	39	44
237	Cuts – all departments	25	14	20	77	48	55	44	32	59	38	41
238	Cuts – least efficient department		67	22	65	33		38	42	32	25	41
236	Increase long-term borrowing	35	45		39	35		52	54	41	21	40
245	Reduce administrative expenditures			15	60	35		67	35	45	32	38
248	Freeze hiring	51	15	5	40	37		70	41	30	41	37
249	Reduce workforce through attrition		22	15	43	43		41	38	50	49	37
250	Reduce expenditure for supplies, equipment and travel			31	11	45	21	37	59	39	36	37
229	Obtain additional intergovernmental revenues				55		25	39	45	20	34	33
228	New local revenues	8	30	2	63	38	15	42	32	25	54	33
233	Sell some assets	22	24	46	14	57		32	13	35	19	30
242	Contract out to private sector		35	6	39	30		22	39	61	27	29
261	Defer maintenance of capital stock	59	9	11	59	36		32	15	13	22	29
247	Freeze wages and salaries		41			8			31	22	22	28

Table 5.1 The 33 austerity strategies, indices of importance and the mean across countries *(continued)*

Var. No.	Strategies	Denmark	Norway	Sweden	Finland	England	Holland	France	Canada	Japan	USA	Mean
257	Keep expenditure increases below inflation		26	27	52	36			5	12	37	28
252	Reduce services funded by revenues	36	9		13				56	28	22	27
260	Purchasing agreements	33	3	15	43	39		56	6	25	25	27
251	Reduce services funded by own revenues	44	14		27				20	32	23	27
255	Eliminate programmes		10	5	34	27	15	9	62	52	26	27
258	Early retirements		2	3	22	36	49		42	23	13	24
235	Increase short-term borrowing		16	37	12	17		35	31	24	19	24
259	Reduce overtime		14	8	15	32			22	24	33	21
234	Defer payments to next year		15		32	42	6	20	27	8	18	21
239	Lay off personnel	26	4	0	30	26	49	4	15	16	30	20
246	Reduce employee compensation		11		22	13			38	13	11	18
241	Contract out services to other units	8	28	7		0			37	5	15	14
240	Shift responsibility to other units of government						4		7	11	16	14
262	Impose controls on new construction to help limit population growth		12	31					13	6	9	9

Source Mouritzen and Nielsen (1988; revised 1992). FAUI surveys of administrative officers in each country.

Sweden seemed a peaceful haven for social democracy and the welfare state as late as 1985, but Swedish localities were changing rapidly. Scholars found quite dramatic results; while few drastic and painful strategies were used in the mid 1980s, the number rose considerably into the 1990s (Figure 5.2).

The Swedes have also sought to incorporate good ideas from abroad. Indeed, in less than a decade, Sweden has dramatically reassessed its commitment to state planning and adopted elements of local market and citizen-driven policy making. It is mounting national experiments with vouchers for citizens to use in purchasing public services, privatising day care (the largest local service and employer) and, in a few localities, as soon as the budget is passed, the council considers bids from private firms for many services.

I note in passing that these same strategy indicators show relatively few changes for US local governments over the 1980s and 1990s, certainly nothing on the scale of the Swedish cities. The system shift in the USA took place a decade earlier, led by the New York fiscal crisis.

These same indicators have been used in Eastern Europe to monitor changes with the rise of democracy there after 1989. In contrast to the USA, monumental change emerges in practically each new survey; turbulence and uncertainty are dramatic (see Bartkowski et al. 1990; Baldersheim et al. 1996; Gabor 1991).

Effects of different strategies? Privatisation/contracting out as critical example

Do market-oriented strategies save money? The claims are clear, especially those of F.A. Hayek and Milton Friedman, but evidence is thin. Miranda (1994) analysed impacts of contracting on expenditures and employment for US cities. His dramatic result is that what matters is *how* cities contract, i.e. with what type of contractor. He compared effects of local government contracting with (1) private firms, (2) other governments (like a regional government), and (3) non-profit organisations (like hospitals). Contracting with private firms or other governments did *not* significantly reduce total city expenditures.

But contracting with non-profit organisations significantly reduced spending in 9 of 12 areas. By contrast, contracting with private firms reduced spending in just one area, and increased it in a second. Contracting with other governments reduced spending in one area, and increased it in three. These data are for spending by city governments. Contracting may have saved them money, but the saving may simply have been used to spend more in that same area on something

76

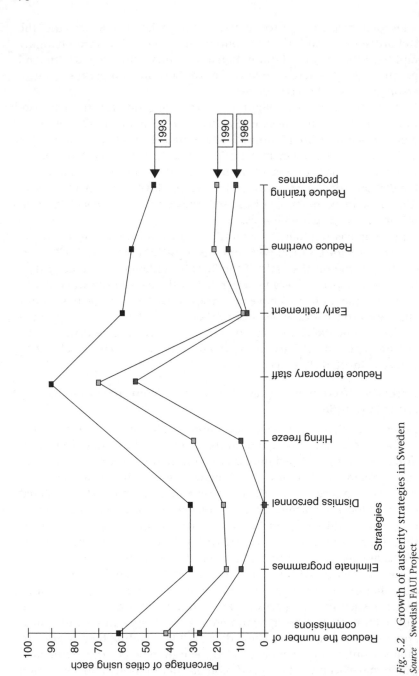

Fig. 5.2 Growth of austerity strategies in Sweden
Source Swedish FAUI Project

else; these data do not permit such discrimination. Indeed, Miranda found that while the number of employees working in each area was cut, their salaries went up with contracting. Thus contracting often lowers staff numbers, especially lower-level staff, while higher-level staff are needed to monitor the new arrangements.

Many theoretical discussions concern preserving competition, and how to police agencies with whom you contract. But Miranda's results suggest that local governments find it costly to police private firms, and often do not trust them. They trust non-profit organisations more, they can and do police them less closely, and save money in the process. Trust saves money. Why? If one contracts with a private hospital that has shown that it wants to provide a service, and has established a good local reputation which it wants to preserve, this trust means that the city government can contract with it and monitor it less. Miranda's results suggest that this approach is more cost-effective and may result in better service than contracting with a private firm. Previously, no one had shown this distinct importance among types of contractors.

Economic development: traditional strategies versus amenities

With cuts in national grants, more fiscal stress and management shifts towards market sensitivity, many local governments seek to expand their tax base. What strategies do they use to seek to encourage economic development? Three types can be distinguished: traditional (tax incentives, land consolidation, etc.); redistributive (minority assistance programmes, etc.); and amenities (historical preservation, sign ordinances, environmental protection, etc.). Many studies report that traditional economic incentive strategies work only weakly (Walzer and P'ng 1984). Instead, amenities are increasingly recognised as critical. Efforts to improve the 'quality of life', via festivals, bicycle paths or culture are recognised increasingly as central for economic development. Amenities are Samuelson-type public goods; they do not disappear the way a payment to one firm does if the firm goes bankrupt. Amenities benefit all firms as well as citizens in the area. They often enhance local distinctiveness (architecture, waterfront, etc.) in ways that differentiate the locality rather than just make it cheaper for one business. If many localities adopt amenity strategies, one should find fewer zero-sum conflicts. Even less developed countries are discovering the huge value of clean vacation areas (across Latin America), and historic sites (China, etc.), which rise in salience with global tourism.

More attention to amenities flows from the gradual recognition that people choose their place of residence often *before or simultaneous with* their choice of job. No longer is the prime mover the job-seeking migrant from rural areas. This still continues for some jobs, especially lower positions. But increasingly important is a new pattern illustrated by students who, for example, move to San Diego to surf, stay a year, find jobs and begin to invest in small businesses. Perhaps extreme, they illustrate the more fundamental points that nowadays personal moves increasingly come first and jobs second. Urban economist Richard Muth has traced this pattern with simulation equation models which show that the path from jobs to people is sometimes weaker than that from people to jobs (Clark and Ferguson 1983; Clark et al. 1986). Both types of migration are statistically important.

Taking this logic one step further leads to the question of whether economic growth brings disamenities. Some cities answer yes, and have adopted local government policies of growth control, reversing normal pro-growth policies. There is very little work on such policies, but San Francisco shows that even a major city can limit the number of skyscrapers to one or two a year, and impose strict controls on all building, stressing environmental and aesthetic concerns like shadows from high buildings. These concerns are traditionally ignored by most US cities in their quest for growth. But in San Francisco, these preservationist policies emerged from the persistent activities of anti-growth groups, via protest demonstrations, and especially lawsuits which the courts have begun to support. Growth controls have been much publicised in areas such as Orange County, California, and nationally, 26 per cent of US cites had an 'anti-growth group' present in 1989. By the Presidential campaign of 2000, 'suburban sprawl' was the first issue seriously addressed by candidate Al Gore.

Ed Goetz and I completed five case studies of cities that were national leaders in limiting growth. We then analysed our US national data and found broadly similar patterns (Clark 1994c). We tested four classes of hypotheses. Two were not supported, those concerning capitalism and competition, and strong business leadership. That there is so much growth control in capitalistic America partially contradicts the first hypothesis. Second, several business leadership measures also consistently showed no impact on local government policies of growth control. This contradicts widespread theories which suggest that business regimes or 'growth machines' dominate American cities, pressing them to grow. Rather, we found support for two other hypotheses. Organised groups played an important role in political mobilisation; having an anti-growth movement in a city was a major factor in explaining adoption of growth control policy. Also supported was our political culture hypothesis. Growth controls are more common in cities where citizens were younger, more highly educated, and were professionals working in high tech fields. Such citizens support a distinct set of preferences – a New Political Culture that stresses consumption and lifestyle issues rather more than traditional workplace and economic production issues. The adherents of the New Political Culture value amenities and pursue them in an activist manner (in waste recycling, bicycle paths, and growth control, etc.).

A New Political Culture

Where and why do policies like user fees and growth controls emerge? This section addresses the paradigm question raised at the outset by stressing that it is not just our theories that have changed, but also the rules of the game by which cities operate. Just as elected officials have had to shift their paradigms to win elections and govern, so do urban analysts need new theories as old paradigms crack.

Small innovations can be smuggled in by anyone – staff, a mayor or council member – with just lukewarm support of other participants. But major policy changes seldom emerge without a shift in political leadership: a new mayor and council majority, committed to new policy directions. Schneider and Teske (1992) report that in over 1000 US cities, 43 per cent of major policy proposals came from mayors, 26 per cent from city council members, 23 per cent from top staff, and the rest from civic or business leaders. Some 'new rhetoric' is just that. But after they win, leaders with programmes like 'reinventing government' or 'responding to new challenges' are driven not just by their rhetoric, but the media and their supporters, to implement real changes in specific policy outputs.

One major development, termed the 'New Fiscal Populist' in Clark and Ferguson (1983), found great resistance among political commentators and analysts to the concept. Resistance was greatest in Europe. In 1983 we organised a conference on 'Questioning the Welfare State and the Rise of the City' at the University of Paris, Nanterre. A forceful and articulate New Fiscal Populist mayor, Bill Morris, mayor of Waukegan, Illinois, talked about his policies. He was a leftist Democrat in background, who had grown conservative on fiscal issues while remaining progressive on social issues of race, gender and the like. He appealed in populist manner to individual citizens – not to traditional parties and organised group leaders. The mayor stressed productivity and improved service delivery to respond to the disadvantaged, while reducing costs to the taxpayer.

In Nanterre, Bill Morris was politely treated as an alien visitor. He might have come from Mars. The French and other European participants clearly felt there was nothing like this on European soil. 'We have a Left and a Right which are far more explicitly defined and consistent with our history.' Still, one participant, Milan political sociologist Guido Martinotti, thought there might be lessons for Italian mayors, and published an article to that effect in the *Corriera della Serra*. A curious phenomenon, but clearly non-European.

Things changed just a year later. A small number of French mayors and younger politicians with national ambitions were making waves. One press account even referred to them as 'the New Mayors'. This is reminiscent of 'the New Philosophers' of years earlier who had similarly broken with the traditional left. Some saw this as a rise of a new right, interesting more for its dynamism and popular success than for any new programme. There was much ferment on both right and left. But a decade later, the clear importance and popular appeal of many new types of leaders are increasingly recognised, in France and around the world. By the 1990s hundreds of mayors and national leaders articulated new themes: from Blair, Schroeder and Clinton nationally, to mayors of the largest three US cities, Giuliani, Daley and Riordan, to new mayors who revolutionised Italian politics in the 1990s, from Genoa's Mayor Sansa in the north to Mayor Orlando of Palermo in the south (Clark 1999).

A New Political Culture is emerging, but its recognition is long overdue – largely because many intelligent persons wear analytical lenses which do not focus on it. Class politics is not dead, but increasingly inadequate. Clientelism is also weakening in many locations. Social stratification is expressed in new ways. Class never explained all the variance, yet was often the 'best tool in the tool box' and seemed adequate from the late nineteenth to mid-twentieth century. Since the 1970s, new non-class cleavages have emerged concerning gender, race, regional loyalty, sexual preference, ecology and broader citizen participation. These social issues are distinct from fiscal/economic issues. They may even cost government nothing; they concern new social patterns, lifestyles – cultural norms about how people should live. Most social issues began earlier, but their cumulative combination brings a fundamental change, a New Political Culture. The New Political

Culture is distinct in seven key respects and we now consider each in turn.

1. *The classic left–right dimension has been transformed.* People still speak of left and right, but definitions are changing. Left increasingly means social issues, less often traditional class politics issues. In Eastern Europe the polarity of left and right so changed that in the late 1980s the term 'left' sometimes referred to those who support increasing private ownership and *less* state intervention in the economy. The change is less dramatic in the West, but increasing the role of government is no longer automatically equated with progress, even on the left; and the most intensely disputed issues no longer deal with ownership and control of the means of production. Many leaders, and citizens, feel disoriented by the shifting meaning of the left–right map.
2. *Social and fiscal/economic issues are explicitly distinguished.* Social issues demand analysis in their own terms. They are not just 'ideological superstructure' or 'false consciousness'. Correspondingly, positions on social issues – of citizens, leaders, and parties – cannot be derived solely from their positions on fiscal issues. Note that we do *not* define 'social issues' as expensive welfare state programmes, although some people do. Rather, we focus more on issues like tolerance for new women's roles or multiculturalism, and other items measured in many citizen surveys on social tolerance. To say that social and fiscal issues should be analytically distinguished does not imply that they do not overlap empirically. Social issues can have fiscal implications – such as providing extra funding for minority students. But social issues can also be pursued with *no* fiscal implications, such as appointing more women and minority lawyers as federal judges. By contrast, the class politics model implies the opposite: (1) fiscal issues dominate social issues, (2) social issue positions derive from fiscal issue positions, and (3) specifically the left is liberal on social and fiscal issues, and the right is conservative. The new New Political Culture pattern is replacing the older class politics due to more general socio-economic differentiation and professionalisation; correlations between fiscal and social liberalism are in decline.
3. *Social issues have risen in salience relative to fiscal/economic issues.* This change is driven by affluence: as wealth increases, people grow more concerned with lifestyle and other amenity issues – in addition to classic economic concerns. Recognition of these changes spurred

some neo-Marxists to rethink socialist theory (e.g. Bowles and Gintis 1987; Harrington 1989). New Fiscal Populism was earlier defined as including fiscal conservatism as it was so clearly central; the New Political Culture does not include fiscal conservatism as a defining element because of the relative decline of fiscal issues relative to social issues, and since not all of the New Political Culture is fiscally conservative.

4. *Market individualism and social individualism grow.* Neither market nor social individualism implies a return to tradition; indeed the New Political Culture is most clearly opposed to the statist European right. Both individualisms foster scepticism towards traditional left policies, such as nationalisation of industry and welfare state growth. But the New Political Culture joins 'market liberalism' (in the past narrowly identified with parties of the right), with 'social progressiveness' (often identified with parties of the left). This new *combination of policy preferences* leads to new programmes, and new rules of the game.

5. *Questioning the welfare state.* Some New Political Culture citizens, and leaders, conclude that 'governing' in the sense of state-central planning is unrealistic for many services – economic and social. While not seeking to reduce services, they question specifics of service delivery and seek to improve efficiency. They are sceptical of large central bureaucracies. They are willing to decentralise administration or contract with other governments or private firms – if these work better. 'Work better' includes citizen responsiveness as well as meeting professional staff criteria. In difficult economic times – like the 1970s stagflation – the New Political Culture can become fiscally conservative. But the culture is clearly far from the traditional right (e.g. Reagan, Thatcher) that focuses on simply cutting government, and services.

Many observers feel that local governments can serve the public better than nation states. This leads to efforts to develop smaller and more responsive governments and new intergovernmental agreements. This happened in the USA and many other countries in the 1980s and 1990s. In the USA, non-profit organisations have taken a far more visible role, even shaping government policies in their own image, such as in health, education and social service provision. In Eastern Europe local governments are enjoying a renaissance, especially in small towns that had been abolished in the past few decades. Many US cities are criticising their existing service delivery modes and experimenting with such alternative patterns of service delivery as contracting out services, using new technology and the like. Neighbourhood governments, block clubs and other such associations are emerging the world over, simultaneous with declines in turnout and interest in national elections. This new decentralisation and volatility may be more citizen responsive, but it causes problems for provision of large public goods, like national defence or coherent national policies. The new character of leadership and decision making is thus open to criticism by many intellectuals and displaced political leaders. Sometimes these opponents have been successful in displacing initial New Political Culture leaders in Eastern Europe and Italy in the 1990s.

6. *The rise of issue politics and broader citizen participation; the decline of hierarchical political organisations.* The New Political Culture counters traditional bureaucracies, parties and their leaders. 'New Social Movements' and 'issue politics' are essential additions to the political process. These movements encourage governments to respond more directly to interested constituents. By contrast, traditional hierarchical parties, government agencies and unions are seen as antiquated. New demands are articulated by activists and intelligent citizens, who refuse treatment as docile 'subjects' or 'clients'. They thus organise around new issues of welfare state service provision, like daycare or recycling paper. The media grow more visible and important, as new issues and developments rapidly emerge and frequently change, making New Political Culture leadership often volatile and turbulent. New groups seek to participate in general policy formation (rivalling parties and programmes); and may press to participate in service delivery (rivalling government agencies, clientelist leaders, and unions). Advocates of the New Political Culture are thus seen as 'rocking the boat'; they mean to. Conflicts with traditional particularistic leaders whose political support depends on clientelist patronage are particularly acute – for example, such as in southern Italy or Chicago.

7. *These new views are more pervasive among younger, more educated and affluent individuals, and societies.* The New Political Culture has emerged with basic changes in the economy and the family, and is both encouraged and diffused by less social and economic hierarchy, broader value consensus and spread of the mass media.

Space limits elaboration, but the transformation we describe with mayors and the New Political Culture is also profoundly changing the roles and dynamics of parties, organised groups, staff and citizens. It implies a weaker role for at least traditional political parties, unions and organised groups, and a stronger role for citizens, the media, and outside experts who can encourage policy innovations. Traditional 'class politics' was undercut by a shift towards fiscal conservatism by left parties like the Italian, Spanish and East European communists. Similarly, dozens of socialist leaders around the world have shifted towards market and citizen-responsive themes, and away from state central planning, with Bill Clinton and Tony Blair continuing this pattern. We do not posit the same changes everywhere, but specify characteristics likely to promote or retard this New Political Culture. For instance, socio-economic hierarchy should maintain class politics; but as hierarchies, the New Political Culture should grow. Figure 5.3 shows how we mapped these processes with data for some 7000 FAUI cities in 20 countries. For instance, cities with fewer blue-collar and more professional workers have more female mayors and weaker political parties, which support more socially progressive issues like abortion and sex education.

At the mayoral level, big city mayors in the USA like Giuliani in New York, Daley in Chicago and Riordan in Los Angeles all articulate these new themes, even though only Daley is a Democrat; all three stress management specifics and details on *how* rather than they *why* do things. (How to reduce crime? What makes buses cheaper to operate? How to attract more tourists?) This new style of pragmatic implementation is more common in the USA and many northern European countries. By contrast, the new mayors of Italy in the 1990s share many of the same policy outlooks, but they are rather more ideological and sometimes charismatic than their predecessors – due largely to their being elected directly rather than chosen from party caucuses. Leaders such as Blair proposed similar direct elections in England in the late 1990s, perhaps to help reinforce the New over the Old Labour approach, as the new seems more popular with citizens (Hambleton 2000). Similar efforts to change legal patterns and all manner of governance procedures to respond more to citizens are found in democracies around the globe in the 1990s. These themes are elaborated in two books and related work (Clark and Rempel 1997; Clark and Hoffmann-Martinot 1998; Clark et al. 1993).

Globalisation spreads the New Political Culture. Western-oriented media diffuse egalitarian themes and undercut hierarchy in news as well as (even more?) entertainment, from rock music to Hollywood movies and TV soaps. Social criticism has mounted across the USA via advocacy journalists from the *New York Times* to CNN. The media grow

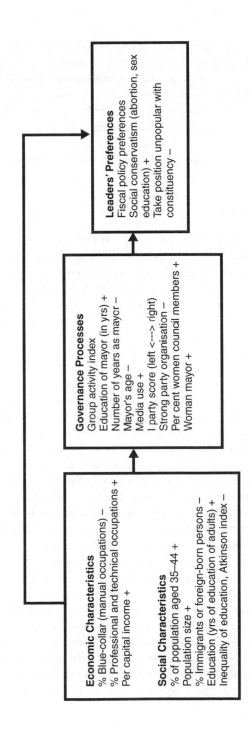

Fig. 5.3 Global model of processes generating the New Political Culture

Notes: A plus sign after a variable indicates that a higher value on it measures or should encourage the New Political Culture. Three variables have no signs as their effects are more complex. I party is the International political party score ranging from conservative to liberal on a 0–100 scale, based on expert judgements and citizen self-placement (Clark and Hoffmann-Martinot 1998, pp. 179ff)

Source Variables from the Fiscal Austerity and Urban Innovation (FAUI) Project. Data are incomplete for some countries. More detail is in Clark and Hoffmann-Martinot (1998, Ch. 4)

more central as global interpreters, and links to new ideas for political actors – as traditional left and right parties decline. Markets similarly rise with globalisation, which undercuts clientelist economic and political foundations of competing political styles. The internet takes these tendencies one step further, empowering potentially each individual citizen to access a world of information. From students around Tienanmen Square to cyber cafés in Warsaw, the internet offers a vast expansion of contacts and a source of critique of the traditional and local.

Citizens: a new active role

A core component of the New Political Culture is the rise of citizens. This is a major trend around the world, as pressures towards more egalitarian democracy increase. Our FAUI survey asked mayors and council members about their views of citizens and citizen inputs to government. One revealing item asks how often leaders 'vote against the preferences of the majority of their constituents'. Leaders most likely to vote against citizens were those in pre-1989 Poland and in Italy – governments which subsequently collapsed. The most citizen-responsive mayors were in Israel (Figure 5.4).

How can we capture citizen preferences? The major political movement of the late 1970s in the USA was the taxpayer's revolt, illustrated by Proposition 13 passed in 1978 in California, which cut property taxes (e.g. on all individual homes) by about half. Its passage shocked most observers, and spurred questions as to how widespread such opinions were among citizens. Most contemporaneous studies (e.g. Mushkin 1979 and Lipset and Raab 1979) concluded that citizens really wanted more, not less, spending. But these studies were flawed, as they omitted a budget constraint. They simply asked citizens do you want more, less or the same services, or a variation of this question. Most citizens naturally answer more. This was an area where public choice theory could sharpen survey analysis. The simple idea was to use a budget pie format in an interview, for instance, saying here is the total budget of your government. Can you please show us how you would cut each piece? Or you can make the whole pie larger (which would imply increasing taxes)? The pie format acts as a budget constraint in that it forces one slice to be smaller if another is larger, and citizens can see this directly. Result: more fiscally conservative answers. And more realistic answers, closer to how citizens vote in referenda (Clark 1974). A further specification adds information on the cost of each

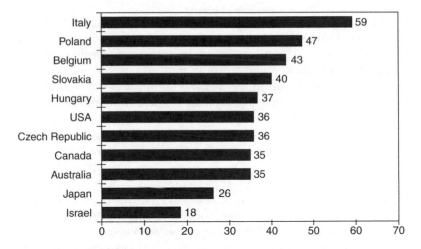

Fig. 5.4   Citizen responsiveness by local officials varies across countries
Note   These are national averages for mayors and council members to the question:
'Sometimes elected officials believe that they should take policy positions which are
unpopular with the majority of their constituents. About how often would you estimate
that you took a position against the dominant opinion of your constituents?' Responses:
0 = never or almost never 25 = only rarely 50 = about once a month 75 = more than once a
month 100 = regularly
Source   Fiscal Austerity and Urban Innovation Project surveys by national teams; most
surveys conducted 1985 to 1988; Czech Republic, Hungary and Slovakia in 1990 to 1992

service; the result is that more information leads citizens to answer
more conservatively (Simonson 1994).

Decentralisation, metropolitan government and local democracy

Several paradigms intersect here. Two types conflict: first, those paradigms focused on economic 'efficiency', favouring big government,
versus, second, those concerned more with democracy, favouring small
government. First the pro-big government views. In the 1950s the 'suburban exploitation thesis' emerged, suggesting that suburbs exploit
their central cities by using them for jobs and shopping, but not
paying taxes, hence exploiting them fiscally (Hawley 1951; Kasarda
1976), although other more precise work doubted even the fiscal
results (Neenan 1972). Suburbs have also been blamed for taking jobs
from central city poor (Kasarda 1985; Wilson 1987). Service delivery
costs are raised, some hold, since suburbs are too small to realise

'economies of scale' that metropolitan government permits. And suburban population growth undermines the central city tax base (ACIR
1976; Hawley and Zimmer 1970). Metropolitan government is the
solution commonly proposed to these multiple problems. Note the
dependence of this 'solution' on a key assumption: each central city
and its suburbs are a (semi) closed system, isolated from other locations
across the nation and the world. As national and global interdependence rises, all theories and policy prescriptions assuming isolated metropolitan areas grow increasingly inadequate. People and firms now
move out and subcontract out more easily. These national and global
changes undermine many metro-type analyses.

Globalisation undercuts nations, but spurs localities. Just as citizens
have grown more legitimate, so have local governments. In many countries, national governments have delegated more powers, if not money,
to local levels in the last decade. This reverses the tendency of the 1960s
and 1970s, which was to centralise in regional authorities planned and
controlled by national governments (e.g. in France and Italy). But the
most dramatic cases are in East Europe, where like West European
national governments, communists found small, local governments
troublesome. So they abolished many in the 1960s. But in 1989, one of
the very first major actions following restoration of democracy, was
restoration of small local governments. Local governments in Hungary
and Czechoslovakia, for example, doubled in number.

The country where local governments are most 'oppressed' by
national government has been the UK. Margaret Thatcher vigorously
decentralised many policies to individual citizens and public authorities, but often not to general purpose 'local authorities', since many
were controlled by Labour Party councils. This continues the Anglo-
Saxon tradition of strong individualism derived from Adam Smith's
writings, countering the organic continental conception of local community life, *Die Gemeinschaft* from Toennies. In past decades this atom-
istic individualism facilitated consolidating small local governments
more than in other countries, so that Britain today has large metropolitan governments, including central cities as well as suburbs. Local
policy makers in countries like France and the USA who look to 'metropolitan government' as a solution to urban problems should examine
the British case closely. Many British observers lament that local
democracy has been substantially undermined since metropolitanisa-
tion (Chandler and Clark 1995).

Do local governments foster democratic participation as Tocqueville
long ago proclaimed? Probably. But specifics clearly vary from place to

place. The most citizen-responsive country seems not to be America, but Switzerland. It has no national government at all, rather a federation of cantons; charismatic leaders are so distrusted that few communes have mayors. Instead they have 'executives' comprised of several council members who keep out of the press. Council members regularly consult with citizens, in cafés, on street corners, in offices. In council meetings, the major organised groups are officially represented in many committees. But unlike France, the USA or most countries where they aggressively pursue narrow interests, groups are constrained by a frequently used instrument: the referendum. In Switzerland the referendum has become so regular a part of the policy-making process that it is used for annual budgets in many communes. On salient public issues, the threat of a referendum constrains many pressure groups to consider broader interests, like those of taxpayers, and not just increase spending for the most active groups as in most other countries. For these reasons, Switzerland had much lower taxes than almost anywhere in Europe (Jeanrenaud and Clark 1989). The Swiss can help us by comparing their own patterns more internationally to help spread their messages of citizen empowerment, regional government and democratic decision making. Tocqueville missed Switzerland, but policy analysts could still discover it.

Conclusion: an illustrative general proposition

What reformulations are implied for the paradigms with which we began? Our review suggests that globalisation is transforming urban dynamics. Specifically:

1. *Land use and land value analyses* have seen concentric zones and density gradients diminish in power with global markets for goods, services and subcontracting of production by firms. Residents conceived as consumers have grown more important, and their amenity concerns often lead them to exurban-type locations, rather than central areas. Amenities like mountains and vistas thus rise in explanatory power of land values.

2. *The growth machine* has declined in many locations, as production and jobs have been superseded by consumption and lifestyle decisions. This shift is clear in the issues stressed by political candidates and in citizen surveys of salient issues. 'Human capital' concerns reinforce a focus on public education even for large employers. Anti-growth machines, environmentalists of all sorts, pursuing amenity

agendas become visible political actors. They reinforce related changes in the political rules of the game. Cities are decreasingly growth machines and increasingly entertainment machines.

3. *Class and race cleavages* are critical in some locations, but politically insignificant in others. This is not an anomaly, but an instance where city contexts provide valuable data for more general theory building. Locations with more working-class persons (in Europe) and more non-whites (in the USA) have more class/race politics and less New Political Culture (as measured by women elected officials, importance of the media, etc.) Hierarchies perpetuate class and racial conflicts; yet as hierarchies decline, so do the old cleavages. Post-class politics is not consensus: new cleavages will arise on new issues, but they are diverse, splitting divisions in numerous directions.

4. *Clientelism (patronage, nepotism)* is declining even in its strongest bastions: Chicago, southern Italy, Ireland and, albeit more slowly, less developed countries. The visible hand of globalisation can be seen operating quite directly here, as international accounting standards and written contracts are forcing Third World subcontractors to accept First World rules against clientelism. World Bank loans in Asia and Russia also come with strong pressures in this direction. This is not to say that clientelism fully disappears, but that more strict market cost pressures help keep it under control. The value of patronage jobs declines as media advertising, polls and other professional activities rise.

5. *Local autonomy has been invigorated* as the critical roles of active citizens and local politics have been rediscovered by leaders from Prague to Mexico, illustrated by works like Putnam (1993, 2000) on Italian regions and civic groups in America. The political culture of local democracy has become a global priority. This has reinforced arguments against 'metropolitan' government in the traditional hierarchical sense, but encouraged voluntary agreements in multiple, distinct service areas among localities near one another. As democracy has spread across virtually the entire globe, its quality is more closely watched and criticised. Federalism is being forged globally.

6. *A New Political Culture is spreading.* Weaknesses in several other paradigms take on meaning in contrast with the emerging New Political Culture. But the complexities of cities and neighbourhoods are far from homogeneity: class and race cleavages endure in some areas, clientelism in others, which stand as clear contrasts to the New Political Culture. Still, what was seen as a short-term aberration by

many a decade or so back, has grown more mainstream. Whatever one's normative views, it is increasingly important to clarify how and why leaders, organised groups and citizens, change their rules as they shift towards the New Political Culture. The volatility of New Political Culture politics, illustrated by the complexities and roller-coaster fluctuations of President Bill Clinton, is a common theme replayed, if less dramatically, in thousands of local governments around the world. With Britain's Blair and Germany's Schroeder following France's Mitterrand, the New Political Culture is clearly not just American and not just local, these were just its roots.

I conclude with a general proposition. If we make the reasonable assumption that uncertainty about citizen preferences should increase with the number and diversity of citizens, then a proposition follows: *larger and higher level governments, ceteris paribus, are less responsive to citizens and more responsive to organised groups.* This should hold across governments: groups should rise over citizens in larger cities compared to small towns, metropolitan governments compared to their subsidiary units, or national and international governments compared to local governments.

The consequence is clear for citizen-based democracy. Over time, leaders in bigger governments, acting with less information and more lobbying pressures from organised groups, are more likely to alienate citizens than are smaller governments. Consequences can be disruptive, like the taxpayers' revolts in the USA in the 1970s (following the turbulence of the late 1960s), or the paralysis of established leaders in Italy in the early 1990s, followed by the rise of anti-government leagues, new parties and candidates. These are just extreme cases; more sensitive survey data on citizen preferences should document variations for more normal local governments.

Similarly, governments like the United Nations and European Union are most apt to be swayed by aggressive and rich pressure groups, and weigh citizen preferences less. Given the huge diversity of citizens under such large entities, responding to them seriously is less possible than for smaller governments. This suggests that as global forces grow, via markets and international governments, local governments and their associated democratic processes should also grow in importance due to local efforts to balance distant global forces. We see this new localism all around us in the last decade, just as we see more globalisation. This chapter has shown how specific components of local democracy and globalisation reinforce one another.

Part 2

Cities at Risk – Challenge and Opportunity

6
Rapid Transformations in Post-Socialist Cities: towards an Uncertain Future

Margaret F. Reid

Introduction

More than a decade after the first major efforts of societal and institutional transformations were launched in former socialist countries of central and Eastern Europe, the outcomes of these systemic changes are far from certain. Budding economic and social structures to support a capitalist system had emerged in virtually all of the central European countries during earlier decades of the twentieth century, but experiences with a civic culture that Western democracies normatively assume as indispensable for the functioning of their societies had evolved only in the most rudimentary ways (Wiatr 1980), and were in any instance seriously diluted, almost eliminated, under the communist regimes of recent years.

On a regional scale, the homogenisation efforts of a Soviet-style system of governance were far from total, however. Traditional historical differences between the countries of central and Eastern Europe (Poland, Hungary, the Czech Republic, Slovakia, Slovenia, Romania, the Baltic countries and to some extent the former German Democratic Republic, GDR) are beginning to re-emerge (Wollmann 1994). This must dampen any expectations that a single political or economic approach can be advanced to explain the transformation from a state-led to a market-based political economy in these countries.

Without proper regard for the political and social changes still ongoing, the economic responses of cities to these challenges cannot be fully appreciated. While a number of excellent assessments of the transformations of urban areas are available, a compelling normative model has as yet to be advanced (Baldersheim 1996; Coulson 1995; Wollmann 1994).[1] To evaluate the transformations solely on their economic merits would disregard the ideological legacies of the state-planned systems and overestimate the transformational and integrative capabilities of rational economic forces that some models are premised on (Sachs 1990).

The chapter adopts Poznanski's (1993) contention that the restructuring process is an evolutionary one, just as the former communist regimes were not impervious to changes (Eichwede 1994; Szücs 1990). In the same vein, taking advantage of opportunities as a result of the reforms will depend on a host of factors. The governments' ability to strengthen civic institutions, and thus trust in the newly formed regimes, hinges to a great extent on the development of capacities of the national and local governments to modernise their physical and social infrastructures after decades of neglect under state socialism.

While most countries in central and Eastern Europe have made considerable strides in transforming their economic structures, the institutional and social changes to *sustain* these changes and to strengthen fledgling democratic institutions are quite a different matter (Kaminski 1991; Hankiss 1990; Swianiewicz 1996; Setnikar-Cankar 1998). The resulting strains and divisions in those societies coupled with nascent political and social institutional restructuring have already resulted in widespread disaffection with the changes after the initial euphoria over the transformation subsided (Ferge 1996). Therefore, both national political culture and political institutions and various aspects of local governmental systems must be considered in order to appreciate and understand the differences in the emerging styles of local governance (Pickvance and Preteceille 1991). Finally, to compound the complexities of the domestic challenges, these countries are now also fully exposed to international market dynamics for which their decision makers are insufficiently prepared.[2]

This chapter addresses the issue of how former socialist countries (excluding Russia from these discussions) have responded to these challenges. The chapter opens with a brief synopsis of the conditions predating the transformation. Changes that appear to a non-expert observer as revolutionary were preceded by efforts of the communist regimes to inject reformist elements. The chapter advances the argument that the interpretation of these prior conditions is critical to the analysis of choices available to national and local decision makers. As the institution-building processes are still in flux, it is impossible to project success or failure in individual countries. An important related issue is how forces of internationalisation can be harnessed without further exacerbating a tense domestic situation. Those who claim that processes of 'globalisation' are bound to force these countries to 'reform' themselves more quickly, are oblivious to the systemic inertia that does not favour a rapid process (Ickes 1990; Szablowski and Derlien 1993; Reid 1999). Established elites and institutions will make accommodations with the new systems, but will also continue to rely on their networks of friends and suppliers to maintain their positions. The chapter concludes with an attempt to synthesise some key criteria that can assist in assessing the capacities of local governments to deal with these challenges. The argument is predicated on the assumption that the role of cities in the rebuilding of their countries must be viewed in a differentiated fashion; not all cities and towns are equally situated in dealing with these problems nor will their responses be the same.

From state socialism to capitalist accumulation regimes

Models of transformation for the countries under discussion have not been fully developed (Szablowski and Derlien 1993; Riese 1995). Even fewer studies are devoted to the effects of these changes on urban areas, certainly an integral, if not determining, factor in these change processes. Even the term 'local government' is not easily translated (Coulson, 1995, p. 1), and often has no direct counterpart in many newly formed institutional frameworks. In all of these countries local elections are now held on a regular basis, but local self-governance is still in a nascent state.

The reasons for the relative neglect of urban areas in the transformation process are twofold. One is the previous subordination of local administrations to the central state and the attendant absence of independent political and economic decision-making mechanisms. The other is the ideological emphasis of Western-inspired reforms advocating the adoption of a market system in which the city would emerge as one of many rational economic actors in a global market place (Lambooy and Moulaert 1996). Those who look to cities to emerge from this era of neglect have favoured 'shock therapy'. Poland adopted such an approach and German reunification imposed a rapid economic transformation on the former GDR. Those advocating such an approach have contended that it minimises not only suffering for the citizens but also the chances for entrenched apparatchiks to sabotage the process of marketisation (Kemme 1991; Frydman and Rapaczynski

1994). The legitimacy of the new regimes in the eyes both of their citizens and of foreign investors will thus be increased by quickly establishing the requisite institutional conditions in which trade and investments can flourish (Wagner 1993; König 1993; Wollmann 1997).

Poznanski (1993) argues, however, that such contentions fail to recognise that some of the socialist regimes in central and Eastern Europe had been experimenting with reforms long before the eventual collapse of their systems. Many of these reforms were resisted or only partially implemented. Yet each reform cycle contributed to the weakening of state control over the system. In the end, the state's inability to reform socialist planned systems contributed to the ultimate collapse of socialist regimes. A second argument against the likely success of shock approaches rests in the question of who or what can steer such a complex process. The difficulties of the German *Treuhandanstalt*, a privatisation agency created in the wake of unification and charged with disposing of eastern German state property, illustrates the problems with such an approach (Donges 1991; Reid 1999). Finally, another point needs to be mentioned. Socialism engendered different responses in all of these countries; indeed socialism itself experienced different developments in all of these countries (Prybyla 1990). The countries discussed here had some prior experience with market systems, experimented with democracy movements, and most certainly have had vibrant larger cities throughout their histories with rich civic and commercial traditions (i.e. strong local and cultural identities).

Challenges confronting urban areas

Conceptually, what constitutes effective urban governance in Western countries has undergone some significant changes in the 1990s (Peters 1996). Gaffkin and Warf (1993) postulate that conservative 'post-Keynesian' policies (including among others a retreat of the state from economic management, privatisation of welfare functions, heavier reliance on deregulated markets instead of public planning) have clear urban policy implications. Their effects on US cities have been well documented in the literature (Keating 1991; Goetz and Clarke 1993; Judge et al. 1995; Pierre 1997). New public management (NPM), in a complementary fashion, advocates devolution of national responsibilities to lower levels of governments (Pollitt 1990) and a 'substitution of economic for social criteria for development' (Gaffkin and Warf 1993, p. 77). The NPM, however, is silent on the issue of the role to be accorded to democratic principles and citizen participation (Frohlich and Oppenheimer 1997). Furthermore, it is doubtful if these policy components can be successful or sufficient if links between organisational and geographic, technological, demographic and economic forces are not explored.

As many international funding agencies increasingly mirror these post-Keynesian approaches, transformation processes thus place extreme demands on urban elected and appointed officials (Coulson 1995). Germany's reunification was largely inspired by similar criteria, and many of the same post-Keynesian blueprints have found their way into urban policy preferences in post-socialist cities elsewhere (Swianiewicz 1996). Many cities initially embarked on extravagant spending programmes, in many cases exceeding by far what they could reasonably expect from their central governments or what they were able to raise from their own sources (Baldersheim 1996; see e.g. Eichwede 1994 and Szücs 1990).[3] The socialist legacy of central party control of all aspects of governance is difficult to shake (Owen 1994). Consolidation of very small communities for the purpose of creating greater administrative efficiencies was rejected in many countries throughout the region, especially in the initial phase (Coulson 1995). In a few years, many cities began to realise that these freedoms were accompanied by significant sacrifices (Ferge 1996). Struggles between the central and the local governments for control over fiscal decisions, struggles to improve housing and social services (many of which were low-priority items under the former communist regimes, despite the official socialist rhetoric), and uncertainty how best to encourage local business activities are typical examples of quandaries shared across the region (Myant 1995).

Socialist regimes intent on rapid growth created a system of forced industrialisation, sometimes in very remote regions. Industrial monostructures with intense vertical integration 'created significant power bases in core enterprises with a satellite system of branch plants in more peripheral regions' (Smith 1995, p. 763). Capitalist accumulation regimes, however, tend to favour more diversified and self-supporting economies. In Slovakia where both arrangements existed in the late 1980s, it was the latter that made the successful transition to a market-based system and are now experiencing lower unemployment rates as well (Smith 1995).

A major break with communist-era policies has been the reintroduction of private property rights as a central component of establishing market systems in these countries. Theoretical discussions about preferred methods of privatisation aside, most countries have chosen a gradual transfer of assets (Poznanski 1993; Frydman and Rapaczynski 1994; Reid 1999). Even under the most favourable of conditions (as in eastern Germany), the process has lasted a decade. Residual assets remain unsold and some property restitution cases continue to languish in the courts. Similar situations are found in neighbouring countries (Frydman and Rapaczynski 1994).

The challenges of increased autonomy and internationalisation

New opportunity structures are emerging that should provide these transforming urban systems with avenues to strengthen their political independence while rendering them more competitive with other cities in the larger Euro-Asian region (Clarke and Gaile 1997). The question is what can those cities do to counter strategically the forces of exclusion and polarisation as a result of the new political and economic structures while also taking advantage of access to regional and international markets. Specific strategic choice behaviour can only be determined on the basis of sophisticated analysis of local and regional institutions and their capacities, and surveys of local decision makers in these countries (Clarke 1989). In their absence we can, however, outline available strategies and their likelihood of success based on factors known to exist.

One of the more problematic consequences of introducing Western-style institutional arrangements has been the emergence of new social, spatial and economic schisms. Despite the socialist egalitarian ideology, all of the region's old regimes had targeted selected urban and regional development programmes through their planning mechanism (Gorzelak and Szul 1989). Planning occurred in a top-down fashion but often with little inter-regional or inter-sectoral coordination and only nominal citizen participation was undertaken. Linkages to other planning efforts in the technological, social and economic areas were not always successful. Consequently, shortages in housing, economic development breakdowns, and inadequacies in social service delivery were quite common (Pensley 1995).

In the abstract, the transformation promised cities greater decision-making autonomy. In many of the countries comprehensive legislation to re-establish local autonomy was quickly passed but without much concern for the division of labour between central and local governments. Poland, for example, abolished traditional intermediate governing authorities (*powiaty*).[4] Some eastern German states preferred not to re-establish intermediate administrative districts (Coulson 1995, pp. 18–19). These may be temporary phenomena, and as historic institutions are rediscovered and the need for intermediate or regional co-ordinating devices recognised, some of these decisions may be reversed.

It is the unresolved issue of equity versus administrative efficiency, however, that has placed many local government officials in a quandary (Owen 1994; Fabian and Straussman 1994). The opportunity for dialogue between citizens and elected officials in the many towns and villages may conflict with pressures from national and international actors to spur on the progress towards a market economy. Polls in the middle of the 1990s document the pessimism of populations across the region that their economic conditions will soon improve (Rose and Seifert 1995). Persistent funding constraints severely limit options available to all cities, especially in smaller or rural communities. The shift from older forms of industrial production that were typical for many countries of the region, to service and knowledge-based production requires not only a massive infusion of new capital and the revamping of local infrastructure, but also a significant reorientation in the countries' school and educational systems many of which are now local (Myant 1995; Rondinelli et al. 1998). These developments can be illustrated by reference to a number of spatial, social and economic schisms and their consequences for urban areas.

Spatial imbalances

Even with the demise of socialism, the legacy of its institutions lingers. Diversifying the economy and identifying region-specific opportunities is the largest challenge facing these countries and their cities (Gorzelak 1992; Blazek and Kara 1992; Smith 1995). The resulting migration of populations to new places with better employment potential, schools or social services is coupled with rising unemployment in smaller towns or areas with low productivity or competitiveness of traditional socialist industrial sectors. It is thus quite important to examine the urban areas in a disaggregated fashion to develop a full appreciation of the effects of the transformation on various types of communities, especially the development of medium and intermediate size cities in their roles as potential regional growth centres. These cities are distinct from their larger cousins (City of Speyer 1990; Leimbrock 1997).

However, if they are to serve as engines for economic growth, their administrative and fiscal capacities must be strengthened to offer a range of services commensurate with such a role. They are small enough to retain a cultural and social identity for their citizens. Leimbrock (1997) notes that medium-sized cities are often assumed to be 'big cities in waiting', if only they were endowed with appropriate resources. His discussion of transforming eastern German cities, however, clearly shows that many of them lack both regional and economic advantages typical of the larger cities. Even when propped up by external funding, they lack the diversity, the economic and administrative capacities to serve such a role. Medium-sized cities need to find a niche in their region that matches their abilities to innovate and to grow while addressing the needs of local populations for participation and inclusion in political decision making. This being said, it must be noted that cities of this size are rarely considered in the discussions by urbanists. They are vital, however, as a reservoir of innovation and have a potential for strong civic identity formation.

Social exclusion

A second emerging schism in the newly transformed countries involves the social realm. One of the more noteworthy consequences of the transformation is the increased exclusion of women from economic and political life, the other is the potential for severe ethnic strife (Ladanyi 1993). The curtailment of civil and political rights in many of the socialist countries coupled with a strong welfare state produced a hollow state: '... In the absence of rights and entitlements, the individual members of society could not become *citizens* and active agents, but remained *subjects*' (Ferge 1996, p. 104). The formation of a new civil society produces an interesting dilemma: the absence, or slow emergence, of a third sector that could perform some social services and address a strong expectation of citizens for the delivery of social services (Eisen 1996). Local social service agencies are central to the speed and direction of the transformation as they serve as potential bridge builders between the old and the new systems (Backhaus-Maul 1993).

One of the more disconcerting developments in the larger cities, however, is the undefined role of women in the new social systems of central Europe. In many countries, women's organisations contributed to the system transformation in the 1980s and early 1990s, with eastern Germany being a case in point (Kamenitsa 1997; Einhorn 1991). After the initial changes, these groups have been less activist or they have been marginalised. With limited financial resources, a political agenda that demanded more rather than fewer social services, and a prolonged economic recession, many groups now find themselves isolated in a corporatist economic and political structure. Those groups that were able to adjust have found ways to attract governmental or private resources to the point that they have served as models for their less activist Western counterparts (Kamenitsa 1997).

Economic transformational challenges

Economic challenges resulting from the regime transformations are twofold. One is domestic, the other international. Both result in differential impacts on urban populations and businesses. Taking advantage of international economic opportunities does not occur in a policy or institutional vacuum. It is closely tied to the ability of national and local governments to mobilise and focus resources that are already scarce. Moreover, all governments have to be sensitive to the effects of such reforms on large portions of the working-age population that constitute the majority of potential voters. Societies are not malleable entities, but they are the result of long-standing historical processes and experiences that tend to shape their willingness to embrace innovations more or less willingly or energetically (Szücs 1990). Socialist administrations and public actors did not have to deal with pluralist interest constellations, or be concerned about stakeholders or other external actors (Möller and Reissig 1996). The differential speed with which reforms have been accepted, even among elites, across central European countries is clear evidence of this contention.

Relationships between public and private economic agents that are now typical for Western urban settings are still viewed with some suspicion. Many cities have difficulties in developing long-range plans because of acute shortages in material and human resources that demand their constant attention. In the same vein, local political and administrative actors, initially emboldened by what they might have viewed as unlimited opportunities, have been forced to curtail their expectations. Central European local actors must find definitions of their problems that reflect and blend their own past experiences with the expectations of domestic and foreign investors. Thus, the ability to take advantage of the international opportunities is limited in many ways. It is cities that are advantaged by spatial and capacity advantages that are likely to be the primary beneficiaries of international markets.

The neglect under socialist regimes both of domestic infrastructure and of the less well-known cultural artefacts and heritage sites limits the ability of transforming economies to develop a flourishing tourism industry – often seen as a quick way to attract foreign currency. Administrators face the unenviable task of trying to perform a kind of 'cultural triage' in an effort to ascertain what to preserve or refurbish and what to destroy to make way for new economic ventures. Preserving the identity of local places in the aftermath of socialism can be vital to restoring residents' belief in a future for their country, an opportunity to become actively involved with their communities.

In sum, economic activities cannot be viewed in isolation from other social policies and political institution-building efforts. To do so would certainly risk the deepening of already existing social and political fault lines. Traditional liberal economic models are predicated on individual preferences rather than central control or communal decision making. In the absence of fully formed institutions to channel individual social and economic choice behaviour, societal fragmentation cannot be overcome by any advantages that governments, businesses or communities might seek from involvement in international economic activities.

Assessment of future opportunities

The opportunity structures and problems discussed above are by no means equally distributed among all municipalities. Case studies and other research that have accumulated over the 1990s clearly indicate that uniform prescriptions are by no means justified. While the problems as outlined affect more or less all the transforming societies, neither the degree nor the type of responses can be identical. A framework for future development needs to incorporate at least two policy dimensions: a domestic policy dimension and an international competitiveness dimension.

Differentiation along a domestic policy axis

This policy arena must address the *development of internal capacities* to deal with the ongoing changes: administrative–legal, political–democratic and economic. The new political environment of the late 1990s makes resolution of these issues even more complex, as the political coalitions that were instrumental in initiating the changes are beginning to crumble. Poland's most promising efforts towards a civic society and openness towards international markets began to disintegrate quickly by mid-decade (Tatur 1995). Privatisation policies in post-*Solidarność* governments were struggling to balance internal clientele pressures with the demands of international market actors. Similar developments can be observed in eastern Germany, albeit muted by the German government's efforts to downplay the societal costs of unification (Heilemann and Reinicke 1995). Cities are thus constrained by their national policy climates. Only the largest or the capital cities are in a favourable position to respond in a semi-independent fashion to national or international challenges.

It is self-evident that a recycling of local elites is inevitable, especially in the mid-management ranks. Reformist mentality plays a significant role in the differential interpretation of Western and Eastern actors (Möller and Reissig 1996). Social consequences of the transformation were of little concern for the Western reformers but were of imminent concern to the central European decision makers. Administrators are only now beginning the difficult process of relating to their relevant publics. The vestiges of the old regime are difficult to jettison.

Differentiation along an international competitiveness axis

Each city is not equally equipped to become a regional or international economic actor. It is important to appreciate the varied roles that cities are capable of playing for their respective regions. International investors have often exploited the weaknesses in laws and administrative capabilities or the naivety of local politicians for their own ends (Kovacic and Thorpe 1996). This is a phenomenon that has been widely observed during the privatisation of state-owned enterprises across all countries of the region.

Governments intent on reforming their local structures have delegated new and quite extensive social and economic responsibilities to their urban areas (Fabian and Straussman 1994). Those cities that were able to rapidly reform their antiquated industrial base while also attracting new firms or encourage the formation of small businesses, have experienced fewer problems with unemployment (Kudrin 1997). Other less knowledgeable local governments or those disadvantaged because of their weakened fiscal condition or unfavourable location have found themselves exploited by foreign investors attempting, first, to establish monopolies once they gained access and foothold in their new markets, and thereafter to push local and national legislators to establish favourable conditions for their ventures (Török 1996). Monopolistic positions of foreign investors lessen the chances that cities can influence the investment or employment strategies of those firms. Thus, differentiated treatments will allow for more specific analyses in search of suitable governance arrangements that address the desires of local populations for more policy input, the need for appropriate economic responses in support of fledgling market systems, and the need for administrative and legal support structures to allow these systems to develop further.

Conclusion

In post-socialist cities much attention has focused on marketisation and privatisation. The importance of developing other societal institutions to respond to both domestic and international challenges has become quite apparent from this chapter (Stiglitz 1998). Visible remnants of the old regimes continue to remind citizens and public officials alike of what was wrong with socialist systems. The challenges remain overwhelming: deteriorating housing conditions, clamour for more self-governance coupled with central government's desire to retain control, continued weaknesses in the economic sectors coupled with uneven planning activities to privatise state-owned land and property have combined to create social and economic dislocations.

The examples cited here have also demonstrated the limits of self-governance for the smaller urban areas and rural communities. Cities are not firms. They exist as places in which to live and work and they remain dependent on the central state to resolve problems that are beyond their abilities (such as poverty) or over whose existence they have little control. The most obvious divisions exist between the large metropolises or capital cities and medium-sized cities. But size in itself does not tell us all about the response capacities of these cities. Opportunity structures are a complex mix of geography, ability to manage institutional innovations during times of high uncertainty and in the presence of severe internal crises while attempting to sustain support from local citizens and businesses.

The larger urban areas have been the quickest to make adjustments, but even here we see many maladies from the old regime continue and new ones emerge. As other chapters in this volume have shown, citizens' pressures for greater participation in political, economic and planning decisions have not always been met with great enthusiasm from political and administrative officials. The Czech Republic manifests a potentially worrisome trend to privatisation of public planning activities, with estimates showing public planning contributing less than 15 per cent of all planning activities (Hoffman 1994, p. 694). The premature shrinking of the public sphere before adequate capacities in the urban areas have been created, may eventually lead to a backlash as citizens become disenchanted with the promises of marketisation and democratisation. The emergence of extreme political parties or reinvented socialist ones may be the first precursor of things to come if social and economic gaps continue to widen.

Notes

1. Systematic research of urban transformations in this region is hampered by a lack of comparative assessments despite the wealth of case study and anecdotal material. The difficulties of collecting empirical data and disseminating it widely throughout the region, coupled with the dearth of journals focused on these issues, makes this a difficult enterprise both for practitioners and academics. The European Urban Research Association (EURA) held a workshop in Prague in 2001 on 'Strategies for revitalising East European cities', and this confirmed the need for efforts to strengthen urban research in Eastern Europe.
2. The term 'internationalisation' rather than 'globalisation' is used throughout. For a critique of the concept of globalisation, see Hirst and Thompson (1996) and John (1998).
3. Setnikar-Cankar (1998, p. 143) reports that the public sector in Slovenia consumes almost half of the GNP. Slovenia is one of those transitioning countries that quickly realised that its reform benchmarks had to be set high in order to achieve its goal of being competitive within the European context. Its reform aimed at the establishment of efficient administrative and legal procedures and the introduction of effective democratic features at all levels of government. Poland's communities, on the other hand, raise a large percentage of their resources through local taxes and fees. According to Wollman (1994, p. 119) this figure was 42 per cent, with the rest coming from the central government in the form of tax sharing and state subsidies of about 14 per cent.
4. They were reintroduced for the largest urban areas in 1994/95.

7
Managing Urban Ethnic Conflict

Scott A. Bollens

Within a globalising world has come a re-emergence of the local in addressing issues of coexistence, interaction and democracy. This is so because societal fragmentation has been a common companion alongside the economic integration of globalisation (Rosenau 1990). At the same time as we experience the 'mega-narratives' of modernisation (economic growth, high technology, education), we bear witness to subversive 'micro-narratives' that fuel oppositional movements, together with the breaking by electronic mass mediation and transnational mobilisation of the monopoly of nation states over the project of modernisation (Appadurai 1996). In cities, unprecedented migration, emerging multicultural citizenship, postcolonialism, and the rise of minorities and civil society challenge current ideas and methods of urban governance, planning and policy (Sandercock 1998). At the same time, globalisation of economic production and control has created the paradox that while economic activities now have a wide range of locational advantages, small differences in city characteristics and quality can have a decisive influence upon locational choice (Amin 1992). This chapter, while discussing several different cities in the world, derives many of its conclusions regarding the role of the city amidst globalisation from a study of Jerusalem (Israel/Palestine), Belfast (Northern Ireland) and Johannesburg (South Africa). That study involved extensive interviews with urban professionals and non-governmental officials in 1994 and 1995, investigating the role of urban policy and governance amidst broader ethnic/nationalistic conflict (Bollens 1998a, b, 1999, 2000).

Cities at risk

A disturbing number of cities across the world are susceptible to intense intercommunal conflict and violence reflecting ethnic or nationalist fractures. Cities such as Jerusalem, Belfast, Johannesburg, Nicosia, Montreal, Algiers, Sarajevo, New Delhi, Beirut, Karachi and Brussels are urban arenas penetrated by deep inter-group conflict associated with ethnic or political differences. In some cases, a city is the focal point for unresolved nationalistic ethnic conflict. Jerusalem is at the spatial epicentre of Israeli–Palestinian conflict which during the five years of the *intifada* cost over 1600 lives (Human Rights Watch 1993). In other cases, a city is a platform for the expression of conflicting sovereignty claims. Belfast is the capital of contested Northern Ireland, which has borne witness to over 3000 Protestant and Catholic deaths over the 25 years of civil war. Other examples (such as Brussels and Montreal) indicate that some effectiveness in defusing nationalistic conflict through cooperative communal governance and law-making is possible (Levine 1990; Fitzmaurice 1996). In today's world, such effective management applied to war-torn cities may hold the key to sustainable coexistence of warring ethnic groups subsequent to cessation of overt hostilities. In the former Yugoslavia, the cities of Sarajevo and Mostar are critical elements in whether enemies can spatially coexist in a workable reconstruction of a war-torn Bosnia that has suffered over 200,000 dead and 1.7 million refugees. Johannesburg is the economic powerhouse and largest urban region in the new democratic South Africa, a country where over 15,000 people have been killed since the mid-1980s in political violence between the former white government and blacks, with thousands more dead from black-on-black hostilities (Human Rights Watch 1993). The physically partitioned city of Nicosia is the focal point of the United Nations-managed settlement between Greek and Turkish Cypriots who engaged in a civil war that cost over 10,000 lives in the 1960s and 1970s. And, the Lebanese political capital and cultural centre of Beirut is undergoing physical and social reconstruction after a 15-year civil war that cost over 15,000 Muslim, Christian and Druze lives.

Common to many of these cities is that ethnic identity[1] and nationalism[2] combine to create pressures for group rights, autonomy or territorial separation. In conflict-prone cities, the machinery of government may be controlled by one ethnic group and used to discriminate against competing and threatening groups. In other cases, a third-party mediator may be brought in to govern the urban setting. In either case, the legitimacy of a city's political structures and its rules of decision making and governance are commonly challenged by ethnic groups who either seek an equal or proportionate share of power (such as blacks in South Africa) or demand group-based autonomy or independence (such as Palestinians in Jerusalem or the Quebecois in Montreal). Ethnically 'polarised' cities host a deeper, more intransigent type of urban conflict than found in most cities. In the most intense cases, these cities are battlegrounds between 'homeland' ethnic groups, each proclaiming the city as their own (Esman 1985). Conflicts commonly involve one group seeking autonomy or separation (Gurr 1993). With any consensus regarding political power-sharing problematic, political means are seen as incapable of effectively resolving urban ethnic differences (Douglas and Boal 1982; Romann and Weingrod 1991). While doctrines of collective rights, pluralism or autonomy are invoked by those on the outside, the politically dominant group views resistance by the subordinated group as obstacles to 'natural' processes of city-building and assimilation (Gurr 1993; Horowitz 1985).

Cities and intra-state conflict

Urban centres of ethnic proximity and diversity are assuming increased salience to those studying and seeking to resolve contemporary conflict because the scale of world conflict has shifted since the 1960s from international to intra-state. Sixty-nine of the 94 wars recorded between 1945 and 1988 have been intra-state conflicts (INCORE 1995). Gurr and Harff (1994, p. 6) identify 49 'protracted communal conflicts' in the world in the mid-1990s, involving confrontations between 'ethnic groups and governments over fundamental issues of group rights and identity'. In addition, military strategists are increasingly focusing on ethnically based animosities that are often intra-state in nature (Gibbs 1989; Schultz 1991; Hoffman 1992). As a result of international migration and substate ethnic divisions – oftentimes exploited and exacerbated by governing regimes and political leaders seeking to maintain or achieve power (Brown 1996; Lake and Rothchild 1996) – the nation state is decreasingly viewed as the territorial answer to the problem of human political, economic and social organisation.

Within ethnically tense and fragmenting states, urban management of ethnic competition can have profound consequences for the national, and ultimately, international level (Ashkenasi 1988). Urban areas and their civilian populations are 'soft, high-value' targets for broader conflict (Brown 1993). They can become important military and symbolic battlegrounds and flashpoints for violence between warring ethnic groups seeking sovereignty, autonomy or independence. Cities are vulnerable organisms subject to economic stagnation, demographic disintegration, cultural suppression, and ideological and political excesses violent in nature. Cities are also focal points of urban and regional economies dependent on multi-ethnic contacts, social and cultural centres and platforms for political expression, and potential centres of grievance and mobilisation. They are suppliers of important religious and cultural symbols, zones of inter-group proximity and intimacy, and arenas where the size and concentration of a subordinate population can present the most direct threat to the state. The proximity of urban living means that contested cities can be located on the fault line between cultures – between modernising societies and traditional cultures; between individual-based and community-based economies and societal ethics; between democracy and more authoritarian regimes; and/or between old colonial governments and native populations.

Cities as catalysts

Cities are not simple reflectors of larger societal tensions and dynamics but rather capable through their physical and political qualities of exerting independent effects on ethnic tension, conflict and violence (A. Shachar, Hebrew University of Jerusalem, interview). The inter-group proximity, social interaction, symbolic centrality and economic interdependency characteristic of cities can bend or distort the relationship between broader ideological disputes and the manifestations of local ethnic conflict. Depending upon how a polarised city is governed, the urban arena can be a catalyst encouraging either inter-group tension or inter-group tolerance. Figure 7.1 outlines the chapter's discussion, showing the relationships between broader ethno-nationalist conflict, the city, and the stability or volatility of ethnic relations.

Governing ideology and urban policy

An ideology is a comprehensive political belief system that embraces an inner logic and seeks to guide and justify organised political and social actions (Bilski and Galnoor 1980). The emphasis in this study is on *governing ideology* because public authorities operating amidst ethnic unrest must adopt an explicit doctrine that justifies and defends their

NATIONALISTIC ETHNIC CONFLICT
Cultural and political foundations
of competing claims in urban arena

↓

GOVERNING IDEOLOGY
Ethno-nationalist or civic

↓

URBAN POLICY
Urban policy and governance strategies

1. Neutral
2. Partisan
3. Equity
4. Resolver

↓

URBAN ETHNIC CONDITIONS

1. Control of land
2. Distribution of economic benefits/costs
3. Access to policy making
4. Maintenance of group identity

↓

URBAN STABILITY/VOLATILITY
Political resistance and mobilisation

Fig. 7.1   Ideology, urban policy and ethnic relations (adapted from Yiftachel 1992 and Gurr 1993)

policies amidst societal fragmentation. The governing ideology in a polarised city constitutes an intake or gatekeeper function, either allowing or barring a single ethnic group's claim to penetrate and frame public policy. A state's urban governing ideology can either be ethno-national or civic (Lijphart 1977). When there is a single dominating ethnic group in control of the government apparatus, the morally based doctrines of that ethno-national group regarding sovereignty and cultural identity will merge with the state's urban policy. In cases where a third-party overseer may govern the city, or after the resolution of political conflict, government goals may pursue a civic ideology that seeks to accommodate or transcend ethno-national ideologies. Governing ideologies have been ethno-national in post-1967 Israeli Jerusalem and apartheid Johannesburg, and civic in post-1972 Belfast and post-apartheid Johannesburg (Bollens 1999, 2000). Ideology, to be actualised, must be translated into technical prescriptions that seek to move a society, or in this case a city, towards those final goals or vision.

Ideology in an urban system is implemented primarily through urban planning and policy decisions. City planners and other administrative implementers seek to give concrete meaning to ideological goals such as political control, ethnic separation, security or fairness. Four *urban policy* strategies are possible under conditions of polarisation (Table 7.1). They differ in their substantive goals, the extent to which they address root causes or urban symptoms of inter-group conflict, and in the degree to which they incorporate ethnic criteria or not.

A *neutral* urban strategy employs technical criteria in allocating urban resources and services, and distances itself from issues of ethnic identity, power inequalities and political exclusion. The urban symptoms, not root causes, of sovereignty conflict would be addressed. Residents are treated within local planning processes as individuals rather than members of ethnic groups (Smith 1969). Thus, planning acts as an ethnically neutral, or 'colour-blind', mode of state intervention responsive to individual-level needs and differences. This is the traditional style of urban management and planning rooted in an Anglo-Saxon tradition, and commonly applied in liberal democratic settings (Yiftachel 1995). A government espousing a civic ideology of ethnic accommodation or transcendence would likely utilise this reform tradition. A neutral urban strategy of benevolent reform would

Table 7.1 Models of urban policy strategies

Strategy	Tactics
Neutral	Address urban symptoms of ethnic conflict at *individual level*
Partisan	Maintain/increase disparities
Equity	Address urban symptoms of ethnic conflict at *ethnic group level*
Resolver	Address root causes/sovereignty issues

Source Adapted from Benvenisti (1986).

seek to depoliticise territorial issues by framing urban problems as value-free, technical issues solvable through planning procedures and professional norms (Torgovnik 1990; Forester 1989; Nordlinger 1972). Disagreements and negotiations between ethnic groups would likely be channelled by government towards day-to-day service delivery issues and away from larger sovereignty considerations (Rothman 1992).

A *partisan* urban strategy chooses sides and is a regressive agent of change (Yiftachel 1995). It furthers an empowered ethnic group's values and authority and rejects claims of the disenfranchised 'out-group'. City residents are identified through their ethnic group affiliation, which is the main lens through which urban policy is directed (Smith 1969). Domination strategies are applied to land use planning and regulation in order to entrench and expand territorial claims or enforce exclusionary control of access (Lustick 1979; Sack 1981). Public policies are endorsed which substantially restrict out-group economic, political and land-based opportunities. Monopoly or preferential access to the urban policy-making machinery is provided for members of the dominant group (Esman 1973). Partisan urban strategies are intentionally repressive, such as in apartheid South Africa. Nevertheless, partisan planners may use many of the same tools as ethnically neutral strategists. Many urban planning techniques emphasise regulation and control of land use and thus can supply important means to implement partisan goals of territorial control and subjugation (Yiftachel 1995). Planning may also provide partisan policy making with a mask of objectivity behind which discriminatory intent can be hidden.

A third model, the *equity* strategy, seeks to decrease inter-group socio-economic disparities by using criteria such as an ethnic group's relative size or its need in allocating urban services and spending (Davidoff 1965; Nordlinger 1972; Esman 1973). An equity planner is more aware than a neutral planner of group-based inequalities and political imbalances in the city, and will recognise the needs for remediation and affirmative action policies based on group identity. This model is 'one infinitely more politicised, committed, and relevant than that offered by the pseudo-professionalism of contemporary practice' (Kiernan 1983, p. 85). Basic human needs – public services, human rights, employment opportunities, food and shelter, and participation in decision making – would be assured by urban development and planning policy.[3] Equity planning applied to politically polarised cities aims to reduce the urban symptoms of the root conflict, such as inter-group disparities in public services, housing, education and employment opportunities. This approach assumes that the causes of ethnic conflict and tension reside, at least partially, in the objective economic disparities of the urban landscape.

The final model – a *resolver* strategy – seeks to connect urban issues to the root political causes of urban polarisation – power imbalances, subordination and disempowerment. It is the only strategy of the four that attempts to resolve the conflict, as opposed to manage it (Burton 1991). As part of broader efforts to build peace in polarised environments, the resolver urban strategy seeks to reconceptualise the planning of cities and urban communities. Its mechanisms and goals are to be restructured and transformed in order that city-building facilitates mutual empowerment and peaceful urban coexistence. This strategy seeks not incremental reform of basic parameters, but rather emancipation and basic structural change that can confront and contradict neutral and partisan urban strategies. The model goes beyond the equity-based allocation of urban resources – with its focus on urban symptoms – to connect city issues and policy making to root political and territorial issues. Planning arguments are brought to bear to outline the basic parameters of a sustainable and peaceful urban system, one which meets each side's needs for territorial jurisdiction, control of population movement, and access to resources and to adequate supplies and distribution of labour. The resolver urban strategy is essentially confrontational of the status quo in its attempts to link scientific and technical knowledge to processes of system transformation. Such a strategy will not likely come initially from within a bureaucratic state, but would be created through the actions of non-governmental planners, cross-ethnic political groups and the subordinated out-group. It demands significant change from urban professionals, asking them to transcend each of the stances – professional neutrality, narrow partisanship and urban equalisation – of the previous three strategies. The impact of urban policy on ethnic conditions and thereafter on urban stability/volatility is outlined in Figure 7.2.

Urban policy and ethnic conflict

The relative deprivation theory of ethnic conflict posits unjust disparities and unmet human needs as a primary motivational force of political action (Gurr 1993; Burton 1990). Urban ethnic conditions reflect social, cultural and economic deprivation and the unfulfilment of basic human needs for identity and purpose. Four types of urban conditions can be identified – territoriality, economic distribution, policy-making access and group identity – each of which can be affected by urban

GOVERNING IDEOLOGY

URBAN POLICY

URBAN ETHNIC CONDITIONS

1. Control of land/territorial jurisdiction

Settlement of vacant lands; control of settlement patterns;
dispossession from land; control of landownership; determination
of planning boundaries; ethnic boundaries and identities

2. Distribution of economic benefits and costs

Allocation of 'externalities'; magnitude and geographic distribution
of urban services and spending

3. Access to policy making

Formal and informal participation processes; inclusion/exclusion
from political process; influence of non-governmental organisations

4. Maintenance of group identity and viability

Maintenance or threat to collective ethnic rights and identity;
education, religious expression, cultural institutions

URBAN STABILITY/VOLATILITY

Political mobilisation and resistance
Actual and potential organisations for and commitment to joint
action in pursuit of group interests

Fig. 7.2   Urban ethnic conditions and urban stability/volatility

policy. City policy and governance, and the urban conditions they
create, may dampen or energise an out-group's political mobilisation
and resistance, which is the key measure used here to measure the stability or volatility of the urban system. Figure 7.2 illustrates the point.

Urban policy most concretely affects the ethnic conditions of the
urban environment through its significant influence on *control of land
and territoriality* (Murphy 1989; Yiftachel 1992; Gurr 1993). Two common techniques of territorial control amidst ethnic tension aim (1)

to alter the spatial distribution of ethnic groups and (2) to manipulate jurisdictional boundaries to politically incorporate or exclude particular ethnic residents (Coakley 1993). The combination of a government's regulatory and developmental efforts can significantly affect in a polarised city the demographic ratios between the two sides, change the scale of focus of planning efforts, and reinforce or modify the ethnic identity of specific geographic subareas. An urban government involved in active territorial policies may seek penetration or dispersal of an opposing ethnic group in order to diminish its group coherence and ability to coalesce politically (Murphy 1989). Penetration and dispersal entail two contrasting projects, and illustrates that there is no clear line from the goal of city political control to specific territorial policies. Penetration involves placing members of the dominant ethnicity into areas having an opposing group majority. This seeks to fragment or contain the opposition group geographically and to increase the dominant party's surveillance of the out-group. In contrast, a dispersal territorial strategy seeks to spatially displace and disconnect the out-group from the urban system. In this case, separation of ethnic groups, rather than co-mingling, is viewed by the governing regime as politically stabilising and capable of excluding the subordinate group from a city's system of electoral and material benefits.

In addition to its tangible effects on land and territory, urban policy substantially shapes the *distribution of economic benefits and costs* and the allocation of urban service benefits (Yiftachel 1992; Stanovcic 1992; Gurr 1993). Urban land use and growth policies affect such aspects as the accessibility and proximity of residents and communities to employment, retail outlets and recreation; the distribution of land values; and the economic spin-offs (both positive and negative) of development. Economic nodes, depending upon their urban location and intended beneficiaries, have the ability to either integrate or separate the ethnic landscape. Urban service and capital investment decisions – related to housing, roads, schools and other community facilities – directly allocate urban advantages (and disadvantages) across ethnic communities. These may consolidate inter-group inequalities across a polarised city's ethnic geography by distributing benefits and advantages disproportionately to the ethnic in-group. Alternatively, activities and spending can be allocated so as to equalise urban benefits (and costs) across ethnic areas.

The nature of urban policy and planning processes can have substantial effects on the distribution of local political power and *access to policy making* (Yiftachel 1992; Stanovcic 1992; Gurr 1993). Unequal access to policy making is a core ingredient of ethnically polarised cities which translates into unequal urban outcomes dealing with local communities and their built environment. Usually, there is no access to the formal machinery of city government by one of the ethnic antagonists (or by both, in the case of a third-party intervenor). Along with poor or no representation in legislative deliberations, an ethnic group is concurrently marginalised in terms of access to urban planning processes and administrative rule-setting. Models of governance commonly applied at national levels (summarised by O'Leary and McGarry 1995) illuminate different participatory and political options at city level. 'Hegemonic control' by one ethnic group occurs when the opposing group is excluded from the political decision-making process. 'Third-party intervention' removes contentious local government functions – such as housing, employment and services – from control by *either* of the warring parties and empowers a third-party overseer to manage the urban region. Urban 'cantonisation' occurs through the devolution of some municipal powers to neighbourhood-based community councils or boroughs, which would advise the city government on 'own-community' affairs. 'Consociationalism' is based on agreement between political elites over a governance arrangement capable of managing ethnic differences (Lijphart 1968; Nordlinger 1972); elements of urban consociational democracy can be found in Brussels and Montreal.

In those circumstances where access to policy making is substantially curtailed for one urban ethnic group, pressure for change is often redirected through non-governmental channels. The web of non-governmental and voluntary associations that deal with urban issues such as community development, land and housing, cultural identity, social service delivery and human rights protection constitutes a polarised city's 'civil society' (Weitzer 1990; Friedman 1991; Partrick 1994). This organisational web can be an important source of glue holding together a threatened or disempowered minority, providing access to international organisations and their funding, and otherwise advocating change in the urban system through documentation, demonstrations and protests.

Maintenance of group identity is critical to the nature of inter-ethnic relations in a polarised city. Collective ethnic rights such as education, language, press, cultural institutions, and religious beliefs and customs are connected to potent ideological content. Collective identity is connected to relative group worth and is more psychological than other urban ethnic conditions. For an urban subgroup which

feels threatened, these psychological needs pertaining to group viability and cultural identity can be as important as territorial and
objective needs. The social–psychological content of urban group
identity can be enhanced or disrupted through urban policy. Public
policy, for instance, can affect important forms of ethnic expression
through its influence on public education (particularly dealing with
language). Urban service delivery decisions dealing with the location
of proposed new religious, educational and cultural institutions, or
the closing down of ones deemed obsolete, can indicate to urban
residents the government's projected ethnic trajectories of specific
neighbourhoods and can substantially threaten ethnic group
identity.

Urban policy and stability/volatility

These urban ethnic conditions – land control, economic distribution,
policy-making access and also group identity – can influence urban
stability/volatility (see Figure 7.2). City conditions affected by urban
policy may inflame or moderate inter-ethnic tension and conflict at
the urban scale. An indicator of a city's stability or volatility is the
magnitude and prevalence of *political mobilisation* on the part of the
subordinated group. Mobilisation refers to an ethnic group's capacity –
in terms of organisation and commitment – to engage in political
action and resistance (Tilly 1978). Such actions run the gamut from
non-violent actions such as verbal opposition, demonstrations, strikes
and rallies, to violent protests such as symbolic destruction of property,
sabotage and rioting, to active rebellion in the forms of terrorism, guer-
rilla activity, and protracted civil war (Gurr 1993).

Urban policies are capable of both producing a widely shared sense
of deprivation conducive to sustained communal resistance and of providing a platform for the purposeful and rational actions of inflamma-
tory ethnic group leaders. In the early stages of organised political
resistance, objective urban conditions related to deprivation may be
critical causes (Gurr 1993; Gurr and Lichbach 1986). However, once
collective political action is under way, these objective conditions can
pale in significance to factors related to out-group organisation and
leadership (Gurr 1993). In other words, political organisation related to
ethnic conflict can reach a point beyond which betterment of objective
conditions through urban policy would have only marginal effects on
the amelioration of urban ethnic tension. This means that the internal
political dynamics and needs of the out-group's political organisation,

as well as the urban needs of its city residents, must be accommodated in efforts to secure urban stability.

State urban policies can structure the local political system in ways that either restrict or enable out-group political opportunities, and they can frustrate or cultivate the development of out-group organisations and networks that comprise the collective building blocks of political capacity (McAdam et al. 1996; Tarrow 1994; Tilly 1978). Urban policies can forcefully repress political resistance, as well as internally fragmenting the out-group's urban political community through planning regulations that spatially separate the out-group neighbourhoods and through the preferential channelling of urban benefits to more 'moderate' subgroups. Alternatively, urban policies can provide political opportunities for the out-group through electoral representation, provision of multiple and decentralised layers of local governance, or by nurturing non-governmental organisations aligned with the out-group. Because material grievance and political disenchantment can both contribute to urban instability, urban policies seeking stability need to address both the physical city and the political relationships within it.

Flashpoints or buffers?

Cities may be either flashpoints or buffers for inter-ethnic conflict. Urban living can exacerbate conflict due to the proximity and economic interactions that are a necessary part of a functioning urban system. The economic centrality and/or religious symbolism of a city within a national hierarchy and the close juxtaposition of antagonistic neighbourhoods would lead one to anticipate exacerbation of the general level of inter-ethnic tension and the increasing frequency of violent actions. Proximity can intensify feelings of group-based relative deprivation and threats to collective identity. Urban policies that have direct effects on territoriality, material well-being and cultural expression can help mobilise an urban-based political opposition that can then energise or solidify national-level resistance. Planners manipulate ethnic territoriality in a polarised city at a substantial risk to urban and political stability. In particular, policies by an empowered ethnic group that aim to penetrate out-group-controlled urban territories, or otherwise change relative ethnic proportions, will likely foment ethnic mistrust and conflict (Yiftachel 1992). To the extent that a city is a flashpoint, it can act as a major and independent obstruction to the success of larger regional and national peace processes.

Cities, on the other hand, may act as buffers or mitigators of inter-group conflict to the extent that the city's daily interconnectedness and forced coexistence thrusts upon intimate urban enemies some modicum of mutual tolerance (Ashkenasi 1988). The extension of material benefits (urban services; social security or unemployment insurance; urban employment) may moderate the relative deprivation effect. A co-optative relationship between city government and out-group community elites may act as a wall preventing broader hostil-ities from entering the urban arena. Further, a territorial separation of opposing ethnic groups in an urban system that is mutually agreed upon may enhance urban political stability. Even if such mitigative effects are present in the urban system, however, one must ask whether they simply suspend inter-group tension temporarily or truly amelio-rate it. The possibility exists that urban-based ethnic arrangements and compromises may, under certain conditions, radiate outward to help pacify conflict at national and international levels. However, lacking resolution of deep-rooted issues of identity and sovereignty, the best that we may expect from urban policies may be an abeyance of overt signs of conflict and a buying of time that may enable willing political leaders to negotiate the root causes of conflict before the city explodes.

The challenge of urban coexistence

This chapter has outlined a process whereby nationalistic ethnic conflict is filtered through an urban system. A state's governing ideol-ogy regarding the urban arena is either derived from one group's politi-cal claims, or seeks to transcend or integrate competing ethnic visions. This constitutes an important gatekeeper function that influences the extent that ethnicity will or will not penetrate governmental goals and actions. Urban policies that operationalise a governing ideology then affect the spatial, economic, social and political dimensions of urban space. This urban effect can intensify or lessen inter-group hostility through its impacts on objective urban conditions, social–psychological aspects of urban group identity, and place-specific forms and dynamics of political resistance and mobilisation.

A central contention here, based on research in three cities formerly or currently contested politically, is that there exists an 'urban' ef-fect on inter-ethnic relations that acts semi-autonomously from the broader ideological causes and organisational dynamics of ethnic polarisation. Urban policy is not simply derivative of broader ideology, but operates at a specific level of analysis and interaction having dynamics, participants and consequences potentially different than found at regional or national levels. A city can act as a prism upon ethnic tension and conflict rather than a mirror. Whether urban policy moderates, exacerbates or simply mirrors the broader historical conflict is dependent upon the policy strategies chosen, the spatial, economic and psychological conditions and contradictions they generate in the built landscape, and the organisational and mobilisation qualities of the oppositional group. Urban policy is not necessarily impotent in the face of ideological dictates (or global trends), but rather gains importance due to the complexities of cities through which such ideologies and extra-local forces are filtered and upon which it operates. Cities appear to have important mediating effects on the relationship between ideological and place-specific conflict, and in ways that are complex and not easily predicted.

In order for urban policy to advance peace, the process and practice of city-building must be reconceptualised so that it explicitly accounts for the importance of ethnic community identity, territoriality and symbolism embedded in urban landscapes. It must be able to manage not only the material, but also the psychological and identity-related, conditions of its antagonistic groups. It must contribute practical principles which foster the coexistent viability of antagonistic sides in the urban setting and connect these efforts to larger peace and reconstruction efforts. Such an urban strategy may require an engagement in equity policy that disproportionately targets territorial and material benefits to the objectively disadvantaged ethnic group while tending to the psychological needs of the materially advantaged, in terms of their security, ethnic identity and neighbourhood vitality.

Policies and principles of urban coexistence are not to be a substitute for larger political negotiations. Rather, tangible urban-level efforts and diplomatic national-level negotiations should constitute an inseparable peacemaking amalgamation. Urban accommodation without a national peace would leave the city vulnerable and unstable, while a national peace without urban accommodation would be one unrooted in the practical and explosive issues of inter-group and territorial relations. Local policies aimed at the basic needs and coexistent viability of competing ethnic groups are capable of contributing the sole authentic source of inter-ethnic accommodation amidst a set of larger diplomatic political agreements that may otherwise be susceptible to ethnic hardening and fraying. National and international agreements over political power and control, while absolutely essential, impose abstract and remote sets of rules and institutions upon the urban landscape. Local

political arrangements such as two-tier metropolitanism or consociational (power-sharing) democracy that might emerge respond to the
basic dual needs for sovereignty and political control, but represent
agreements at the political level, not that of daily interaction between
ethnic groups and individuals. Progressive and ethnically sensitive
urban strategies can anchor these formal local agreements over power
by fostering interaction between semi-autonomous ethnic governments, hindering a de facto separation, and providing positive-sum
policy outcomes that can obstruct the development of a mentality of
policy gridlock and ethnic vetoes.

The challenges of urban policy making in politically contested cities
inform policy makers and planners in the growing number of multi-
ethnic cities across the world that are not polarised, but nonetheless
reside close to the ethnic breaking-point. The ethnic fracturing of
many of these non-polarised urban populations creates a 'public interest' that bears signs of fragility and cleavage similar to polarised situations. When public discourse and governmental techniques in cities
adopt territorial and physical means to increase security and segregate
classes or races, they move towards the polarised circumstances studied
here. The common goal of urban management in cities – whether they
be contested politically or 'only' divided socially – is to accommodate
plural needs without sacrificing the soul and functionality of urban
life. Policy makers and planners in multicultural cities must address the
complex spatial, social–psychological and organisational attributes of
potentially antagonistic urban communities. They must be sensitive to
the multi-ethnic environments towards which their skills are applied
and to the ways that empowered groups legitimate and extend power.
The problems and principles of city-building in deeply polarised cities
provide guidance to all those who cope with multiple publics and contrasting ethnic views of city life and function.

Notes

1. Ethnic groups are composed of people who share a distinctive and enduring
   collective identity based on shared experiences or cultural traits (Gurr and
   Harff 1994). Such group awareness can be crystallised through shared struggle, territorial identity, 'ethnic chosenness' or religion (Smith 1993).
2. Nationalism is a doctrine wherein nationality overrides or subsumes alternative criteria such as social class, economic class or patronage (Snyder
   1993).
3. The idea that there should be minimum standards dealing with basic
   human needs and rights has been endorsed by the United Nations in 1966

in its *Covenant on Economic, Social and Cultural Rights* and *Covenant on Civil and Political Rights*, both of which are legally binding on those countries ratifying them. The International Labour Office (1977) has also proposed and defined a human-needs approach to economic development.

8
Urban Policies in the Netherlands: from 'Social Renewal' to 'Big Cities Policy'

Robert Kloosterman and Dennis Broeders

Introduction

The Dutch economy was relatively hard hit by the economic recession of the 1980s. Unemployment soared, especially in the larger cities. In these cities, unemployment was unevenly distributed with some neighbourhoods experiencing concentrations of economic decline. Unemployment was also more prevalent among immigrants (Burgers and Kloosterman 1996). In the 1970s and early 1980s, the Dutch government had embarked upon an ambitious programme of urban renewal financed, to a large extent, by the profits from the natural gas production in the north of the Netherlands. This programme was almost exclusively focused on the housing stock, however, and proved insufficient to sustain renewal when economic recession struck. To prevent further decline, two important policy initiatives were taken in the 1990s, the first being the *Social Renewal* initiative during the first half of the 1990s, and the second the *Big Cities Policy* launched in 1995.

In this chapter we examine these two policy initiatives by looking at a specific neighbourhood in The Hague – The Hague Southwest. This post-war neighbourhood consisting of two adjacent areas (Bouwlust and Vrederust), was a pilot project for Social Renewal and is also now included in the Big Cities Policy. These two initiatives are examined in turn, but first we describe the neighbourhood. The following section analyses the Social Renewal policy in The Hague Southwest, particularly with regard to the pilot project of the early 1990s. In the next section the contours of the current programme of the Big Cities Policy are sketched. The final sections offer some more general findings on urban policies in extensive welfare states.

The Hague Southwest as a local community

The Hague Southwest, a post-war medium high-rise neighbourhood, has a layout somewhere between that of a high-density city and that of a suburban neighbourhood. It was explicitly designed to incorporate the *Gemeinschaft* ideal of community. According to Dudok, the architect who designed The Hague Southwest, the modern city lacked 'a meaningful arrangement, a clear structure'. His carefully worked-out city–borough–neighbourhood hierarchy was actually based on a clearly anti-urban point of view (van Doorn 1955). The intention was to establish a sense of *Gemeinschaft* in the urban environment of the post-war neighbourhoods based on the pillars of 'family', 'neighbourhood' and 'friendship' (Hall 1988). Since many of the first residents found themselves in a similar stage of the life cycle, that is mostly families with children, there was the possibility that this *Gemeinschaft* could actually be realised. Schools, small local shopping centres and courtyard gardens were the obvious places where women with children could meet. Thus, networks of personal contacts could actually develop and extend in the post-war urban neighbourhoods.

In the past 40 years, however, many occupants of the monotonous high-rise buildings in The Hague Southwest who could afford to do so, have moved to single-family houses in the surrounding suburbs (Oerlemans 1990): 'As soon as they could, they all moved away. It became the largest clearing-house in The Hague.' The post-war housing shortage then attracted many households whereas now it is much more low rents that draw people towards The Hague Southwest. However, this does not mean that the *social* heterogeneity as such has decreased. In the mid-1980s, when the housing corporations had to abandon their allocation policies, the influx led to a gradual change in the composition of the population. By that time residents were mainly 'stayers', those of the first generation who could not or did not want to move, young starters, mothers on social security, the disabled, migrants and those who had to leave their previous homes because of urban renewal.

From an economic point of view, the current population is more homogeneous than that of 40 years ago. Then income levels and socio-economic status varied but there were other features held in common. Newcomers were desperately looking for a home in the very tight immediate post-war housing market and most of them were about the same age and had just started families. Nowadays, the population is predominantly at the lower end of the socio-economic scale, either in low-paid jobs or without a job. They differ, however, in many other respects, such as age, stage in life cycle, country of origin and cultural outlook. Consequently, these residents do not have the common characteristics to restore the sense of *Gemeinschaft* from days gone by. The differentiation between lifestyles, so characteristic of the post-modern era, exaggerates the current differences in the population as compared to the first generation of the 1950s (Blokland-Potters 1997). The schools, local shops and courtyard gardens, which once were the obvious meeting places especially for families with young children, have lost their function as locations for contact between neighbours. Many current residents do not have any children of school age. In other cases the language barrier makes communication between the parents difficult. Since many households now own cars, mobility has increased enormously. This seriously undermines the carefully planned hierarchy of service provision in The Hague Southwest. As a consequence, most of the small local shops have closed down. The distance travelled for shopping has become much greater than 500 metres (which was considered to be the maximum distance that a woman with a perambulator was able to cover on foot). The decrease in the number of children, the introduction of television and the generally increased orientation towards the private sphere have reduced the role of the communal courtyard gardens as meeting places and play areas (Kloosterman 1995).

As a result there is no longer a broad social basis for *Gemeinschaft* in the neighbourhood. Ironically enough, this part of the city, explicitly designed to create a non-urban sense of community, is now characterised by the atomised, anonymous relations that are common in large cities. The presuppositions with respect to family, mobility and employment, which underpinned the construction of The Hague Southwest and other post-war neighbourhoods, proved to be too much the products of their time. Thus, a large part of the social cohesion in this neighbourhood has disappeared, and as a consequence, many of the social norms to be expected in the public realm are sustained by those specially assigned to this task, for example police officers, neighbourhood wardens and social workers, instead of by the residents themselves.

'There's hardly any community spirit.' 'The people here don't identify themselves with the neighbourhood they live in.' 'We don't belong

together.' These are three statements from key persons who are profes-
sionally involved with the neighbourhood. Community now seems to
be enjoyed somewhere else, in communities people choose themselves,
for example, at the camping site where they have stationed their
caravan more or less permanently. The sociologist Blokland-Potters
(1997), who has analysed a comparable neighbourhood in Rotterdam,
has called them 'privatised communities'.

With the disappearance of community spirit, The Hague Southwest
seems to be stuck with the disadvantages of the conscious denial of
urbanity in the design of this city neighbourhood. Urbanity, however,
does not necessarily have to lead to a situation of Durkheimian anomie
or a lack of social control. In the still fascinating *The Death and Life of
Great American Cities* (1961), the New York geographer Jane Jacobs set
out the requirements an urban environment has to fulfil in order to
remain habitable. According to her, high density, mixture of functions
(residential, work and recreation), a combination of old and new buildings, and a diverse street pattern contribute to the habitability of a city
neighbourhood. This holds true from an economic as well as social
point of view, but The Hague Southwest is almost exclusively a residential area (hardly any bars, restaurants, shops or other economic activities) with a relatively low density and predominantly post-war
buildings, and a street pattern that is all but diverse. As a city neighbourhood, it is practically the direct opposite of the Jacobs notion of
urbanity.

A 1992 survey confirmed this conclusion – see Table 8.1 (Kruize and
Kroes 1992). Social cohesion in The Hague Southwest is indeed less
than the average for the city of The Hague as a whole. There is more
anomie, less identification with the neighbourhood and most people
do not want to stay there.

Table 8.1   Characterisation of the neighbourhood (per cent of respondents
that agree with statements)

Statement	Southwest	The Hague
Hardly know each other	57	46
Good social interaction	42	50
There are many nationalities	70	44
Attached to the neighbourhood	56	64
Like to keep on living there	67	74

Source Kruize and Kroes (1992).

Social Renewal policy

Towards the end of the 1980s unemployment – both official and hidden – had risen to unprecedented heights and seemed to threaten the social fabric of many cities if not of society itself (Kloosterman 1995). To combat localised processes of marginalisation, the Social Renewal policy was introduced and piloted in a number of areas of which The Hague Southwest was one. Social Renewal was not only considered to be a new policy for the improvement of certain deprived areas, but also as a first step towards *administrative* and *moral* reforms. It advocated in particular the necessity of administrative changes at the local level. The element of moral reform referred to a new balance between the rights and obligations of both citizens and authorities. These administrative and moral reforms formed the starting point for tackling three clusters, or circles, of problems, considered to be the focal points of Social Renewal (Ministerie of Binnenlandse Zaken 1990). These circles – the local environment; employment, education and income; the improvement and effectiveness of local service provision – were to be tackled on a small area basis in such a way that as many links as possible would be realised between the three circles. The fight against petty crime and the degeneration of the physical environment in which people lived was a primary objective linking the first two circles, through establishing a connection between vocational integration and the local environment by involving the unemployed in socially useful activities such as maintenance and management of the local neighbourhood. This could be interpreted as a kind of government-instigated process of Max Weber's *Vergemeinschaftung* (cf. Blokland-Potters 1997).

Reference was made to administrative and moral reforms. The human environment circle not only included desegregation and deregulation, the keywords in the administrative reform within the framework of Social Renewal, but also the participation of those involved. Residents were expected to play an active role in improving the human environment in their neighbourhood. They are seen as the ultimate experts when it comes down to the actual problems that exist in their immediate environment. Thirdly, the explicit starting point was the neighbourhood. Social Renewal implied a *territorialisation* of the policy for the improvement of deprived areas.

With these starting points, the Dutch policy of Social Renewal fitted in perfectly with the (inter)national trend of administrative decentralisation (Jacquier 1991). Neighbourhoods are seen as relevant spatial administrative units and one of the goals is to enlarge the role played by citizens in the administration and management of their neighbourhood. Under the Social Renewal policy the local arena had thus become crucial for policies concerning deprived areas. This shift had important consequences for citizens as well as for authorities. Local authorities were expected to be sufficiently receptive to the initiatives of citizens and that they would be able to value these properly, and also that they could respond adequately to the wishes expressed by these citizens. The reliance on citizens' participation was even greater. First of all, they needed to show sufficient involvement with *their* neighbourhood. Secondly, it was expected that they would *act* themselves – whether organised or not – out of their own accord and then make an appeal to the local authorities in order to combat the problems via a joint approach on the basis of mutual consultations. With respect to Social Renewal, it was therefore implicitly assumed that there already existed a *viable and resourceful community* in the neighbourhoods involved. Or more precisely, this kind of local policy involves a kind of local participation that presupposes an identifiable, perhaps even palpable local community.

Social Renewal in The Hague Southwest

Negative influences on the everyday environment such as deterioration or street violence are matters that concern each resident directly. Almost everyone will, hence, have some perception of what is meant by 'the quality of the human environment'. Also the inherent territorial dimension of the everyday environment will be very clear to those directly involved. Nevertheless the notion of everyday environment is more problematic than one would expect. With the deterioration of the *Gemeinschaft*, mainly caused by the increasing individualisation and by the introduction of mass-ownership of cars and televisions, the differences in the perception of the everyday environment have become greater.

First of all, there are differences in the assessment of the relevant spatial scale level of the everyday environment. The spatial conception of the human environment is very subjective and differs from person to person (Hill 1994). The residents' daily activities, level of education and age determine to a large degree their range of action and consequently also their perception of the everyday environment. For some, the doorway will be the first boundary of the everyday environment. For others, this may be the street, the block or the neighbourhood.

Secondly, the assessment of the quality of the human environment is also very subjective. Some things that annoy some residents tremendously, such as noise, graffiti on the walls or weeds poking up between the paving stones, will only elicit a shrug of the shoulder from others. This does not only concern the more material aspects of the built environment, but also the accessibility of the public space. Someone who takes his dog for a walk around the old familiar block at night may not have such a strong feeling of insecurity as someone riding his bicycle through the neighbourhood at the same time of night. The assessment of how safe or unsafe the neighbourhood is, is therefore also very much coloured by personal experience. It should also be mentioned that long-term unemployment, limited financial freedom, or the arrival of new residents – whether or not from Dutch or foreign origin – as well as a pessimistic perspective on the future of the neighbourhood may generate feelings of discontent with the local environment. These feelings may manifest themselves as a general feeling of discomfort and also as an increasing dissatisfaction with the environment, even though this environment has demonstrably not lost quality. Complaints about the human environment are in that case merely symptoms of some other problem.

Thirdly, there is the question of measurability. Even if one has opted for a certain scale level and defined clearly what the quality of the everyday environment exactly is, the question remains how to measure this quality. A simple measurement (e.g. in the case of unemployment) is impossible due to the complexity and high degree of subjectivity. Therefore, other ways have to be found to approach this quality indirectly. The opinions of those directly involved, i.e. the residents themselves, are of central importance in this respect. However, it should also be taken into account that the residents' assessments of that quality are not just determined by 'objective' factors present in the environment, as we have mentioned above. The introduction of Social Renewal in The Hague Southwest might in itself be a factor in the sense that it possibly encourages the residents to observe their environment more attentively and critically. It is therefore important to include not only the assessments of the residents, but also the assessments of key informers.

With respect to the quality of the environment, a distinction has to be made in The Hague Southwest between the Bouwlust area and the Vrederust area. Local experts mention explicitly the blocks of flats called 'De Oorden' and 'De Raden' in the Bouwlust neighbourhood as areas where the nuisance and the deterioration are clearly worse. There are others who point out the difference between the Bouwlust and Vrederust neighbourhoods. In their research report for The Hague police, de Coninck and Westerberg (1991, p. 8) stated that Vrederust is seen as 'a more quiet neighbourhood where the residents come from a somewhat higher social class than those of Bouwlust'. This was partly caused by the fact that Bouwlust has been a refuge for 'urban renewal nomads' for some time now. In particular large families, mostly with an immigrant status, have become eligible for the rather large houses in Bouwlust. This is one of the reasons that the quality of the everyday environment in Bouwlust has come under more pressure. This reveals itself as disturbance of the peace (also due to the thin-walled houses), tinkering with cars on the public road and a general feeling of insecurity in the streets, particularly among the older people in the neighbourhood. This last group experienced the arrival of an increasing number of immigrants to be a degradation of the neighbourhood. According to the police researchers, the problems in Vrederust are evidently of a different nature: the rather homogeneous population of this neighbourhood tend to see 'ghosts', that is to say, each tiny problem is given more weight than would normally be the case in other neighbourhoods. Apart from nuisance caused by parked cars and speeding, the residents here are mainly worried about the problems that the present or future restaurants and bars may cause.

Nonetheless the police pointed out that this rather peaceful façade can be deceptive. 'The problem in this neighbourhood is, it is covered up . . . . looks nice, but [the] mess is hidden behind the doors.' Sometimes the dissatisfaction will surface and then 'the fat's in the fire' as during the notorious riots in this neighbourhood in the summer of 1994. This last example refers also to another characteristic of The Hague Southwest. Compared to the city centre with its many shops, cafés, bars and other places of entertainment, the monofunctionality and lack of meeting places for young people in this neighbourhood make it less suitable for quite a number of criminal offences (van der Leun et al. 1998).

The scores of this part of The Hague in the police survey confirm to a large extent the impression that this neighbourhood does not have any serious problems. Table 8.2 shows the top five of the most frequently mentioned problems in the part that is called Laak/Escamp in 1993. This gives an indication of what goes on in the everyday environment, even though The Hague Laak/Escamp covers a larger area than The Hague Southwest (Bouwlust/Vrederust) and particularly the problems in the Laak quarter may be quite different from those in the Southwest. The

Table 8.2   The most frequently mentioned problems in The Hague
Laak/Escamp (includes The Hague Southwest), 1993

---

1. Dog litter
2. Speeding
3. Litter on the street
4. Burglary
5. Bicycle theft

Source Bevolkingsonderzoek (1994).

fact that 'dog litter is the problem that the respondents most frequently mentioned indicates that this is not really a seriously deprived area. Two other items on the list, i.e. 'speeding' and 'litter in the street', also do not point in that direction. The first three items merely refer to careless or antisocial behaviour, whereas numbers four and five unmistakably give an indication of criminal behaviour. The mentioning of 'burglary' and 'bicycle theft' prove that Laak/Escamp is certainly not free of petty crime. It is rather striking that real urban problems such as drug-related issues or nuisance caused by prostitution are absent from this list.

The nature of the complaints and the reasons people give for feeling unsafe confirm that The Hague Southwest lacks social control and therefore also community spirit. Dog mess, vandalism, litter in the streets and speeding are symptoms that pre-eminently indicate that the residents are not very involved with the neighbourhood and the other residents. This lack of social control and involvement is supported by the fact that only a few residents are inclined to report suspicious situations to the police.

Another indicator of this lack of involvement is the number of non-voters. In the municipal elections of March 1994, no less than 43.8 per cent of those entitled to vote in The Hague Southwest stayed at home. This figure was just slightly above the average for the whole of The Hague. These same elections also gave a clear indication of the dissatisfaction among the residents in this part of the city. The extreme right-wing parties scored no less than 15.8 per cent against an average of 11.9 per cent from the entire population of The Hague.

There was in fact not much wrong with the everyday environment in this neighbourhood, generally speaking, but yet a considerable part of its population seems to have been seized by a feeling of discomfort. This feeling of discomfort had undoubtedly something to do with the lack of social cohesion in the neighbourhood and the resulting problems. However, this feeling also seems to have been reinforced by the pessimistic perspective that some of the residents have concerning the future of the neighbourhood. To dispel this feeling, Social Renewal in The Hague Southwest should not only have been aimed at improving the present situation in which there is little social cohesion and involvement. It should also have contributed to a different perspective on the future of the neighbourhood.

Most important, however, was the fact that a decentralised policy involving the participation of the residents who live in this everyday environment, which is the essence of Social Renewal, has been made difficult by prevailing resident attitudes. As the community spirit is almost entirely lacking, policies could only be successful in those instances where residents were actively induced to participate in matters relating to their everyday environment and thus experience a sense of involvement. Intermediary organisations, the residents' committees in particular, which can mediate between the residents and the local authorities, constituted a rather important factor in the successful realisation of certain concrete aims of Social Renewal. Apart from bolstering the residents' involvement and participation in the neighbourhoods, the local authorities also played a more indirect, albeit very crucial, role in making Social Renewal a success. By becoming more open and receptive with respect to complaints and wishes of citizens, the local arena came to be seen as more relevant. Transparent and accessible locally active government services are therefore very important in making local policies a success.

Big Cities Policy

Though Social Renewal gave a significant impetus to urban policy many observers considered the policy to have failed (SER 1998). The persistence of the problems facing the big city, such as long-term unemployment, dependence on social welfare and the deterioration of living conditions in certain neighbourhoods, had not been countered adequately. In 1994, the Netherlands' four largest cities, Amsterdam, Rotterdam, The Hague and Utrecht, launched a new initiative to reform urban policy. During the formation of the first Kok cabinet (1994–98), they presented a 'Delta plan for the big cities', in which they asked for a new approach to the typical big city problems. According to this plan, 'An unorthodox approach to the metropolitan problem is needed, in which Social Renewal and revitalisation of urban economies go hand in hand.' This memorandum proved to be the kick-start for the Big Cities Policy in 1995 (Amsterdam, Rotterdam, Den Haag, Utrecht 1994).

In many respects, the Big Cities Policy is a continuation of the Social Renewal programme. The three clusters of problems (circles) which were the central focal points in Social Renewal have been taken up in the Big Cities Policy. Many of the practical experiences – project and pilot formats – have now been shifted under the umbrella of the Big Cities Policy. The theory underlying the Big Cities Policy is that all policies aimed at the various metropolitan problems should be merged together into one integral approach. The Big Cities Policy, hence, rests on three 'pillars': the economic, the physical and the social infrastructure of the city. One of the main additions of the Big Cities Policy, when compared to Social Renewal, is the inclusion of the urban economy as an important part of the programme. Boosting the urban economy is considered an important goal and a means to revitalise the city both economically and socially (by creating new jobs in the city and its neighbourhoods).

Whereas Social Renewal was intended to be both a substantive and a procedural reform, and has in retrospect at least been praised for creating a new wave of enthusiasm among professional fieldworkers, the emphasis in the Big Cities Policy was and is mainly on administrative reform. The cities argued that a change of administrative structures is a necessary condition for developing a new urban policy. Further decentralisation and deregulation of the relation between central and local government, should open up possibilities for municipalities to come up with creative solutions for the problems within their city limits. Payments from the central government to the municipalities should become 'lump sum' payments with broad definitions of the goals to be achieved, instead of the usual 'earmarked' payments restricted by departmental instructions. The administrative reform also included high ambitions for cooperation between all the public and private players in the Big Cities Policy. First and foremost, a new cooperation between central and local government, but also between provinces (the Dutch middle layer of government), regions, municipal bureaucracies, welfare organisations, local businesses and citizens. The new cooperation between the central government and the cities was laid down in so-called 'covenants', a kind of charter in which the mutual rights, obligations and expectations concerning the Big Cities Policy were drawn up.

Big Cities Policy also meant an intensification of two of the major starting points of the Social Renewal policy: the expectation that residents would play an active role in improving the human environment in their neighbourhood and the territorialisation of policy for the improvement of deprived areas. Even more than before, the 'local' approach was deemed vital for solving the problems of the so-called disadvantaged neighbourhoods. Problems are to be identified, defined and solved on the scale of the neighbourhood, preferably in close cooperation with community organisations and residents. The localisation of policy, however, presents problems.

Firstly, the spatial scale on which a problem is identified is not necessarily the proper scale to try to solve the problem. The problems of a neighbourhood characterised by large groups of long-term unemployed, for example, are not necessarily solved by a policy which is grounded in a spatially defined neighbourhood. Combating unemployment can be better addressed on the scale of the city or the urban region as the institutions dealing with job creation and employment provision in the Netherlands are organised on a regional scale (Priemus et al. 1998; De Boer 1999).

Secondly, critics question the implicit policy assumption that there is a sense of community feeling in these problematic neighbourhoods, an assumption already present in Social Renewal. The appeal to the community and the possibilities of using community feelings and participation of residents as 'policy instruments' are often seen as a misconception (Blokland-Potters 1997; Boomkens 1999; Duyvendak 1998).

Initially development of the policy was plagued by differences over coordination, responsibilities and finance between central and local governments and within the municipal organisation. Desegregation, one of the main objectives of the administrative reform, seemed hard to deliver at both the level of central government and of the municipality. The so-called 'Visitation Committee Big Cities Policy' emphasised additional points of criticism as they concluded their work in 1998. They were critical of the lack of long-term vision and of the absence of innovative and creative new policies; in most cases the cities had merely brought forward existing projects and there was insufficient attention given to migrants from non-industrialised countries.

Dissatisfied with the general lack of coherent programmes that were able to rise above an accumulation of existing projects during the first covenant period (1995–98), the central government and the cities decided to try and turn the tables. In the *doorstartcovenant* (which roughly translates into 'restart plan') of December 1998 they agreed to develop structural long-term plans for the Big Cities Policy. Every city was to present a new, more programmatic plan for the period 2000–4 within the guidelines laid down in the *doorstartcovenant*. This plan should also contain an indicative vision for the city's urban policy until 2010.

In October 1999, the city of The Hague published its policy document for the Big Cities Policy for the period 2000–4 under the title *The Strength of The Hague* (Gemeente Den Haag 1999). The city presents a three-pronged plan, which largely follows the approach of the three pillars of the Big Cities Policy. The plan focuses, firstly, on the strengthening of the local economy by means of improving the business climate, the quality of public space and the internal and external accessibility of the city. Secondly, it aims to enhance the housing and living conditions by means of improving the position of certain neighbourhoods in the regional housing market and improving the quality of public space and the human environment. Thirdly, it sets goals to strengthen the social and educational climate of The Hague. This track includes education and youth policies as well as programmes for 'special groups' and the improvement of safety. The term 'special groups' is a kind of 'new-speak' for underprivileged groups such as migrants from non-industrialised countries, the elderly and the long-term unemployed.

Just as under the Social Renewal policy, The Hague Southwest has been selected to be the frontrunner in the new plans for the Big Cities Policy. It will again be one of two pilot areas where the city will experiment with an 'integral territorial approach'. This approach embodies the high and long-standing ambitions of achieving effective cooperation between public and private partners. Municipality, police, housing corporations and welfare organisations should develop a joint vision on a specific area and mutually fine-tune their activities. In this sense, Big Cities Policy is a clear continuation of the earlier Social Renewal. The emphasis, however, remains on housing and the quality of the housing stock. Priority has been given to large-scale transformation of the housing stock in the area: more than 13,000 houses are considered too small and are to be consolidated or replaced by new dwellings. The transformation is intended to break the negative spiral towards a deteriorating position of the neighbourhood in the regional housing market. The city of The Hague has since 1995 been plagued by an increasing outflow of residents which is expected to continue until 2010 (Priemus et al. 1999). For a relatively unattractive neighbourhood as The Hague Southwest, the soon to be completed VINEX[1] locations near by may produce a further exodus of even more residents in the future. These new neighbourhoods are being constructed just outside the built-up area of the existing larger cities to accommodate the increasing demand for housing. They constitute an important plank of the national spatial planning scheme. Many observers, however, are afraid that they will not strengthen the existing cities, but instead threaten them as they will contribute to a renewed exodus of middle-income households from the older, more central neighbourhoods. In order to prevent this, new housing in The Hague Southwest will be to a large extent housing for the middle- and high-income groups in order to keep these groups for the neighbourhood. This strategy is connected with a lively debate among academics as well as policy makers in the Netherlands about 'mixed neighbourhoods', that is creating neighbourhoods with different priced dwellings, both in the rented and in the owner-occupied sector (Blokland-Potters 1997; Duyvendak 1998). This should lead to a more mixed *social composition* of the neighbourhood population. One of the central questions in this debate is whether or not mixed building has an 'uplifting' social effect on, primarily, the lower-class residents by means of countering an existing or foreseen 'culture of poverty' (Noordanus 1999).

A further interesting feature concerns the role of residents in the new territorial approach. In Social Renewal there was great reliance on the participation of residents. Residents were required to show active involvement in their neighbourhoods. In the new plans the expectations with regard to the residents are more modest. They are now first and foremost seen as clients. Local arenas should be created to give residents the opportunity to join in the debate about the plans and initiatives for their neighbourhood. They are invited to think along with the policy makers and other organisations involved, but they are not expected to play an autonomous *initiating* role. Residents are to be regularly informed about the development and execution of policy plans but the professionals take the lead. In the words of the policy document: 'They (the residents) are not co-directors, but they do act as a "sounding board".' This may be a result of past experiences during Social Renewal. In the *Progress Report Pilot-project Bouwlust/ Vrederust*, published by the city of The Hague in January 1994 (Gemeente Den Haag 1994), it was concluded that citizens' participation was great in the case of concrete projects, yet marginal in the case of subjects beyond the direct self-interest of the neighbourhood residents.

Social Renewal and Big Cities Policy compared

We will now look at the situation in The Hague Southwest in 1998 in order to gain some insight into the neighbourhood after the period of

Social Renewal and the first years of the Big Cities Policy and at the
starting point of the new city plans. In order to get an impression of
the social 'state of the art' in the Bouwlust/Vrederust area in 1998 we
will look at some figures of the so-called *Omnibus enquête* (Gemeente
Den Haag 1998). This is a large-scale survey conducted for the city of
The Hague and is also partially developed for the purpose of measuring
developments within the framework of the Big Cities Policy. The
figures in Table 8.3, from the section on 'living conditions', provide
insights on the problems and the social condition of The Hague
Southwest as perceived by the residents. For reasons of comparability,
the table contains the figures for the Bouwlust neighbourhood, the
city district of Escamp (which includes both the Bouwlust and the
Vrederust area) and the average score of the city of The Hague as a
whole.

If we look at the results for the Bouwlust neighbourhood, the figures
in Table 8.3 paint a somewhat surprising picture. They do not indicate,
as might have been expected, that the residents in this neighbourhood
have a grim outlook on their living environment or their fellow

Table 8.3 Residents' perception of the quality of life in The Hague Southwest
and The Hague as a whole, 1998

	Bouwlust	*Escamp*	*The Hague*
1. General opinion of the neighbourhood	7.6	6.9	7
2. Degree of degradation of living environment	4	5.4	7
3. Degree of nuisance in the neighbourhood	2.1	3.1	3
4. Cleanliness of the neighbourhood	79	46	50
5. Perception of insecurity in the neighbourhood	21	18	23
6. Degree of social cohesion in the neighbourhood	5.9	5.4	5.6

Notes
1. 0 = unfavourable, 10 = favourable.
2. 0 = little degradation, 10 = much degradation.
3. 0 = little nuisance, 10 = much nuisance.
4. Percentage that agrees with the proposition 'My neighbourhood is a clean neighbourhood.'
5. Percentage that agrees with the proposition 'I sometimes feel unsafe in my own neighbourhood.'
6. 0 = little social cohesion, 10 = much social cohesion.
Source Gemeente Den Haag (1998).

residents. In the perception of the residents of Bouwlust their neigh-bourhood is relatively free of degradation and nuisance and is consid-ered to be rather clean. When asked about their general opinion of the neighbourhood they value it with a score of 7.6, substantially higher than the scores of Escamp (6.9) or the average score for The Hague (7). The indicator of 'social cohesion', composed on the basis of proposi-tions such as 'The people in this neighbourhood hardly know each other' and 'I feel at home with the people that live in this neighbour-hood', gives a similar impression; again the residents of Bouwlust value their own neighbourhood slightly higher. These positive feelings may of course be a consequence of the Social Renewal project, showing that the attention paid by local policy makers to this neighbourhood had raised resident satisfaction.

The odd one out in this array of positive developments seems to be the perception of safety in the neighbourhood. Although it cannot be said that the feelings of insecurity in Bouwlust are disturbingly high (they are still below the average score of The Hague), it seems strange that the score is higher than that of Escamp which has worse scores on all other indicators. This glimpse of social uneasiness in the neighbour-hood surfaces more clearly when we look at the results of the last municipal elections of March 1998. The voter turnout in the Bouwlust area was dramatically low in that year; only 44.13 per cent of those eli-gible to vote took the trouble of doing so. This was substantially lower than the average turnout of The Hague of 48.20 per cent. According to Hill (1994), this indicates a lack of social control and involvement with the neighbourhood. The figures for the number of votes cast for the extreme right wing, and more or less openly racist parties CD and CP '86, seem to support this indication of dissatisfaction. This is especially noteworthy, since the election year of 1998 showed a landslide defeat for the extreme right-wing parties (they lost all three seats in the national parliament and an enormous amount of seats in the munici-pal councils throughout the country).

As mentioned earlier, there were important distinctions between the Bouwlust and the Vrederust areas during the period of Social Renewal. In the Bouwlust area the nuisance and deprivation were clearly worse and the status of a refuge for 'urban renewal nomads' produced in-creasing pressure on the quality of the everyday environment and feel-ings of insecurity. The area of Vrederust, on the other hand, was characterised by more or less covered up problems of dissatisfaction, which were not so much related to the physical environment. During the period of Social Renewal many of the projects were aimed at improving the quality of the physical environment. The same might apply for the early years of the Big Cities Policy, as many cities merely continued existing projects. Improving the public space by means of enhanced green areas, cleaning street litter and the removal of graffiti may be held responsible for the more positive evaluation of the Bouwlust neighbourhood in 1998. It is evident that a cleaner and better maintained neighbourhood generates a more positive opinion of the physical surroundings. The election results and figures for insecurity on the other hand seem to indicate a feeling of dissatisfaction that is probably beyond the possibility of repair by means of improving the physical environment. Feelings of insecurity and dissatisfaction are usually a lot harder to pinpoint and address and require special policies.

Big Cities Policy has been under way since 1995 and at the same time is at the beginning of a second lifetime. The new programmes that are meant to 'restart' the Big Cities Policy have only just been completed and will be implemented in the future. Fearing a deteriorating position in the regional housing market, the city of The Hague has chosen to emphasise the aspect of urban renewal in their pilot project in The Hague Southwest. This effort to prevent a decline in population may indeed be pressing in view of the current trend of 'moving out of the city' and the coming completion of the VINEX locations which is expected to accelerate this process. The social fabric of the neighbourhoods involved is, however, not as strong as one might hope for after a decade of policy attention in Social Renewal and Big Cities Policy. Underneath comforting developments concerning the residents' evaluation of the physical environment of the neighbourhood, a more hidden feeling of dissatisfaction and insecurity still seems to be present. From this point of view a more robust social programme is needed. This also raises the question of how the ambition of an integral approach combining the city's physical, social and economic infrastructure (central to the Big Cities Policy) will materialise in the future.

Urban policies in the Netherlands

Only a few years ago, it seemed as if permanent (high) unemployment was an almost natural phenomenon that had to be accepted. As all social phenomena, unemployment was unequally distributed. Those with lower levels of education were especially hard hit, and among them were many immigrants from less developed countries living in the larger Dutch cities. The unemployed were, notwithstanding the extensive Dutch welfare system, severely limited in their options in the urban housing market. The danger that the categories of 'recent immigrants', 'those living in deprived neighbourhoods' and those at the bottom of the social pyramid, would overlap so much that they would become an identical excluded group created a major challenge for Dutch cities as for cities elsewhere.

We have described the successive policies Social Renewal from 1992 and Big Cities Policy from the mid-1990s. Social Renewal differed from the preceding urban renewal policy in not only focusing on housing but also including the people living there. This urban initiative was supposed to deal with housing, public space, labour market policies and education. To deal with these different fields, a so-called integrated territorial approach was taken. Neighbourhoods were the target of these policies, and it was expected that residents of these neighbourhoods would actively collaborate in these policies. Apart from the usual infighting between the different branches of government (both local and national) that were not geared towards a neighbourhood approach, Social Renewal suffered from two fatal flaws. The first was the fact that different problems have to be dealt with on different spatial scales. Making the neighbourhood safer is all very well as a neighbourhood policy, but labour market policies transcend city boundaries. The second flaw concerns the role of the local population. Precisely from those neighbourhoods that were already deprived in some respects, the government expected all kinds of initiatives from the population. The community that might have existed in earlier industrial times is, in many cases, no longer there. The pilot project in The Hague Southwest is a testimony to the fragility of the post-modern community.

Social Renewal was dropped and replaced by Big Cities Policy. This policy builds upon its predecessor. Again we see administrative reform aimed at enlarging the room for manoeuvre for cities by giving them a lump sum of resources. Again we see that neighbourhoods are the prime targets of the policies. This time, however, the role of the residents is more modest – they are redefined not so much as actors but as clients. Moreover, the current Big Cities Policy aims at restructuring the deprived neighbourhoods not just physically, but also socially by reintroducing middle-income groups. To achieve this, owner-occupied housing is being constructed in the neighbourhoods as a kind of government-induced programme of gentrification. This latter element is a matter of much contention as many observers doubt that this will lead to a strengthening of the local community. Nevertheless offering higher-quality housing will stop neighbourhoods from a further slide downwards, especially in the light of competition from new VINEX neighbourhoods.

Social Renewal has shown the resistance and the entrenchment of the different branches of both local and national government to decentralisation, but decentralisation has, evidently, helped to fine-tune policies at a local level. However, one should always keep in mind that for urban policies to be effective, one needs an effective national welfare system, national labour market policy and a national educational system. Now the Dutch economy has been growing so fast that unemployment has finally been reduced to almost frictional levels, the backdrop for urban policies has changed fundamentally. The threat of a truly divided city in which ethnicity, social disadvantage and living in deprived neighbourhoods are different sides of the same equation seems to have been thwarted. This will significantly help to create and maintain *open* and, perhaps even to borrow Jonathan Raban's (1974/1998) phrase, *soft* cities that are accessible and malleable for a whole range of people. That is what urban policies, embedded within a comprehensive, efficient and activating welfare system, should aim at.

Acknowledgement

We would like to express our thanks to E.J.J. Lanoye for her comments on an earlier version.

Note

1. VINEX neighbourhoods are now being built in close proximity to existing cities such as The Hague. They derive their name from a national planning memorandum from 1993 (Vierde Nota Extra). They are specifically intended to accommodate population growth in the Netherlands while preserving the countryside and preventing further urban sprawl. Cities fear that the completion of these VINEX neighbourhoods will lead to an abrupt exodus of middle-class households from the city centres.

Part 3

Innovations in Urban Governance

9
The New City Management
Robin Hambleton

Introduction

In many countries traditional approaches to local government leadership and management are being transformed. Long-established practices and procedures are being questioned and innovations in democratic and managerial practice now proliferate. More than that, the very role and purpose of elected local authorities are being reconsidered and reshaped. In this chapter it will be suggested that these changes amount to the emergence of a 'new city management'.[1] As we shall see, there are connections here to what has been described as the 'new public management' (Hood 1991; Dunleavy and Hood 1994). But the new city management is about much more than the development of an array of managerial tools for urban governance – such as customer-driven decision making and the contracting out of public services to private companies. It is also concerned with the changing roles of politicians, managers and citizens in the governance of localities – it promotes innovation in the politics of place as well as innovation in public service management. It will be suggested that successful city management in the twenty-first century must be concerned with democratic renewal as well as with management innovation. Coalition building with local economic and social interests as well as new approaches to community development need to be seen as part of a new management agenda which creates space for able officers to transform the effectiveness of service delivery to citizens.

There are significant differences between different countries in the way local government has grown and developed over the years. These need to be taken into account in any cross-national analysis of city management. Thus, the constitutional position of local government

147

varies across nation states, as do the powers and functions of elected local authorities (Humes 1991). National legal traditions and cultures also vary (Goldsmith and Klausen 1997). Moreover, local politics may, or may not, be dominated by powerful political parties. Local political power structures can vary remarkably even within a particular country, let alone internationally. It follows that it is dangerous to generalise too freely about international trends in local government leadership and management. It is hoped, however, that the value of the new city management perspective set out below is not that it simplifies the rich complexities of local politics and policy making in diverse countries into a single international agenda for local government modernisation. Rather the aim is to provide a framework, or set of pointers, which might aid understanding of the way processes of governing localities are changing and how they might be expected to change in the future.

The change drivers

Two sets of change drivers underpin the development of the new city management. First, the forces of globalisation discussed in earlier chapters are putting new pressures on all local authorities to be more efficient and effective – to do more for less. This does not necessarily mean reducing public expenditure. Certainly the integration of the world economies has introduced new competitive pressures into all public as well as private organisations. Clearly this means looking for 'efficiency savings', but the renewed interest in the effectiveness of public services also reflects changing views about the appropriate role for government, including local government, in modern society. Reformers argue that government should be able to achieve more by working in a different way (Osborne and Gaebler 1993). That is, it may be that government can be more successful in achieving its aims by working with other actors to achieve social outcomes rather than by trying to do everything itself (Rhodes 1997).

The second change driver is public opinion which, in turn, reflects wider changes in society. A more confident and well-informed citizenry is putting new demands on local government, as well as other public agencies, to be more open, more responsive and more accountable (Goss 1999). The old 'leave it to us, we know best' approach adopted by some local councillors and public service managers in the twentieth century is now simply unacceptable to local citizens and communities. Demands on governments to become more customer-oriented and citizen-centred can be expected to grow. Certainly, citizens now expect their local authority to deal effectively with a growing number of 'quality of life' issues which cut across departmental boundaries and perspectives. For example, citizens have concerns about: the perceived deterioration in public safety; the need for more sustainable forms of living and urban development; the social exclusion of disadvantaged groups; and the importance of providing job opportunities for all. None of these concerns – concerns that have been described as 'wicked issues' because they are difficult to resolve (Rittel and Webber 1973) – can be adequately addressed by the traditional approach of separate service departments and agencies working in relative isolation. They need 'joined up' thinking and 'joined up' action (Stewart et al. 1999).

It can be argued that these two sets of change drivers – those seeking improvements in efficiency and effectiveness, and those pressing for improvements in responsiveness and accountability – are not particularly new. Over the years local government reformers have commonly attempted to reconcile managerial and democratic objectives (Keating 1991). Thus, there has been pressure in different countries over several decades to improve professional public service management and delivery in order to enhance government efficiency and effectiveness (Pollitt 1990; Osborne and Plastrik 1997). At the same time the banner of democratic renewal has also been waved at the head of many local government reorganisation campaigns. Reformers have often advocated changes in the belief that they would make city hall bureaucracies less paternalistic, ensure elected representatives became more accountable to local citizens and generally enhance civic traditions (Putnam 1993; Ranson and Stewart 1994; Phillips 1994; Tam 1998).

In this chapter it will be suggested that three factors associated with the new city management distinguish it from previous reform efforts. First, the pace of change expected is much faster – partly because of rapid advances in new information technology, but also because public expectations about speed and customer responsiveness have grown. Second, the impact of the changes on the role and purpose of local government is potentially more far-reaching. This suggests that tinkering with traditional models will not suffice. Third, the potential for achieving synergy between managerial and democratic objectives has never been greater.

The analysis is divided into three interrelated parts. The first two discuss two significant shifts in thinking relating to local government and public services – the change from local government to local governance and the shift from public administration to new public management. These moves have profound implications for the role and culture of elected local authorities as well as the roles and practices of all those engaged in the local democratic process. The third part examines the changing roles and relationships of the three main groups of local actors: elected politicians, appointed local government officers and citizens at large. The modernisation agenda for local government emerging from this review suggests that elected local authorities need to develop better approaches to political and managerial leadership and more inventive approaches to citizen participation. These requirements have significant implications for local politics as well as the institutional design of local government.

From local government to local governance

As mentioned in Chapter 1, there is some confusion over the terms 'local government' and 'local governance'. Certainly the term 'governance' is used in a variety of ways (Rhodes 1997; Andrew and Goldsmith 1998; Pierre and Peters 2000; Stoker 2000). For the purpose of this discussion it is sufficient to use these words in the way they are commonly used in practitioner as well as academic debates. *Government* refers to the formal institutions of the state. Government makes decisions within specific administrative and legal frameworks and uses public resources in a financially accountable way. Most important, government decisions are backed up by the legitimate hierarchical power of the state. *Governance*, on the other hand, involves government *plus* the looser processes of influencing and negotiating with a range of public and private sector agencies to achieve desired outcomes. A governance perspective encourages collaboration between the public, private and non-profit sectors to achieve mutual goals. While the hierarchical power of the state does not vanish, the emphasis in governance is on steering, influencing and coordinating the actions of others. There is recognition here that government cannot go it alone. In governance relationships no one organisation can exercise hierarchical power over the others. The process is interactive because no single agency, public or private, has the knowledge and resource capacity to tackle the key problems unilaterally (Kooiman 1993).

Moving to the local level, *local government* refers to democratically elected councils. *Local governance* is broader – it refers to the processes and structures of a variety of public, private and voluntary sector bodies at the local level. It acknowledges the diffusion of responsibility for collective provision and recognises the contribution of different levels and sectors (Andrew and Goldsmith 1998; Wilson 1998). In most situations the elected local council is the only directly elected body in the local governance system and this is of critical importance. Some take the view that the new emphasis on local governance is a subtle or, perhaps, not so subtle, device for managing cutbacks in public expenditure. Certainly, the rhetoric about governance can be viewed as a way of shifting responsibility from the state onto the private and voluntary sectors and civil society in general. This displacement of responsibility can also obscure lines of accountability to the citizen, and the shift to governance certainly poses a major challenge to local democracy (Kearns and Paddison 2000). More optimistically, the movement to local governance can be welcomed as an overdue shift from a perspective which sees local government simply as a vehicle for providing a range of important public services to a new emphasis on community leadership. This interpretation envisages the role of the local authority being extended beyond the tasks of service provision to embrace a concern for the overall well-being of an area (Clarke and Stewart 1998). This shift from government to governance is not just a UK phenomenon. It is visible in other countries, for example Germany (Banner 1999).

In terms of the government/governance dimension the new city management is at the governance end of the spectrum. It requires leading politicians and senior managers to adopt an outward-looking approach and, crucially, to engage with the economic and other interests which influence the current and future well-being of the locality. Clarence Stone, a leading American urban political scientist, argued in 1980 that local politicians operate 'under *dual pressures* – one set based in electoral accountability and the other based in the hierarchical distribution of economic, organisational and cultural resources' (Stone 1980, p. 984, emphasis in original). Stephen Elkin refined this approach, arguing that the division of roles between the state and the economy means that government must continually deal with the mandates of popular control and economic well-being. The way the division of roles develops and is handled gives rise to specific 'regimes' (Elkin 1987). These depend, basically, on the strength of political elites relative to economic elites. Put bluntly, in some cities – in the US context at least – it is big business which virtually runs the city with the elected leaders having relatively little influence. Dallas (Hill 1996) and Houston (Feagin 1988) provide striking examples. In European cities too, the power of business elites to influence local decisions should not be underestimated (Pierre 1998; Kleinman

1999; Harding et al. 2000). The new city management acknowledges the reality of these local power structures but is not cowed by them. It uses the unique positional power of local government to intervene in these processes.

The academic study of urban politics and local power structures has benefited in recent years from valuable research on 'urban regimes' carried out, initially, by scholars in the USA (Stone 1989; Lauria 1997). More recently, cross-national research on urban regimes suggests that the approach can illuminate modes of urban government in the European context, although account needs to be taken of the different history of relations between the state and the private sector. Di Gaetano and Klemanski (1999) in their thoughtful comparative analysis of Birmingham, Bristol, Boston and Detroit develop a categorisation of four approaches to local governance: (1) pro-growth, (2) growth management, (3) social reform, and (4) caretaker. Pro-growth agendas focus on the importance of encouraging business development. Growth management agendas are developed to protect or improve the urban physical environment. Social reform agendas concentrate on community development rather than business development and centre on redistributive justice. Caretaker agendas seek to minimise public spending and, therefore, limit the tasks of governance to essential service provision. These are not, of course, watertight categories, but they do point in different directions when it comes to governing strategies and policy making as well as the nitty-gritty of priority setting in the practice of city management.

The central purpose of regime theory is to explain how governmental and non-governmental elites form alliances around governing tasks. One insight which emerges from this approach to urban political analysis, which will be of particular interest to practitioners, relates to conceptions of power. In the traditional approach to city government power has stemmed, as often as not, from the formal legal authority of the state. The law of the land gives elected authorities 'power over' various functions and activities. The regime approach, and Stone's work in particular, suggests that the power to command or dominate over others under modern conditions of social complexity in cities and communities is illusive: 'The power struggle concerns, not control and resistance, but gaining and fusing a capacity to act – *power to*, not *power over*' (Stone 1989, p. 229; emphasis in original). In other words, power is structured and exercised in an effort to obtain results through co-operation, not to gain control over other agencies.

Subsequent chapters explore various aspects of this governance theme in more depth. Inter-agency networking in economic governance is explored by Collinge and Srbljanin, the reform of metropolitan governance is then examined by Jouve and Lefèvre, and the internationalisation of local governance through cross-border cooperation is considered by Church and Reid. In various ways all these chapters point to new opportunities for political leaders and their senior managers. But, as mentioned earlier, there are problems with the shift towards a governance approach. How open to public scrutiny are these new governance arrangements (Burns 2000)? How can the people operating in these increasingly important multi-agency partnerships be held to account? Does governance inevitably widen the gap between power holders and citizens? A major challenge for those involved with the development of the new city management is to ensure that the new collaborative models of governance now being developed do not build up a dangerous democratic deficit in the eyes of the public.

From public administration to new public management

In parallel, and overlapping with, the movement from government to governance there has been a significant shift in the way public services are organised and run. It is possible to discern two overlapping phases of change in local government: from public administration to corporate management; and from corporate management to new public management. There is a good deal of rhetoric about these changes. Bold claims have been made about the virtues of private management practice and about the desirability of developing a more businesslike approach to the running of public services. But there is considerable confusion in the debate. In particular, the phrase 'new public management' has several meanings and there is a risk that management-led reforms may come to lose sight of the underlying social purpose of public services.

In order to make sense of current developments it is helpful to step back and examine the evolution of public service management thinking over time. Modern public services, and the associated profession of public administration, have their origins in the expansion of state-run services in the nineteenth century. Pollit (1990), in his useful analysis of managerialism in public services in the USA and the UK, tracks the way different management ideas and concepts have filtered into public administration for over a century. A particularly significant wave of management thinking hit local government in the 1960s and 1970s. Corporate management involved:

> . . . taking an overall view of a local authority's activities and the way they relate to the changing needs and problems of its area. More specifically it involves the authority developing management *and* political processes and structures which will enable it to plan, control and review its activities as a whole to satisfy the needs of the people in its area to the maximum extent consistent with available resources.
>
> (Hambleton 1978, p. 45, emphasis in original)

Two well-established traditions of public administration were challenged by corporate management thinking. First, the view that the local authority is the passive administrative agent of central government – an agent incapable of mapping out its own future – was called into question. Second, the view that the local authority was a vehicle for delivering separate services directed at essentially separate problems was also confronted (Stewart 1971). In the UK the movement led to lasting organisational changes. Out went the old town clerk who 'administered' local services and in came the new chief executive who was appointed to 'manage' the local authority on behalf of the elected members. Local authorities created policy committees and councillors developed distinctive policies suited to local circumstances. Fresh management practices were imported from the private sector – for example, management by objectives (MBO) and planning programming budgeting systems (PPBS) – and policy analysis and performance review work expanded.

It can be argued that the shift from public administration to corporate management was a significant breakthrough. Certainly local authorities started to address the cross-cutting or 'wicked issues' referred to earlier (Rittel and Webber 1973). Critics, however, argued that the corporate management changes of the 1970s led to a centralisation of power. In many councils a joint elite of senior councillors – usually those on the central policy committee – and senior officers were seen as running the place (Cockburn 1977). Certainly, in the UK context at least, the management changes of the 1970s were not sufficiently far-reaching. By 1979, the year Mrs Thatcher led the Conservative Party into government, councils were widely seen to be in charge of large, unresponsive public service bureaucracies. More radical change was bound to come.

Figure 9.1 shows the three currents of change which have characterised public service reform strategies in the last 20 years or so.[2] The first broad alternative, associated in the 1980s with the radical right, seeks to challenge the very notion of collective and non-market provision for public need (Walsh 1995). Centring on the notion of privatisation, it seeks to replace public provision with private. The second alternative, shown on the right of Figure 9.1, aims to preserve the notion of public provision, but seeks a radical reform of the manner in which this provision is undertaken. Thus, it seeks to replace the old, bureaucratic paternalistic model with a much more democratic model, often involving radical decentralisation to the neighbourhood level (Burns et al. 1994).

Interestingly, advocates of both these major change strategies of the 1980s agreed in many ways on what was wrong with 1970s-style corporate management. The shared perception was that the big bureaucracies had become remote and unaccountable – they needed to be shaken up, they needed to be stimulated into developing more cost-effective and responsive approaches and, above all, they needed to be exposed to countervailing pressures *from outside* the organisation. Both the right and the left took the view that public service bureaucracies were incapable of transforming themselves. In Hirschman's terms, the right sought to give individuals the power of *exit* and the left sought to give citizens the power of *voice* (Hirschman 1970). In the market model the consumer, dissatisfied with the product of one supplier of a service, can shift to another. The democratic model recognises that many public services cannot be individualised – they relate to groups of service users or citizens at large. Such collective interests can only be protected through enhanced participation and strengthened political accountability (Barber 1984). Hirschman is at pains to point out that, while exit and voice may be strongly contrasting empowerment mechanisms, they are not mutually exclusive.

The third broad strategy for public service reform shown in Figure 9.1 attempts to distinguish a managerial as opposed to a political response to the problems confronting public service bureaucracies. This response borrows from the competing political models in a way which simulates radical methods but in a form which preserves existing power relations between the producers and users of services. In place of the sometimes violent and unpredictable signals of exit and voice, a panoply of techniques (market research, user satisfaction surveys, complaints procedures, customer care programmes, focus groups, call

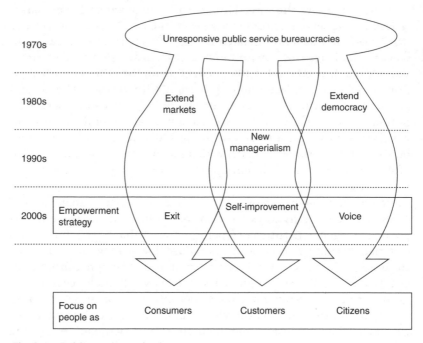

Fig. 9.1 Public service reform strategies

centres, interactive websites, etc.) are introduced to provide more gentle and manageable 'feedback'.

On this analysis the new public management can be seen to be associated with two of the strands in Figure 9.1 – the market and managerialist reform strategies. This interpretation is consistent with the analysis put forward by Hood (1991) who suggests that new public management involves a marriage of two streams of ideas: the new institutional economics and business-type managerialism. New public management also implies giving much more attention to shaping the culture of the organisation – for example, strengthening support to front-line workers, encouraging risk-taking and emphasising the commitment to quality (Burns et al. 1994, pp. 104–7).

There are important links between the development of new public management and the shift towards governance discussed earlier. Both envisage a shift from 'rowing to steering'. In their influential book on 'reinventing government', Osborne and Gaebler (1993, p. 35) draw a distinction between policy decisions (steering) and service delivery (rowing): 'Steering requires people who see the entire universe of issues and possibilities and can balance competing demands for resources. Rowing requires people who focus intently on one mission and perform it well.' They do not, contrary to a popular misconception, advocate the contracting out of all public services as ideologues on the political right have argued in the past (Ridley 1988). They believe that government agencies will often remain as service providers – although they will often have to compete with private producers for that privilege.

The new public management ideas have been taken up with considerable enthusiasm by local authorities around the world. Many US city mayors claim to have moved in this direction – for example, the mayors of New York City (Weikart 1998), Milwaukee (Norquist 1998) and Indianapolis (Goldsmith 1997). More broadly the Bertelsmann Foundation, based in Germany, has documented examples of local authority innovation with new public management in a dozen or so countries (Prohl 1997). However, John (2001) notes that, because local government traditions vary, there has been variation in the take-up of new public management ideas in Europe. At this stage, he argues, it is more a feature of northern local government systems than those in southern Europe.

As mentioned in the introduction, the new city management involves *more* than the application of new public management approaches to local governance. It is concerned with democratic renewal as well as with public service effectiveness and, as such, it is concerned with all of the three change strategies outlined in Figure 9.1. There are strong links here to the efforts being made in some countries to deepen and widen democracy. For example, Giddens (1998), in his discussion of the third way, suggests that the crisis of democracy comes from its not being democratic enough. He notes that: 'Reinventing government certainly sometimes means adopting market-based solutions. But it should also mean reasserting the effectiveness of government in the face of markets' (Giddens 1998, p. 75). This is an important development in the debate for, as various critics have argued, the new public management can result in changes which weaken rather than strengthen local democracy and local accountability (Hoggett 1991; Greer and Hoggett 1999). Giddens argues that government can re-establish more direct contact with citizens, and citizens with government, through experiments with democracy – local direct democracy, electronic referenda, citizens' juries and the like. Again, considerable innovation in local democratic practice is now taking place in various countries and we now turn to consider these developments in more detail.

The changing relationships between politicians, officers and citizens

Earlier, in the discussion of governance, reference was made to the need for local authorities to shape the behaviour of economic actors impacting on their locality. We now focus on the democracy agenda and consider the three main groups of actors in local governance – politicians, officers and citizens. Figure 9.2 suggests that there is a triangular relationship between these three interest groups. Each corner of the triangle can generate important contributions to the local policy-making process, although the relative influence of the three groups can vary enormously. The diagram is a drastic simplification of a more complex reality. There are huge differences of view within each interest group and, more than that, individuals can appear in more than one corner – for example, politicians and officers are also citizens. However, the triangle is useful as it points up the different sources of

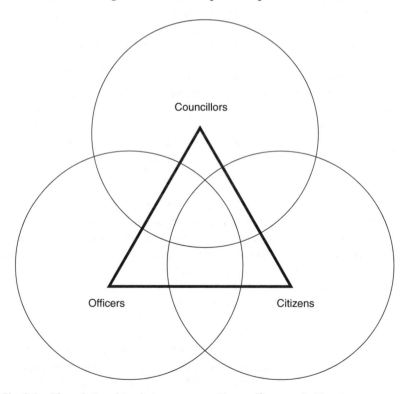

Fig. 9.2   The relationships between councillors, officers and citizens

legitimacy which underpin the contributions of different actors – elected members enjoy a political mandate from local citizens, officers bring managerial and professional skills as well as impartiality, and citizens have a democratic right to be heard and to hold government to account.

The new city management sees interaction on all three sides of the triangle as offering major learning opportunities not just for policy and practice but also for organisational development. However, before we consider each of the groups it is important to draw a distinction between local-authority-wide deliberative and decision-making arenas and local settings relating to parts of the city. The substantial body of literature on area management and neighbourhood decentralisation suggests not only that devolved management can enhance service responsiveness to localities within a city, but also that new settings for enhancing citizen participation – neighbourhood committees, community forums and the like – can strengthen local democratic accountability (Yates 1973; Hambleton 1978; Hoggett and Hambleton 1987; Pollitt et al. 1998). It is certainly the case that many citizens feel more attached to their immediate 'home area' than, say, the city as a whole and are more attracted to participating in decision making about issues which have an impact on the area where they live. Local authorities in various countries have responded to these preferences by introducing various forms of area-based decision making. There are interesting examples in several Scandinavian cities (Back et al. 2000), in the UK (Taylor 2000) and in New Zealand (Forgie et al. 1999). In the USA there is a long and well-researched history of neighbourhood-based community action which is also relevant to current European concerns relating to urban deprivation and social exclusion (Keating and Krumholz 1999). There is great potential for area-based working to improve both service quality and democratic accountability.

The changing roles of politicians

Citizens elect councillors to serve as their representatives, and it is accountability at the ballot box which distinguishes local government from local administration. Councillors are usually elected on a ward (or district) basis and, to varying degrees, have strong links to the area-based communities which elected them. The following roles for councillors have been well established in UK local government for many years:

- Policy making for the local authority as a whole
- Policy making for particular services

- Voicing concerns about the effective operation of local authority services
- Voicing concerns about the performance of services
- Responding to the grievances of constituents
- Voicing concerns about the needs of the area they represent

It is a simplification, but it can be suggested that the traditional role of the councillor focused on *representing* the interests of citizens – speaking out on their behalf and trying to ensure the local authority and other agencies were responsive to their needs. Where party politics is significant the representative role also involves attempting to implement a party programme that has been put to the electorate as a whole. Studies of the way councillors use their time have suggested that local politicians take their responsibilities seriously, put in long hours and are expected to manage many competing pressures (Barron et al. 1991). Reviews of the role of the councillor carried out in the 1990s in the UK suggested, however, that the representative role had become weakened over the years. This is partly because councillors, mainly through their service on numerous committees of the council, were spending an increasing amount of their time on the internal management of the local authority (Audit Commission 1990, 1997; Young and Rao 1994). Councillors found themselves servicing the decision-making system rather than giving a political lead, and many expressed concerns that their time was not always well spent in committees.

Updating and modernising local political management to meet new challenges necessarily involves councillors in a rethink of their roles. In 1995 UK national guidance on local authority management suggested that councillors were wanting to give more attention to four emerging roles (Hambleton and Holder 1995):

- Strengthening the approach to civic leadership – involving promoting the image of the area to outsiders as well as developing a more proactive approach to local leadership
- Developing the ward councillor role – involving decentralisation of power and innovations in neighbourhood-based decision making
- Introducing a scrutiny role – with some councils setting up scrutiny committees to examine the performance of other agencies in their area
- Enhancing joint working – involving the creation of a variety of new forms of partnership arrangement

These four roles have received increased attention in recent years and have been given a significant boost in the UK context by the Local Government Act 2000. The new political management arrangements now being introduced in England and Wales are intended to help councillors develop a more outgoing and inclusive style of operation as well as underpin a more effective approach to community leadership. Goss (1999) has identified five possible new roles for councillors in this changing context: listener/advocate; ring-holder; broker; facilitator; and empowerer.

The new city management is concerned to support the development of a *range* of councillor roles. It recognises that councillors, from the most experienced to the brand new, need help and support in developing new skills to take on new challenges. Managers, too, need to develop their political awareness, to recognise the diversity of councillor roles and to develop creative ways of enhancing the skills of both members and managers. The new era requires good understanding and close working not just between the top officers and the political leaders, but also between ward councillors, the local managers and front-line staff working in the neighbourhoods.

The changing roles of officers

The shifts from government to governance and from public administration to new public management outlined earlier set down important challenges for local government officers. Local government is well served by hard-working and committed officers at all levels – from those interacting directly with the public in day-to-day service delivery through those in middle management to chief officers and chief executives. Moreover, local government officers have a good record as effective managers and a well-deserved reputation for maintaining political neutrality. A public service ethos underpins the way most of them go about their work. This remains a fairly intangible concept but some of the key values of this ethos are:

- A respect for the democratic political process
- A commitment to fair, defensible procedures in public decision making
- A belief in high standards of staff conduct with an emphasis on honesty, integrity, impartiality and objectivity
- A respect for the rights of the individual citizen regardless of that person's purchasing power

- A belief that public servants hold the wider concerns of the public at heart
- A motivation among the workforce which is not driven by the pursuit of profit

These are fine beliefs, but a new city management perspective suggests that the way they are operationalised needs updating. A study of local government management in the UK carried out in the mid-1990s proposed that the 'public service ethos' should be complemented by the development of a 'public innovation ethos' (Hambleton et al. 1996). Table 9.1 suggests that the five pillars of the public service ethos in local government have been a concern for: sound procedures; good control mechanisms; conforming behaviour; consistency of treatment; and service for the public. These are values which remain important for local government today. They are, however, in tension with the public innovation ethos which gives weight to: getting results; steering; enhancing the performance of people and systems; responding to diverse needs in a flexible way; and working with local communities.

There is no suggestion here that public service managers should switch allegiance from the values on the left to those on the right of

Table 9.1   Public service and public innovation in local government management

The public service ethos	The public innovation ethos

1. Procedures
  – fairness
  – propriety
  – accountability
	1. Results
	  – quality of service
	  – efficiency and impact

2. Controlling
  – centralised accountability
  – seeks to avoid mistakes
	2. Steering
	  – clear guidance
	  – local autonomy
	  – valuing staff

3. Conformance
  – obedience
  – reliability
	3. Performance
	  – creativity and inventiveness
	  – risk-taking

4. Consistency
  – uniformity
  – equity
	4. Diversity
	  – responsive to differences
	  – customised
	  – flexible

5. Working for the public
  – caring
  – professional
	5. Working with the public
	  – listening
	  – supportive

Source Adapted from Hambleton et al. (1996).

Table 9.1. There are great strengths on both sides of this table. It may be helpful, however, for individual local authorities to consider, in relation to particular issues and services as well as strategic management as a whole, whether it currently has the right balance between the 'service' and the 'innovation' ethos. Those committed to the new city management may not wish to question the core beliefs of the public service ethos outlined above. But they will want to challenge practices, habits and routines which discourage learning and innovation. In many local authorities there is still a 'watch your back' attitude in the officer corps which works against creative problem solving. The new city management fosters a culture which values informed risk-taking, celebrates successful innovations – small and large – and reaches out to local communities.

What about the role of the top officer – the chief executive? A study of managerial leadership for the UK Society of Local Authority Chief Executives (SOLACE) suggested that chief executives have a key role in leading change and developing the organisation of the authority (Hambleton 1999). Four leadership roles were identified: providing strategic advice to councillors; managing processes relating to decisions; taking decisions on behalf of the council; and influencing other agencies. Chief executives interviewed for the research suggested that the fourth role was expanding quite quickly, and this chimes with the shift from government to governance discussed earlier (Travers et al. 1997). The development of continuous learning opportunities for chief executives has identified five key capacities: working with the political dimension; leading the organisation; developing self-knowledge; developing effective external relationships; and maintaining a focus on strategic and long-term issues (Broussine 1998).

Cross-national comparative research on the roles and functions of chief executive officers has uncovered useful insights on alternative approaches to managerial leadership (Klausen and Magnier 1998). The researchers drew a distinction between two kinds of chief executive – the classical bureaucrat, whose approach aligns closely with the public service ethos outlined above, and the political bureaucrat, who is more committed to learning from the public and whose stance is more in line with the public innovation ethos. Again it would be unwise to suggest that features of the classical bureaucrat are now old hat and can be discarded in favour of the more political approach. But the new city management certainly envisages the chief executive (or city manager) as a dynamic executive leader who is capable of working closely with elected members and brokering community interests.

Changing approaches to citizen involvement

At the beginning of the chapter it was suggested that one of the driving forces underpinning the development of the new city management is an increasingly well-informed citizenry putting new demands on all public agencies. In a series of cross-national studies Terry Clark and his colleagues have suggested that a 'New Political Culture' is developing which contrasts with the class politics that have dominated local politics in many countries for more than a century (Clark 1994c; Clark and Rempel 1997; Clark and Hoffman-Martinot 1998). *Inter alia*, and as discussed more fully in Chapter 5, this body of work points to the rise of single-issue politics and the growth of new social movements (e.g. concerning civil rights, environmentalism or feminism). Certainly, in the period since the 1960s and 1970s, there has been growing public pressure for participation and new forms of democracy and citizen activism have emerged (Held and Pollitt 1986).

Figure 9.1 referred to the growth of voice as an empowerment mechanism and, in practice, local governments have developed a wide array of approaches designed to enhance representative democracy and/or encourage participatory democracy (Lowndes et al. 1997). Table 9.2 refers to four broad strategies councils have developed for strengthening the voice of the service user or citizen in local decision making. This is not a comprehensive listing of the options. Rather it gives an impression of the sorts of innovations that are taking place. Goss (1999) has developed another typology which relates 30 or so

Table 9.2 Ways of strengthening voice in local governance

---

1. Improving representative democracy:
   e.g. voter registration drives, experimenting with voting methods, open government rules, citizens' rights at meetings, better support to local councillors, council debates on the internet, electronic polling, interactive websites
2. Extending representative democracy:
   e.g. area committees of councillors based on wards or groups of wards, strengthening parish councils, community boards, neighbourhood forums, user panels
3. Infusing representative with participatory democracy:
   e.g. community visioning projects, citizens' juries, deliberative opinion polls, community representation on committees and partnership boards, consensus conferences
4. Extending participatory democracy:
   e.g. funding of non-statutory groups, community development, delegation to neighbourhood and/or community groups, referendums, citizen ballots

---

methods of consultation/participation to five main reasons for engaging the public: giving information; consultation/listening; exploring/innovating/listening; judging/deciding together; and delegating/supporting decision making.

The language used by politicians, officers and others often symbolises how they perceive the public, and this perception goes some way to explaining the nature of the different democratic initiatives that they adopt. In the era of corporate management discussed earlier, service users were often referred to as *clients*. This has a paternalist ring, implying that the individual accepts the superior judgement of the professional officer. As shown in Figure 9.1, modern managers, while they refer to users, often use the following terms, sometimes interchangeably (Burns et al. 1994). This usage may mask power relationships. *Consumers* shop around, they are in the market to find a good product and have little loyalty to the service provider. The word *customer* has become a more popular term than consumer in public service management because it implies developing a more lasting relationship between those giving and those receiving services. Customers may even develop a sense of loyalty to the provider. The *citizen* has political rights and responsibilities and is concerned with the public good as well as with the quality of services to individuals and households. The new city management recognises the appropriateness of treating people as consumers, customers and citizens in different settings. This reflects the fact that new-style managers are wanting to respond sensitively to the needs of different people which, quite naturally, will vary.

Mention must be made of yet another 'c' – *community*. The new city management is certainly concerned to promote community development and community leadership. This involves working with local communities of interest as well as communities having place-based identities (Taylor 2000). It involves drawing communities directly into the decision-making arrangements relating to, for example, urban regeneration (Purdue et al. 2000; Atkinson and Larsen 2000) or social care (Means and Smith 1998). There is a risk, however, that some of those involved in the modernisation of public service management lack sophistication when they talk about community involvement. Certainly, as in the 1970s, too many governments seem to use the word 'community' as if it were an aerosol can, to be sprayed onto any policy or service in the hope of giving it a more progressive and sympathetic cachet (Cochrane 1986). In practice, as Hoggett (1997) demonstrates, 'community' can provide a vehicle for dominance by powerful groups as well as a platform for emancipatory politics. Social exclusion has grown in Western democracies in recent times and a new enthusiasm for a community-based approach to public policy making, which is more inclusive and community based, has gained momentum (Etzioni 1994; Giddens 1998; Tam 1998). This is to be welcomed, and the new city management recognises the importance of working closely with communities. But it also understands that modern communities are fragmented and fraught with conflict.

Conclusions

This discussion of the new city management suggests that, if they are to cope with the new challenges which now confront them, local authorities need to develop a much stronger approach to community leadership as well as more effective approaches to citizen involvement. The importance of strengthening city leadership is increasingly being recognised (Judd 2000). This is partly because leadership is vital to attract investment and compete for growth and, more important, because strong local leadership is essential to deal with the social and environmental dilemmas which now confront people wherever they live. Outgoing leadership by elected politicians and their senior managers is now needed to orchestrate the actions of a wide range of public and private actors to achieve desired outcomes. Useful research on urban leadership and alternative styles of political leadership can help here (Svara 1990, 1994; Leach and Wilson 2000). Examples of bold approaches to leadership in difficult settings can also inspire, for example, the imaginative leadership of Philadelphia by Mayor Ed Rendell (Bissinger 1997).

In the UK the Labour government, elected in 1997 and re-elected in 2001, has given considerable attention to the development of new institutional forms which can provide not only a platform for more visible and outgoing approaches to local political leadership, but also a basis for more accountable decision making. The Local Government Act 2000 requires all local authorities in England and Wales to modify their constitutions, and three main options for the future have been provided for in the legislation: a directly elected executive mayor with a cabinet; a directly elected mayor with a council manager; and a council leader, elected by the full council, who heads a cabinet. All these models provide for a separation of powers between an executive, charged with taking responsibility for exercising leadership, and an assembly, which focuses on policy development, representation and scrutiny roles (Hambleton 2000). These proposals, as with the legislation creating the directly elected mayor for London and the Greater London Authority, have stirred up wide-ranging debate about the future of local democracy in the UK. It is early days, but the signs are that the legislation will help to spur a significant wave of innovations with new city management ideas in the coming years.

Does the new city management differ that much from previous reform efforts? Earlier it was suggested that a response to this question should consider three factors. First, the pace of change, spurred by advances in new information technology, is surely more rapid than before. Take the internet – it is estimated that by the end of 2001 half the British population will be on-line. The take-up of the internet is faster than for previous technological advances, such as the telephone and television. The implications for the way the local authority inter-acts with the public are only starting to be grasped. But it is not just the breakthroughs in technology which are speeding up change – the key driver is public demand for enhanced responsiveness. Citizens used to obtaining instant money from bank cash machines on a 24-hour basis and to paying their bills via the internet at the press of a button will become impatient with public service providers who fail to operate at similar levels of speed. Public services are responding. For example, the UK Improvement and Development Agency has, via a new na-tional land information system, cut the length of time taken to con-duct a legal search on a property from six weeks to six hours and is aiming for six minutes (Larner 2000).

Second, the changes discussed in this chapter imply a radical rethink of the role and purpose of the local authority. If the global economic forces and new social challenges are to be met head on, bold new approaches to leadership and management are needed. Take young people – many of them are choosing not to vote in local elections because they cannot see the point. The imaginative local authority does not recoil in horror, rather it takes steps to reach out and engage with young people in new and inventive ways – it takes risks, it listens, it tries out new approaches. In the language used earlier, it emphasises the importance of developing the public *innovation* ethos alongside the well-established public *service* ethos. Many in local government welcome the opportunity to break new ground and lead the way on the issues concerning local people but they have been held back. The new city management, by bringing about a major change in the culture of the organisation, can free these energies.

Third, there is an opportunity to move beyond the old and sterile local government debate which has pitched political leadership against managerial leadership, members against officers. The new triangular relationships between members, officers and citizens discussed earlier provide real opportunities for disaggregating decision making and empowering all parties. Well-supported politicians able to pursue their various political roles will value managers who work closely with them and deliver results on the ground. The reputation of both politicians and officers is well placed to go up if new policies and new approaches lead to improvements in the local quality of life, more so if local people have a real say in the decisions that matter most to them.

The analysis of trends in public service management set out in Figure 9.1 suggests that three empowerment strategies will continue to be important in political and managerial practice in the future: the power of exit, the power of voice and the power of self-improvement. Those involved in the new systems of local governance have growing experience of all three and, in addition, can relate to communities 'in the round'.

In conclusion, there is no suggestion here that the movement to new city management represents a well-defined shift in local government in all Western democracies, still less an international paradigm shift in the nature of local governance and/or public service management. Rather by outlining the main contours of the new city management, the chapter aims to show how local governments in different countries are responding creatively to powerful shifts in their external environment. If political and managerial innovations can be integrated more successfully in the future, communities as well as the institutions of local democracy will benefit.

Notes

1. The phrase 'new city management' is used here to refer to political and managerial innovation being taken forward by elected local governments. These innovations are relevant to suburban and rural areas as well as urban areas.
2. I would like to acknowledge the contributions of Danny Burns and Paul Hoggett in developing this framework in the early 1990s (Burns et al. 1994, p. 22).

10
A Network Paradigm for Urban Governance?

Chris Collinge and Alan Srbljanin

Introduction

It has been argued over recent years that we are now witnessing the emergence of a new approach to local and regional governance based upon institutional networks and partnerships (see, for example, Cooke and Morgan 1993; Stoker and Young 1993; Benington and Harvey 1994; Castells 1996; Cooke and Morgan 1998; Tödtling 1999; Morgan et al. 2000). It has, in particular, been suggested that public authorities in successful cities and regions are following the private sector in adopting a 'network paradigm', and forging strategic alliances which transcend existing territorial or sectoral boundaries in the pursuit of economic development. Apparently this new paradigm is part of a more general movement away from hierarchical relationships, towards flatter structures and more flexible methods of working.

But while there is no doubt much circumstantial evidence, the networking postulate (especially in the context of urban governance) has not as yet been subject to sufficient rigorous examination. On the one hand, the different types of organisational networks, with their different dimensions and attributes, have not been identified and classified sufficiently at a conceptual level. On the other hand, the degree to which these different networks have developed in practice, and the different causes of this development, have not been explored to sufficient empirical depth. The purpose of this chapter is therefore to make a modest contribution by investigating the hypothesis that inter-agency networks and partnerships are assuming a growing importance in the organisation of urban and regional governance, and particularly in economic governance, across Europe.

This investigation is pursued by means of a comparative study of the changing patterns of economic governance in the West Midlands region of England and in the southern German state of Bavaria, two regions which between them cover a wide spectrum of economic circumstances. The chapter begins by sketching out the main parameters of the debate around networks and the network paradigm. This is followed by a detailed account of the changing patterns of governance over recent decades in the two case study regions. The chapter concludes by comparing the main changes in network formation between the two regions, and by assessing the degree to which these can be explained as part of a general paradigm change.

The 'network paradigm' debate

There is now a substantial literature drawing attention to the importance of institutional networking as a form of social coordination. In the context of local or regional governance, the network postulate has been associated with the view that greater autonomy is currently devolving to subnational areas in and beyond Europe. Early statements of the 'new regionalism' case are provided by Sabel (1989) and Murray (1991). Murray, for example, suggests that the development of new industrial districts, together with European economic integration, is encouraging subnational governments to assume a more important role in economic development, and also that successful regions such as Baden-Württemberg and Emilia Romagna are benefiting from this role (Murray 1991, p. 22; see also Morgan et al. 2000).

Cooke and Morgan are interested in what they refer to as 'microregulatory networks' comprising private, semi-public and public institutions which support small and medium-sized enterprises. These networks include trade or employers' associations, chambers of commerce, independent foundations involved in (say) technological diffusion, and governmental bodies at various levels (Cooke and Morgan 1993). They involve 'a thick layering of public and private industrial support institutions, high grade labour market intelligence . . . rapid diffusion of technological transfer' (Cooke and Morgan 1993, p. 562). The quality of the relations in these networks is considered to be of central importance to regional development. In Baden-Württemberg, for example, there are strong institutional linkages which assist firms to remain competitive by renewing their capacity for innovation: 'where market transactions fail the public and private or semi-private institutions in the network provide a substitute' (Cooke and Morgan 1993, p. 557; see also Cooke and Morgan 1998).

A similar observation has been made by the Groupement Européen des Milieux Innovateurs (GREMI). For the GREMI scholars the concept of 'innovative milieu' is used to encapsulate the role of innovative networks and resources held within regions (Crevoisier 1996). 'Institutional atmosphere' is important in conditioning the creation and maintenance of local economic agglomerations. The innovation network comprises a collection of agencies including companies, research and training agencies, trade associations and public bodies. Amin and Thrift likewise use the concept of 'institutional thickness' to refer to the presence of private, quasi-public and public institutions (e.g. financial institutions, chambers of commerce, local authorities) which give support to the economy, together with the quality of co-operative relations between these institutions (Amin and Thrift 1994, p. 15; see also Castells and Hall 1994).

Focusing more within the state system, Benington and Harvey point out that there has been a massive increase in the number of cross-national and cross-regional networks of local authorities based upon shared economic, sectoral and territorial interests (see also Goldsmith 1993):

> In addition to its vertical relationships with member states through the Council of Ministers and national governance, the European Commission also seems actively to be encouraging horizontal relations with cross-national networks of regional and local authorities, and other public, private and non governmental organisations and interest groups.
>
> (Benington and Harvey 1994, p. 28)

The authors conclude by asking whether this indicates 'a paradigm shift in which the very concept of separate vertical 'tiers' of government is being complemented and challenged by a new model of overlapping and interlocking 'spheres' (Benington and Harvey 1994). In a similar vein Stoker and Young (1993) argue that networking represents a new style of governance which contrasts both with the old hierarchical approach to local government and the new emphasis upon market mechanisms.

There are those, however, who strike a more critical note regarding the emergence of a network paradigm in governance. The ability and willingness of cities and regions to form successful networks and to participate in the 'Europe of the Regions' is itself constrained by uneven development and by economic decline (Meegan 1994). Less favoured regions are generally not equipped to emulate successful industrial districts, and the quality of regional networks is quite dependent upon the national context and the attitude of national government (Amin and Tomaney 1995). Networking in the public and quasi-public sectors may grow more readily in regions that are already successful, and may serve the interests of the already powerful at the expense of the rest. Writing from an actor network theory perspective, Murdoch for his part argues that it is not so much the use of networks in practice but the awareness of networks among social scientists that is new (Murdoch 1995).

One criticism of the network paradigm thesis which has yet to be made with sufficient force, however, concerns its rather unqualified and blanket character. There is a noticeable tendency within the literature to postulate a general switch towards networking as a form of social coordination, affecting all Western societies and organisations to similar degrees. There is also a tendency to view this process as the consequence of an overall change from one paradigm of social coordination (or perhaps mode of regulation) to another, a change which is occurring at a broad structural level. But while large-scale changes are undoubtedly occurring, it is important that analysis does not cease at this point, and that efforts are made to develop the kind of conceptual tools that could be used to generate a more precise understanding of these changes. In particular, specific hypotheses about types of institutional networks and their interactions are required, which identify specific proximate causes that operate differentially in different places. Only on this basis can the networking thesis be developed beyond a historicist prophecy.

In this context we can identify two particular features of network relations that require closer attention, their 'direction' and their 'range'. Relations between the tiers of government would not normally be viewed as forming 'networks', but this should not blind us to the possibility that relations between tiers have variable characteristics and can often assume a network quality. Hence it is possible to imagine links between local agencies in one country and national agencies in another, links which are voluntary in character. It is also possible to envisage a network of relations between local agencies and departments of national governments, relations which are adjacent to or embedded within underlying hierarchical structures. An adequate understanding of the state system requires that 'vertical' as well as 'horizontal' relations be taken into consideration (see Benington and Harvey 1994). Indeed, we would argue that it is impossible to understand the evolution of 'horizontal' networks without simultaneously examining the evolution of such 'vertical' relations within and beyond the state system.

Aside from the 'direction' of networking, a further aspect to be considered is the scale or spatial reach of the relationships concerned (Collinge 1999). Some networks – whether horizontal or vertical – are what we might call 'long range', reaching well beyond their region, while others are 'short range' and function mainly within regions. The spatial scale of the network may also differ from the normal spatial reach of the participating institutions. Some international networks, for example, involve institutions with a wider geographical reach (e.g. regional government), while others involve institutions with a narrow reach (e.g. local government). The purpose of the present chapter is to make a modest contribution to the development of network analysis by examining the 'network hypothesis' empirically, through case studies of the West Midlands of England and the state of Bavaria in southern Germany. These case studies focus particularly upon network relationships in and around the state system, and in particular upon those concerned with economic governance.

Governance in the West Midlands

The West Midlands region of England comprises an older industrial conurbation which is surrounded by relatively prosperous smaller towns (such as Telford, Warwick and Redditch). During the 1970s and 1980s the region faced dramatic economic decline, with a loss of manufacturing capacity and a rapid rise in unemployment. In the 1990s, however, the economy staged something of a recovery, with substantial inward investment and new working practices bringing unemployment back down to the national average. Nevertheless, the West Midlands remains very dependent upon metal-related manufacturing, and upon a motor vehicle industry that is largely foreign owned and suffering worldwide overcapacity. Sectors such as information and communications technology remain under-represented despite recent strong growth.

Vertical relations

There are vertical relations within the state system between European, national, regional and local arms of government. These relations can take a variety of forms from strictly hierarchical through regulatory and consultative to collaborative. Extra-regional vertical relations involving the state system in the West Midlands have increased over the medium term as a result of ongoing integration among members of the European Union. The concentration of power and resources in Brussels has inserted an additional tier into government, and encouraged West Midlands authorities to gain direct access to the European Commission. Local authorities in the region have also benefited from European financing, although fiscal links have been controlled by the UK central government and by the Government Office for the West Midlands (GOWM). The City of Birmingham has, for example, taken advantage of European and other resources to redevelop the city centre, to provide communications and facilities for service-based industries, and to attract regeneration funding. Local authorities are also participating (albeit indirectly) in the Committee of the Regions, which is an important if relatively weak arm of the administrative framework of Europe.

Intraregional vertical relations have, however, been diminishing in number since the late 1970s. After a period of central–local tension, the abolition of the West Midlands Metropolitan County Council (WMCC) in 1986 reduced the number of local government tiers and the number of vertical linkages. The review of local government launched nationally in 1990 pointed in the same general direction, removing the county tier of government in some areas. The establishment of ten government offices for the regions in England (in 1994), by internalising previously external relations between government departments in the region, has further reduced the scope for vertical networking on the part of local authorities. More recently this process has been reinforced by the establishment of Advantage West Midlands (AWM), the regional development agency which represents a merger of the regeneration programmes of three pre-existing statutory bodies (Rural Development Commission, English Partnerships and the Government Office for the Regions) and the incorporation of the former West Midlands Development Agency. It therefore appears that the increase in 'long range' vertical network relations (reaching out of the region) has been offset by a reduction in the number of 'short range' vertical network relations sustained within the region.

Horizontal relations

There are also horizontal relations within the state system, linking local authorities and agencies at broadly the same hierarchical 'level' but in different places or performing different functions. Some horizontal relations involving West Midlands authorities are the product of statutory duties laid down by central government, while others are the result of voluntary initiative. Once again, European integration has added to the number of extra-regional horizontal relations. Local authorities in the West Midlands are now involved in a variety of networks with other European authorities including, for example, the Eurocities network, the Telecities network and the European Urban Observatory.

For different reasons, there has also been an increase in intraregional horizontal networking over recent decades. During the 1980s, for example, the four shire counties combined with the metropolitan districts to establish the West Midlands Regional Forum as a consultative and advisory body. In 1985, against a background of economic crisis, these authorities together with the West Midlands Group of Chambers of Commerce and central government agencies in the region, also formed the West Midlands Development Agency (WMDA), a partnership established to attract inward investment. The abolition of the WMCC, although it reduced vertical networking, prompted a further expansion of ad hoc inter-agency horizontal relations within the region. Joint boards comprising delegates from the seven conurbation districts have statutory responsibility for the provision of 'strategic' services such as police, fire and civil defence, passenger transport, waste disposal and other activities (Leach et al. 1990). A West Midlands Joint Committee, comprising the political leadership of the seven district councils, was also established in the late 1980s (apparently at central government's request) to provide a consultative arena for other joint functions.

At a subconurbation level, the four Black Country boroughs (Dudley, Sandwell, Walsall and Wolverhampton) north of Birmingham responded to abolition of WMCC, and the resulting fear of the unbridled power of the city of Birmingham, by establishing a Joint Advisory Group (JAG), comprising the political leadership of each authority. The main focus of this network has been upon urban regeneration and related matters, such as environment, land-use planning, economic development, tourism and European liaison. Despite some useful joint initiatives, however, coordination is limited by the relative absence of political will within the four districts, and by areas of inter-district competition. The growth of local partnerships across England during the 1990s reflected in part the decision by central government to shift responsibility for local initiatives to regeneration partnerships involving local arms of central government (e.g. training and enterprise councils or TECs), the business community (e.g. chambers of commerce), local authorities and the voluntary sector. It can therefore be concluded that the growth of long-range horizontal networks has been complemented and compounded by an expansion in the number of short-range horizontal networks operating within the region.

Public/private relations

During the 1980s Birmingham City Council responded to central government plans to impose urban development corporations by initiating various joint schemes with the private sector. Subsequently the city has pursued a conscious strategy of civic development through strategic alliances and partnerships with private sector partners in a variety of initiatives, including the Birmingham Heartlands Limited, Birmingham Marketing Partnership and the City Pride Partnership (Hall et al. 1996; Collinge and Hall 1997). From a starting point in which this approach was designed to pre-empt government imposition it has developed into a standard strategy on the part of the city.

Outside Birmingham the Coventry and Warwickshire Partnership (CWP) was formed in August 1994 to coordinate economic development activity. The founding partners here included Coventry City Council, Warwickshire County Council, the Chambers of Commerce and Industry, the local TEC and the five surrounding local authorities. But the partnership developed very quickly to incorporate some 60 member organisations from across the subregion. There has undoubtedly been a general increase in the formation of networks and partnerships with a private sector component in the West Midlands since 1985. These partnerships have generally been short-range, operating at a subregional – district or cross-district – level, and have been primarily concerned with regeneration.

Governance in southern Bavaria

Bavaria is a large state with a relatively low population density that contains some of the newest and most advanced industrial regions of Europe (such as Oberbayern and Mittelfranken). It is one of a minority of *Länder* in modern Germany to maintain historical continuity from the pre-war period, and its independent tradition is reflected in its view of itself as a Freistaat Bayern. During the cold war it received an influx of businesses from the uncertain environment of Berlin, and during the 1980s and 1990s it benefited from the growth of high technology activities in search of pleasant rural landscapes. This environment has, however, been challenged recently by new economic pressures associated with reunification, the opening up of East Europe, and competition from the Far East. Traditional manufacturing industries such as glass and ceramics have experienced a decline, and there has been an increase in unemployment which has prompted greater interest in local economic development.

Vertical relations

As in the West Midlands, the number of extra-regional vertical relations involving the state system has grown as a result of the ongoing integration among nations within the European Union, and once again this process has encouraged Bavarian authorities and especially the state government to establish a presence in Brussels, and to participate in the Committee of the Regions. The state has also benefited from European funding, albeit under different budgets and budget headings than the West Midlands.

As regards intraregional vertical relations, Bavaria is divided into seven regions (*Regierungsbezirke* such as Oberfranken in the north and Oberbayern in the south) which are now the constituent units of state control, to which the *Land* government divides and extends its ministerial responsibilities. The system of local government in Bavaria was last reformed over the period between 1971 and 1978, with the establishment of a new framework of local government law whereby some smaller councils were merged to form larger ones. But in the same period 18 planning regions and a number of 'central places' were also established together with the new Bavarian Ministry for Regional Development (Bayerisches Staatsministerium für Landesentwicklung und Umweltfragen).

As in the West Midlands, 'long range' vertical network relations beyond the region have on balance been increased by the process of European integration. But unlike the West Midlands there has been no net reduction in the number of 'short-range' vertical relations within the region. Indeed, despite limited reorganisation of local government in the late 1970s, no tier of local government has been removed, and other steps (such as the establishment of planning regions) have probably added somewhat to vertical networks.

Horizontal relations

Extra-regional horizontal networking has also been increased by European integration. Cities such as Munich have been an active member of the various European city networks and have through this route developed links with other European local authorities including Birmingham. Likewise there has also been an increase in the amount of intraregional horizontal networking over recent years. But for geographical and other reasons Bavarian cities and districts are much more involved than their West Midlands counterparts in cross-border networks. For some time these have been recognised by the European Commission as EuRegio networks, and funding has been available under the INTERREG programme. A network was formed in 1995, for instance, between Berchtesgadener Land and Traunstein in lower Bavaria, and Salzburg in upper Austria. This is seen as re-establishing long-standing economic and cultural linkages across national borders within the Salzburg city region, and as acknowledging the reality of increased cross-border commuting.

A second network called LaRoSa (linking Landshut and Rosenheim in Bavaria with Salzburg in Austria) has also been established, through which the mayors of the three authorities propose to coordinate action in a range of areas including the economy, land use, transportation, technology and lobbying. Both of these networks reflect the concern of Salzburg in particular that it is losing its economic position in the face of competition from Munich and from the Southern Bavaria Economic Area (Wirtschaftsraum Südbayern). They also reflect a recognition of the potential fiscal inequities which derive from extensive cross-border commuting. The future of LaRoSa is however in doubt, and the continuing success of the Berchtesgadener Land–Salzburg cross-border network has encouraged both Rosenheim and Landshut to seek closer relations with Munich.

Links between neighbouring cities are in some cases also being strengthened within national borders. In 1992 the federal government facilitated the networking of cities in its regional action framework (*Raumordnung Politischer Handlungsräume*). These new associations are a significant departure from the previous practice based purely upon formally constituted bodies. The MAI network, for example, was formed in 1992 between Munich, Augsburg and Ingolstat (with finance from the EU Cities network), and was initially intended to develop a coordinated strategy for housing and employment matters, and to act as a powerful subregional lobby within the EU. In part this initiative was a reaction to concerns that development of the eastern *Länder* (particularly Saxony) might in time produce a direct competitive threat to southern Bavaria.

As in the West Midlands, the local authorities in Bavaria cooperate and coordinate their activities at the regional and subregional levels. In the late 1970s 18 planning regions were established which expanded both horizontal and vertical networks by bringing neighbouring authorities and state ministers together at regular intervals. All types of local authorities in Bavaria have state-level associations to press their interests with the *Land* government. But in addition to this, the mayors (*Bürgermeister* and *Landräte*) of the three Frankonian regions (Oberfranken, Mittelfranken and Unterfranken) meet relatively informally to consider regional marketing initiatives – for inward investment and tourism – including relations with Brussels. It seems, then, as though the growth in long-range (extra-regional) horizontal networks has – for a complex set of reasons – been complemented by an increase in the number of short-range (intraregional) horizontal networks within Bavaria.

Public/private relations

The chambers of commerce play a direct role in the administration of public policy in Germany, undertaking functions delegated to them from federal or state level. In Oberfranken, for instance, the Chamber (which is based in Bayreuth) is helping to push forward the Bavaria On-line programme (involving a high-capacity digital highway), to implement initiatives to promote technological change in the hard-pressed local textile industry, and to promote innovation and technological change among small and medium-sized enterprises. Most of these initiatives receive financial support either from the EU or from the Bavarian state government. It is via the chambers of commerce, then, that involvement of the private sector in economic governance networks in Germany is primarily mediated, and thus corporatism is the characteristic form of public–private partnership in Germany.

German local authorities have responded to a reduction in the level of resources from federal or state levels by experimenting with privatisation and with new organisational structures. Cities such as Bayreuth, for instance, have privatised their water, gas and electricity utilities. But rather than putting shares up for public sale as in the UK, the favoured mechanism has been to transfer services to wholly or mainly state-owned independent companies which are able to attract private capital. Once again partnership with the private sector in this case takes a mainly corporatist form. There has therefore been a slight increase in the number of public/private networks in Bavaria over recent years, but this has largely been a product of privatisation rather than of increased public–private regeneration partnerships.

Towards network analysis

The state system in each of our case study areas is overflowing with networks of one sort or another, including many that are concerned primarily with economic governance. Despite the complexity and fluidity of this system it is, however, possible to identify certain significant changes in recent decades, and some important similarities and differences between the West Midlands and southern Bavaria.

We have seen that European integration, and the concentration of political power and economic resources in Brussels, has vastly increased the number of *long-range* vertical and horizontal networks which are sustained by the state systems in both our case study regions, and that this increase has affected each place to approximately the same degree. We have also seen, however, that while the number of *short-range* horizontal networks has increased in both regions, this increase has been more recent and more modest in Bavaria than in the West Midlands. Furthermore, while in Bavaria there has been a limited increase in short-range vertical networks over recent decades, in the West Midlands there has been a significant reduction in such networks. Our first conclusion is therefore that, although each is important for the development of the networking thesis, a clear distinction must be drawn between these four types (two ranges and two directions) of network given their tendency to behave differently from one another.

Furthermore, while the causation of long-range networks of either type has been broadly the same in each place and has produced similar results, the causation of short-range networks has been rather different between the two regions and has produced somewhat different results. Manufacturing decline in the West Midlands prompted the establishment during the early 1980s of joint marketing and other coordinational activities between local agencies, leading to an expansion in short-range *horizontal* networks. It also, however, induced central–local conflict around (for example) industrial and macroeconomic policy, culminating in the abolition of the WMCC. This, combined with the ongoing rationalisation of the local state during the 1980s and 1990s, had the effect of attenuating short-range *vertical* networks. More recently these have been attenuated further by the restructuring of regional government through the establishment of government offices for the regions and then regional development agencies. The reduction of short-range vertical networks is therefore largely a consequence of the general assertion of central government authority – cutting costs, imposing policy agendas and state forms – over UK regions and localities against a background of economic crisis.

Abolition of the WMCC in 1986, however, had its own consequences. In particular, it forced lower-tier authorities to establish a plurality of joint boards and committees to take over coordination of county responsibilities, which led in turn to a further expansion of short-range horizontal networks. But abolition also exacerbated inter-district competition within the conurbation by removing a tier of government responsible for balancing local interests (through a hierarchical political process) across the region. It led authorities concerned at the dominance of the City of Birmingham, in the absence of an overarching authority with responsibility for equalisation of spending, to form networks and associations that could defend their interests. Finally, as part of its drive to constrain elected local authorities, central government in the 1990s pushed through a new approach to regeneration, which obliged councils to pursue their initiatives through the framework of unelected local partnerships. Together these national and regional factors have led to a pronounced expansion of short-range horizontal networks in the West Midlands.

In Bavaria, however, the economic environment has been more favourable since the 1970s, and there has been little or no desire (fiscal or political) to impose a drastic centralisation of the state system. Incremental reforms have therefore been the result, bringing modest changes to the administrative structure over the years, and indeed producing in the 1980s a slight increase in the number of short-range *vertical* networks. During the 1990s, however, the economy began to falter, unemployment grew, and there was mounting concern at the ability of the region to sustain its strength. At the same time, expansion of the European Union to include (among others) Austria, collapse of the Soviet Union and the Warsaw Pact, and the reunification of Germany, led to increased cross-border competition and to increased cross-border interdependence. These factors combined to foster cooperation between neighbouring cities and districts in order to coordinate policy, to promote economic development, and to advance particular definitions of the urban hierarchy. Short-range *horizontal* networks of this sort developed both within national borders and across national borders at an interregional level. But in each case they were driven by similar factors, albeit channelled along some ancient regional affiliations (as for example around Bohemia in the Czech Republic, and from Salzburg to Berchtesgadener Land).

The expansion of short-range horizontal networks in Bavaria and the West Midlands has responded in each case to economic pressures, but to economic pressures that were different in their origins, timing and impact (with the economic crisis being earlier and deeper in the West Midlands). This expansion has also responded in each case to political and administrative pressures within the state system, and to the interactions between these and economic conditions. But once again, these political pressures have been different in their origins, timing and impact. Nation-state restructuring in response to fiscal and political pressures has been a decisive factor in the expansion of short-range horizontal networks in the West Midlands, and indeed this expansion was a direct consequence of the curtailing of short-range networks in the other – vertical – direction. On the other hand, state restructuring – or (more accurately) continued state formation – at the transnational level, and accompanying attenuation of national borders, has been a decisive factor in the expansion of short-range horizontal networks in Bavaria. This factor has had a more recent and more modest impact, however, producing a smaller short-range networking effect than in the West Midlands.

Conclusions

The case study evidence presented above suggests that over recent decades there *has*, on balance, been an increase in the number of networks involving local authorities in economic governance. But the same evidence also shows that this increase has not occurred to the same degree in all dimensions, or in all places, and therefore that it is dangerous to take a blanket approach to network growth. It may well be, then, that concepts such as 'network paradigm' do as much to cloud the issue as to illuminate historical change. This subject should rather be approached in terms of the specific characteristics of networks, and conceptual tools must be developed that will permit these characteristics to be identified with greater precision. The literature so far has stressed what, following Benington and Harvey (1994), we have called short-range horizontal networks. But it has been argued here that at least two dimensions of networking must be differentiated – their *range* and their *direction* – and that differences in causation and impact are to be found both between horizontal and vertical, and between short-range and long-range, networks.

At a more explanatory level, we can also conclude from these case studies that network development is to a considerable extent influenced by structural factors – by prevailing economic conditions, by pressures emanating from the state system and by interactions between these processes. Economic change, for example, has been an important if sometimes indirect influence, and each area has faced economic difficulties which have stimulated forms of network development. It is also true, as suggested by Meegan (1994) and others, that local network growth is affected by the nation state, and the heavy handed, anti-interventionist climate of national government in the UK has had a significant effect, as has the absence of this role in Germany. But really it is the state system as a whole, and restructuring of this system, that has been the decisive factor. In the West Midlands state restructuring has taken place along the central–local axis, with the assertion of national authority leading to a new form of central as well as local government. In Bavaria, too, state restructuring has been important, but here it has occurred along the Europe–nation axis, with continued European state-making and the attenuation of national borders having a direct impact upon the linkages between neighbouring local governments. The analysis of networks must therefore be related to the analysis of social structures, and not (as sometimes happens in actor–network theory) substituted for the latter.

Finally, our evidence suggests that less prosperous cities and regions sometimes have more intense networking, especially in the horizontal dimension, than more prosperous ones. Short-range horizontal networking has increased earlier and to a greater extent in the West Midlands, later and more modestly in southern Bavaria, and seems to be at a significantly higher level in the former than the latter. This is despite the much stronger economic position of southern Bavaria over the medium and long term, and it suggests that the development of such networks should be seen as a consequence and even an index of economic crisis. On the other hand, the performance of the West Midlands economy has improved significantly during the 1990s, after many new local networks were formed. Indeed this recovery was to a considerable extent based upon inward investment, an activity which was promoted by several of the networks identified. So perhaps this does support the view that network development has beneficial economic consequences but (in this case) of a non-indigenous kind.

Acknowledgements

This chapter has benefited greatly from discussions with colleagues from the University of Bayreuth, including Klemens Angerman,

Thomas Goldsmidt, Andreas Rösch and Wolfgang Weber. Particular thanks are due to Professor Jorg Maier for his support of the empirical stage of the research reported here, and also to respondents in Bayreuth, Nuremberg, Munich, Landshut and Salzburg. Likewise the authors would like to thank respondents in Coventry, Sandwell and Dudley. The authors would like to thank the British Council for their support in this research. However, the normal disclaimers apply.

11
Metropolitan Governance and Institutional Dynamics

Bernard Jouve and Christian Lefèvre

Introduction

The last decade has seen the emergence of an apparent paradox. Globalisation of the economy has turned cities into vital centres of growth, while at the same time raising the problem of the transition of capitalist societies to a post-Fordist political and economic mode of regulation, in which the role of the state has had to change (Amin 1994; Jessop 1994). In this general context, the textbooks have clearly indicated the emergence of kinds of urban policies which call into question the traditional forms of the exercise of power based on formal institutions and the use of domination, as evidenced by the new 'growth machines' (Logan and Molotch 1987) and 'urban regimes' (Stone 1989). The exercise of power in today's cities is based on the search for flexibility and a form of partnership between public and private institutions, and on the informal character of the relationship between the latter. The paradox referred to above arises from the fact that, faced with this new form of interaction in which there is a blurring of the distinction between public and private interests, and in which the importance of democratically elected urban institutions is being called into question at a functional level, and even a political level in the case of the UK (Imrie et al. 1995), there have at the same time been numerous attempts to reform the way cities are run throughout Europe.

All those reforms share the common goal of trying to give specific cities new decision-making structures, usually involving very large geographical areas, with the aim of enabling them to play a full role in the new competition which has arisen among major cities. In essence, the aim has been to rationalise local decision-making

processes, which are characterised by a number of hierarchical institutions, the complexity and opaqueness of the political networks and
institutional fragmentation.

It seems necessary to relocate these processes in the wider context of
the relationships between cities and states within Western Europe.
These relationships have often been delicate, even conflictual, inasmuch as the formation of modern states this side of the Atlantic has
been partially based on the destruction or annihilation of the economic, social, cultural and political power which some cities had built
up over the centuries (Tilly and Blockman 1994). According to some
authors (Bagnasco and Le Galès 1997), we find ourselves in a rather
special period offering a genuine historic opportunity, whereby these
relationships could evolve significantly towards a much greater autonomy for cities, particularly the larger ones. There are several different
phenomena which explain this change and this historic opportunity.

Firstly, there is the fact that cities are becoming central to economic
development. They are increasingly taking on the role of focal points
for economic growth. They have become the cradles of innovation and
are responsible for enabling the latter to spread rapidly. This development has come about partly because the elite in the area have become
active in promoting economic and social development, in order to
counter the effects of the economic crisis and to respond to the
changes in attitudes towards the role of the state, brought about by
several phenomena which tend to favour cities at the expense of the
state. For example, globalisation of the economy reduces the scope of
states to implement purely national policies, in particular because of
liberalisation, privatisation and deregulation. Decentralisation, which
has more or less become the rule throughout Europe over the last
15 years, weakens the role of the state as the principal agent for governing societies, as does the rise in importance of supranational bodies,
the most important of which is the European Union, which partially
limit the powers of the state to effect major changes in society. Finally,
the new partnerships which are being formed between democratically
elected urban institutions and private enterprise reduce still further the
ability of states to influence urban politics.

This chapter aims to analyse the socio-political consequences of the
attempts to effect reform of urban institutions in the 1970s, to see
what light they can throw on the nature of the relationship between
European states and major cities, how the processes introduced in such
reforms took account of local democracy and, finally, what they teach
us about the new reconfiguration of urban leadership. A comparison of

the experiences of the eight cities selected for the purposes of this research – Bordeaux, Lyons, Bologna, Turin, Rotterdam, Manchester, Stuttgart and the Geneva–Lausanne metropolitan area in Switzerland – clearly shows the existence of two successive periods in the recent history of urban Europe: the first half of the 1990s saw an increase in the power of the mayors (or political leaders) in major cities to influence the reform of urban institutions and, more generally, an increase in their influence over the local and national political scenes. In contrast, during the second half of the 1990s, we see the control of the reform process of these institutions moving back to the traditional local notables, political parties and certain state bodies. It should also be noted that these attempts at reform were carried out in a basically technocratic manner, which effectively excluded civil society. The processes used, which were justified by the need to give cities more effective decision-making structures which would allow them to cope with the globalisation of the economy and with the competition from other cities, did nothing to revive local democracy – rather the opposite. Finally, this comparison clearly demonstrates that the influence of local economic interests in these institutional dynamics is considerable (Jouve and Lefèvre 2002).

The new economic context requires new urban institutions

As in the 1970s, the vast majority of European states have seen intense activity in the field of the reform of metropolitan governance over the last ten years, the notable exception to the rule being Switzerland. The main differences between these two periods have been the aim of the reforms which have been undertaken and the methods used to implement them.

Globalisation and the search for institutional competitiveness

In general terms, one can say that the main incentive behind the reforms has been the need for a more rational approach to economics in the face of increased competition between major cities. In the 1970s the main thrust of reforms was concerned with questions of town planning, communication infrastructures and housing within urban institutions which attempted to make functional areas coincide with administrative areas within the cities (Lefèvre 1997). While this aim has not disappeared in the 1990s, it has been relegated to a lower order of priority on the part of both local councillors and the various state bodies responsible for the areas in question. What is now considered most important is the search for increased competitiveness on the part of cities through the setting up of institutions able to meet the challenge of the globalisation of the economy. In line with the teachings of economists who analytically formalise the changes occurring in modern capitalism, urban territory and urban institutions have become for the reformers instruments of competition between the major cities.

The approach is basically entrepreneurial: one must create new urban institutions capable of providing cities with facilities capable of assisting companies and of giving rise to genuine metropolitan functions. It is only recently that the political function of these new institutions, that is, the framework they set up between citizens and those who govern them, has been addressed. The same is true with regard to the maintenance of a form of solidarity between social groups and between different geographical areas within cities.

The approaches to the reform of urban institutions adopted during the first half of the 1990s in nearly all European countries have also changed, giving the people on the spot the opportunity to develop the special characteristics of their localities. In contrast to what happened in the 1970s, the responsibility for these reforms has not been monopolised by state bodies, but has been left to local decision makers, first and foremost to local councillors. This is particularly true in Italy, with the passing of Law 142 in 1990. This law introduced the granting of 'metropolitan city' status to the ten largest cities in Italy, and left the regions to implement the project. The same sort of thing happened in the Netherlands, and in the Baden-Wurttemberg *Land* in Germany, where it was the central government which set up, at the beginning of the 1990s, the legal framework for institutional innovation. Similarly, in the UK, where for 20 years successive Conservative governments worked to rid cities of any real status as separate legal and political entities, the debate on institutional reforms was reopened. The urban policies put in place by Prime Minister Thatcher and subsequently by Prime Minister John Major, whereby the clear-cut public/private divide was brought into question, had not managed to solve the problem of creating suitable institutions for mobilising local initiatives and setting up cooperation between them – rather the opposite. In the UK it was often the European Union which, through its regional policy and structural funds, effectively forced local representatives to set up new institutions to represent them in their negotiations with Brussels. The public/private partnership, in all its various forms, seen as a panacea by successive Conservative governments, never really solved the problem of giving cities an adequate form of representation in their dealings with the outside world.

'Does locality matter?' Yes, it is the place for collective mobilisation

There is now a substantial body of literature dealing with the ability of local authorities to come up with adequate local economic development policies. Active participants in the redefinition of the relationship between the centre and the regions clearly indicated, as early as the beginning of the 1990s, that 'these fortunes depend as never before on councils' capacity to negotiate their way around a new political economy in which private financiers, industrialists and European institutions are as important as central government' (Harloe et al. 1990, p. 35). Contrary to a marxist interpretation of the dynamics currently in play, the globalisation of the economy and the competition which has been entered into by many cities in advanced capitalist countries are not something which, in our opinion, has been imposed on local representatives. Localities have not become, through some kind of economic determinism, the new political arena for the reduction of the contradictions of modern capitalism in place of the nation state. On the contrary, local representatives are actively promoting the new economic order. Whereas once local government was basically considered as a political arena for providing local services as part of the welfare state, since the 1990s we have seen the emergence of proactive local authorities initiating economic development (Pickvance and Préteceille 1991). This change in status on the part of local authorities in Europe can also be seen in the nature of the relationships between them and states in matters of town and country planning reforms.

In the 1960s and the 1970s urban institutional policies were devised centrally and then sent out to be implemented in the regions. In the period since then territorial reforms have sought to create agglomeration institutions capable of generating economies of scale in the domain of local public services. Essentially they aimed to rationalise local government by fighting against the fragmentation of basic local organisations. In France, for example, the *communautés urbaines* were created during this period. In the UK metropolitan counties were set up. In Germany they opted for a more radical solution by merging communes.

Nowadays new laws in this area are often passed by central government under pressure for reform from local representatives. Except in Great Britain, where Conservative rule led to a strong centralisation of territorial policies and an attempt to emasculate local organisations by central government, the first half of the 1990s saw a strong trend throughout Europe for central governments to offer a political opportunity to change urban policies at least partly under pressure from local councillors. This represents a significant shift in the decision-making process. Switzerland, which is the only exception to the rule, is characterised by institutional stability, and is sometimes considered as culturally urbanophobic. The local institutions and the method used to select local politicians, who represent mainly rural interests, do not make it easy for the political system to reform urban institutions even in cantons which are largely urbanised, as is the case of the Geneva and Vaud cantons.

There is another important element in attempts to reform the way cities are run, namely recourse to local history. The reconfiguration of the relationship between central government and the regions has led local representatives to seek fresh sources to justify and legitimise what they desire. Among these sources, a favourite one is research into the history and background of local communities. In this way local representatives have (re)awakened a sense of territorial identity, even going so far as to invent myths to support their cause, so as to justify institutional changes. Certain cultural and historical sources have often been used by political leaders to demonstrate that the cities they were responsible for were somehow intrinsically suitable for facing international competition because of their history and their sociological characteristics.

In Manchester, the revolutionary changes brought about by the liberal policies of successive Conservative governments between 1979 and 1997 have, to a large extent, been absorbed and legitimised by local policies implemented by a new generation of local councillors who are members of the Labour Party and who take up a position 'in and against the market' (Cochrane 1988, p. 158). They refer to the history of the economic development of Manchester in the nineteenth century in order to support their claim that the city has the intrinsic ability to embrace neoliberalism. It is the same story in Lyons and Rotterdam, where the archives have been searched for references to local capitalism in order to show that the wealth of these two cities goes back to the sixteenth century, and that this proves that the creation of the Lyons Urban Region or 'Greater Rotterdam', aimed at providing an opening for these two cities onto the international stage, in no way contradicted their local historical roots.

Finally, local reformers have worked towards the creation of new urban institutions and are seeking support for them by invoking groundwork carried out earlier by other people on the theme of urban reform, particularly in connection with fairly old town and country planning procedures. The projects aimed at creating 'Greater Rotterdam', the Metropolitan City of Bologna, Greater Manchester or the Lyons Urban Region are built on the ashes of institutions which indeed did exist in the past. In these various cases the abandonment, for different reasons, of these institutions has not prevented the survival at local level of a technocracy devoted to the theme of the rationalisation of public action by means of the setting up of powerful metropolitan governing bodies capable of imposing, if necessary, collective choices on all local organisations.

In all cases, the reformers are putting forward local experiences and methods of political regulation with a certain historical 'thickness'. This citing of past experiences generally leads their proponents to adopt a political style used originally in different institutional and political contexts. This can lead to visible tension between forms of action inherited from the 1960s and 1970s on the one hand, and contemporary political situations. This tension often shows itself through projects for reforming the way cities are run being dealt with by means of a technocratic approach. The name of the game is to demonstrate that the reform projects are rational with regard to the new economic and political order. To this end, it is thought necessary to put forward as quickly as possible urban policies which prove the validity of the approach. This technocratic approach, which both limits the number of players involved and reduces the likelihood of controversy, thus confers on the projects a legal and rational form of legitimacy.

This obviously reminds one closely of the approach adopted by reformers in the 1960s and 1970s. Projects are always put forward by an enlightened group of technocrats, while the public at large is kept at arm's length from the whole process. There is obviously a price to pay for such an approach: as the general public is not brought on board, this usually results in a democratic deficit when it comes to claiming legitimacy. Indeed, some reformers have paid the price for such a deficit as, for example, in Bologna, and even more so in Rotterdam, where a group of local people hostile to the creation of a new metropolitan institution managed to scupper the reform project by calling for a local referendum on the question.

Behind the international competition of cities lies political competition

The debate on the reform of cities, the buzzwords used in this debate – administrative rationalisation, competition between cities, modernisation of local political life – and the ambitious projects local reformers wanted to implement through the creation of new urban institutions – all these things have created numerous opportunities to try to redefine the longer-term local political leadership. In many cases, a new generation of local politicians have seen this as an opportunity to create the conditions for using these new institutions to create a local stronghold for themselves.

This is the case in Lyons with Michel Noir, a member of the Gaullist RPR Party, who in 1989 was elected mayor and then managed to relegate to a secondary position the Christian Democratic Party which had run the city for the previous 40 years, whereas the RPR was much weaker at local level. Straight from his election Michel Noir set up a system of government which was centralised on himself. As mayor of Lyon and president of the Communauté Urbain de Lyon (a cross-district institution in charge of urban planning and management of the main local public services) he had the power necessary to put this strategy into practice. In doing this he disrupted the balance between the different surrounding district mayors who had accepted the setting up of the Communauté Urbain de Lyon on condition that they could have influence on policy choices and get political resources for their communes.

It is also the case with Braun Pepper, the mayor of Rotterdam, a member of the Dutch Labour Party, a somewhat charismatic figure who, in particular through his admiration of the French presidential system, managed to upset the Dutch political system which was used to consensus politics and to a system where mayors were under the control of the political parties. In effect the Dutch local election system offers an essential place to political parties which present lists of candidates to local elections. The dependence of the newly elected on those already elected is very strong. It is also the case that a number of local councillors in Manchester are typical of the new generation of local councillors belonging to the British Labour Party, whose support was a key factor in Tony Blair's creation of the New Labour Party. We see the same thing in Bologna, where through the setting up of the new metropolitan city, the mayor of Bologna tried to redefine to his own advantage the local set-up at the expense of the Italian Communist Party, which had ruled the town from 1947 to 1999. In these various scenarios, changes in national institutions and on the political scene gave these people the opportunity to gain a firm foothold at local level, while ultimately hoping to become major political figures at national level. What they managed to do, taking advantage of the new urban institutions, was to construct for them-

selves a strong political base, while gaining a large degree of independence from political parties.

On the other hand, it is often the return of the political parties, the
control exercised by the latter over certain mayors of major cities,
which explains the less than total success of some of the projects
aimed at reforming urban institutions. After a period of euphoria, the
last half of the 1990s was characterised by an opposite movement,
namely the regaining of control of the process of institutionalisation
by both the state, the political parties and the local authorities.

Here we see the result of a conservative coalition between certain
state bodies and the traditional local notables. Indeed, the local elected
representatives in favour of modernisation all seem to have in
common the fact that they have represented the ruling classes from a
district in the city centre and have a professional activity within the
higher tertiary sector, i.e. in that part of the economic sphere which is
one of the most concerned with metropolisation phenomena linked to
the globalisation of the economy. When we look at people like Michel
Noir in Lyons, Walter Vitali in Bologna, Braun Pepper in Rotterdam,
the supporters of the application of the 'Paris–Lyons–Marseille Law' to
the city of Bordeaux, or at the newly elected representatives of the
'Verband Stuttgart Region', we note similar social origins and professional careers among the reforming elites. One certainly will not be
able to understand the reactions provoked by their reform projects, in
particular among local institutions representing the interests of rural
districts and social groups (for example, the departmental councils in
France, the province in Bologna or *Kreise* around Stuttgart) without reference to this tension between the tertiary urban elite and the representatives from outlying districts representing rural interests. In
summary, it can be suggested that in many cities a new political elite
has emerged which has attempted to break free from the constraints of
partisan structures. However, these efforts have met with opposition
and local political parties have reasserted themselves. Beyond this
analysis of the emergence of new forms of local power on the construction of innovating government mechanisms, here on the contrary one
may speak of a relatively strong element of stability which deserves to
be highlighted as it constitutes a central point in the exercise of local
democracy.

This return of party politics to the local forefront to the detriment of
the reforming elite was not in step with old practices of negotiation. In
effect under the cover of wishing to lead institutional reforms within a
register of partnership and democracy, it can be observed that a

number of attempts resulted in a centralisation of decisions and an attempt to reshape local leadership through a small number of people. In this context the return of political parties could be seen by the civil society, on a local level, as an attempt to better control the elite which had become disrespectful of the rules of local democracy, or a least a minimum of pluralism.

Dependency on local economic interests

Effective participation of local economic interests in the reform of urban institutions seems to have fallen into a bit of a blind spot and so far escaped serious analysis. Texts on metropolitan governance would at first glance seem to suggest that the local economic organisations are more interested in developing an informal and relatively unstructured partnership with local public authorities than in reforming current urban institutions. However, their role in the setting up of new urban institutions appears extremely important. Whether they drag their heels or are in the vanguard of progress, their participation in the process is usually necessary, as it essentially legitimises the action of local elected representatives and the production of new public policies. It is obvious that when one is reforming urban institutions in the name of the globalisation of the economy and the competition between cities, it makes sense to have the support of those primarily affected by the new policy, namely companies and, first and foremost, their representative organisations.

However, on closer examination we see that the action of those representative organisations varies widely from one city to another. The establishment of a coalition between public institutions and economic interests, whether public or private, is not something one can impose. The creation of metropolitan capitalism, the historical role of public institutions in local economic development, plus the existence of periods of recession, all contribute to the stabilisation, or its opposite, of the various kinds of relationships which can exist between public institutions and economic organisations, both public and private, within cities. It is the long-term nature of these relationships and their confrontation with a new international economic order, characterised by competition between cities, which either supports or works against attempts to reform the way cities are run. It can facilitate or, on the contrary, make difficult the formation of coalitions in support of reform projects, whether or not the latter take on an institutional form.

Whereas in some cases the economic organisations actually initiate the dynamics (as for instance in Bordeaux, Stuttgart, Manchester or Rotterdam), in others they adopt a rather more prudent attitude. In Lyons, for example, the institutional dynamics resulted in an attempt at instrumentalisation on the part of the mayor of the city against the private interests. Their attitude can be reserved as in Bologna or within the new Swiss metropole. In yet other cases they can be totally absent from the debate, as in Turin. There are no discernible national trends at work here. What does seem to directly affect their ability to mobilise and to participate effectively in any reform of metropolitan governance is their level of organisation and the local economic situation.

The organisation of local economic interests is very different from one city to the next. The level of integration of the private individuals and bodies concerned is the key element which decides their political weight and their influence on the local institutional dynamics. Stuttgart, Lyons and Bordeaux are examples of towns where the local employers have for a long time organised themselves around the local chambers of commerce and industry. In contrast, Bologna shows us a situation characterised by a multiplicity of different bodies representing local employers. The situation in Manchester is similar to that in Bologna, as there is a strong tendency, in particular in the context of the current debate on regionalisation, towards fragmentation of the organisation of private interests, the split being basically between urban and regional employers. Where Turin and Rotterdam are concerned, the organisation of private interests has, for some time now, been a low-key issue. Fiat in Turin and the port of Rotterdam, because of their size and weight in the local economy of these two towns, are the only major economic players around.

This level of organisation has a major influence on the effective participation of the various economic interests, whether public or private, in the process of reform of metropolitan governance. Indeed, in some cases the reform project for urban institutions has been initiated by the organisations representing local employers as a response to a situation they consider problematic. This is the case in Stuttgart, for example, where the industrial sector saw a reduction in activity of 15 per cent between 1991 and 1994, with a corresponding reduction in the labour force of 6.3 per cent. Here it was the local employers who put the local elected representatives on notice to devise an institutional response to the economic crisis by giving the city a decision-making structure capable of solving the problem of institutional fragmentation, and by setting up collective facilities capable of enhancing the productivity of the city. This is also the case in Bordeaux, where the end of Jacques Chaban-Delmas's reign as mayor, after holding the office since 1947, was marked by a period of stagnation, where the dossiers which were considered vital for the development of the city were never followed through. This is why the president of the Chamber of Commerce and Industry demanded the application of the 'Paris–Lyons–Marseilles Law' to the city of Bordeaux, whereby the local districts situated around Bordeaux would effectively be taken under the wing of Bordeaux City Council, whose political clout would thereby be greatly increased.

These few examples show that local employers tend only to get involved in the reform of metropolitan governance when the urban system is in a state of crisis, which would suggest the following rule of thumb: urban crisis, in the economic sphere, requires the constitution of new urban institutions. For private actors, urban institutions must answer to a set of collective problems of which theirs is a part. When a situation arises where the economic situation of a city is visibly degrading, where the existing political institutions no longer seem to be capable of responding to the challenge, the private actors become the promoter of metropolitan institutional reforms through public policy adapted to the new situation.

A high level of organisation, as for example in Bordeaux, Stuttgart or Manchester, seems a major factor in getting the question of metropolitan governance put on the political agenda. In contrast, where economic interests are not pushing for such a reform, its inclusion on the political agenda is much more problematic. In such cases, the local elected representatives need to take the initiative in order to mobilise support, by using their influence to reallocate resources so that the latter better serve the interests of the organisations representing the interests of local employers. It is then obvious that the existence of well-organised local employers, whose support needs to be mobilised, constitutes a major factor in this debate. We then see the creation of strategic town and country planning procedures aimed at setting up a framework for the collective mobilisation which is sought. The actual content of such documents is not the main thing; indeed, they often contain little reference to major concrete projects. What is being sought, via the production of collective symbols and references, is the creation of conditions likely to favour the birth of a coalition between public and private interests. In the last resort, what is at stake is the interrelationship between companies, the organisations representing the latter and the metropolitan area. The main problem faced is that recent developments in modern capitalism tend to lead today's companies to see their future development rather on an international than a local scale, which makes it that much more difficult to integrate them fully into their immediate local environment. We see this, for example, in Turin, where the restructuring of Fiat in the 1980s, with a transfer of a large part of their production to certain developing countries, has led this major economic player to view the development of Turin's local public institutions as less and less relevant to the future of the company.

Stuttgart – a 'success story'

Whereas in Europe as a whole we see a remarkable stability in urban institutions in their original forms, plus the general failure of a number of reforms aimed at setting up new decision-making structures, there is one exception to the rule which perhaps deserves special attention, namely the case of Stuttgart which, in 1994, created a new metropolitan institution known as the 'Verband Region Stuttgart'. This institutional reform was made possible by the integration of various factors which, however, evolved in accordance with specific and different principles and timescales:

• The perennial institutional problem in the capital of Baden-Württemberg was that, since the 1960s and in accordance with the by now traditional scenario, the central and the outlying districts were unable to come to an agreement on a fair division of the financial costs of running the central organisation, the outlying districts refusing to contribute to the creation and running costs of certain facilities and services in the metropolitan area (public transport, hospital services, etc.) and expecting the central district to pick up the tab.

• This problem of local taxation was transformed following the economic crisis which severely affected the metropolitan economy at the beginning of the 1990s. The Chamber of Commerce and Industry, which had not got itself heavily involved in this question of local taxation, was to establish a link between the reform of local government and the problems of economic development. Whereas the employers' body had been prepared to put up with the institutional fragmentation and the absence of a clear urban structure, the economic crisis forced a rethink. It highlighted the limits of such an organisation arising from the absence of any body able to implement a real policy of economic development.

- The local political system was enabled to deal with this 'social demand' by means of the constitution of a coalition government at the *Land* level, consisting of the Christian Democrats of the CDU and the Social Democrats of the SPD. The CDU, which for many years had politically dominated Baden-Württemberg and the city of Stuttgart, and which was therefore reluctant to introduce any changes to the local structures, was forced by the SPD to include in the coalition pact the creation of an urban institution elected by direct universal suffrage and by a full system of proportional representation. So far as the SPD was concerned, this would create a metropolitan political arena which, because in Germany it is illegal to occupy more than one major public post at a time, could restore the balance with the CDU by creating conditions for the arrival on the scene of a new political elite.

- Finally, the new institution set up in 1994, the 'Verband Region Stuttgart', to a large extent owes its creation to German federalism. Responsibility for metropolitan institutions does not belong to the federal state but to the *Länder*. The law passed by the Baden-Württemberg *Land*, which set up the 'Verband Region Stuttgart', is in a way perfectly adapted to the political relationship which happened to exist in Stuttgart in 1994. This was not a national law applying to all German cities. There is no doubt that German federalism created the legal and political conditions for dealing with certain problems, taking into consideration the specific situation of each city and the particular nature of the political relationships which exist in that locality. This is mainly what made this reform possible.

Conclusion

We believe that the theory of increasing autonomy for cities needs to be qualified. It presupposes a convergence of European political systems which is by no means certain. Our evaluation of the processes currently in play is founded on four types of argument: the choices made by states in matters of territorial reorganisation; the difficulties of creating genuinely innovative partnerships between public and private interests; the failure to recognise the power of the traditional elite groups in metropolitan governance; and, finally, the importance of institutional contexts.

First, let us examine intergovernmental relationships within Europe. The strengthening of the political capabilities of cities can only be

understood when situated within the framework of the wider rebuilding of European states. In this connection, it is significant to note that
the overwhelming majority of European countries have not chosen to
give cities any special legal and political status in the new institutional
order which is currently emerging, rather the contrary. In France, the
UK, Spain, Italy and Belgium, it is the region which has been recognised as the privileged partner of the state, not cities. In the analysis of
the problematic relationship between European cities and states, we
must include another key decision-making level – the regions – and
increasingly the European Union through its various territorial policies. The increase in the number of 'players' in the game can lead to
very different systems of alliance from one country to the next, and
indeed within a single country.

Second, the strengthening of the political capabilities of cities is
often viewed through the lens of concepts arising from North
American literature on the subject. Metropolitan governance and the
different currents of thought contained in this concept – for example,
growth machine and urban regime – suggest that it is essential that a
coalition between public and private interests should be formed at the
level of the city. Besides the fact that European institutional contexts
hardly lend themselves to this development (Harding 1995), one may
also wonder about the socio-political consequences of such coalitions,
the underlying hypothesis being that we shall see new ways of making
political decisions, in particular by challenging the right of local public
institutions to have a monopoly in this field. However, except for the
UK, where successive Conservative governments tried to create at local
level a new economic elite at the expense of the traditional representative bodies of British employers (Peck 1995), in the other countries
they have kept to the traditional scenario of a dialogue between the
local employers' representative bodies – mainly the chambers of commerce and industry – and the public institutions. If the establishment
of a coalition between public and private interests leads to a strengthening of the capabilities of cities, it seems to us that this is more or less
a reproduction of an oligarchic urban government between traditional
elites. Internationalisation is not likely to lead to any major change,
but rather to a continuation of the status quo in the field of local
government.

This hypothesis is supported by our third point – the fact that the
internationalisation of cities, in particular through attempts to reform
metropolitan institutions, has so far taken place at a technocratic level
only, civil society in general being more or less excluded from this

development. In our view, the internationalisation of cities and local democracy are worlds apart. This technocratic approach has gone hand in hand with an attempt on the part of a new generation of elected representatives to formalise procedures and to become independent of the political parties which brought them to power. We have seen a coalition of interests between state bodies and traditional elites against these reformers, which may help to explain the prospects for future metropolitan reform.

Finally, it seems important to us to include in the explanation a variable which has been largely ignored by researchers to date – the importance of the institutional context. The success of the institutional reform in Stuttgart confirms the fact that the political set-up in any one city depends on a number of variable factors and on the history of that city. This reform was only feasible because the German federalist system made it possible to take account of these various factors. In the process of the internationalisation of cities, the institutional context matters a great deal.

Let us be quite clear: we are by no means invalidating the argument regarding the strengthening of the ability of cities to play an increasingly important role on the international stage. We merely wish to point out that this is not a universal rule, as is demonstrated by the fact that this process does not affect all European cities to anything like the same extent. We are more inclined to put forward the argument that there are major differences in the way this trend has affected European cities. Now that the central role of states in the governance of modern societies has been brought into question, globalisation is taken on board in very different ways from one city to the next. The ability of cities to innovate – in particular where institutions are concerned – depends on the power struggle between the various social groups and is constrained by the nature of the institutional systems.

12
Local Democracy, Cross-Border Collaboration and the Internationalisation of Local Government

Andrew Church and Peter Reid

Introduction and the nature of cross-border collaboration

Local government organisations in many countries are now involved in significant transnational cooperative initiatives. This internationalisation of local governance takes many different forms, ranging from informal cultural exchanges to attempts to influence the actions of foreign state governments. It also has important implications for the politics and the management of local government. The existing evidence suggests transnational exchange may stimulate policy innovation and new thinking, but it can also generate significant problems in terms of accountability, strategic vision, initiative management and policy effectiveness. This chapter takes a critical view of one form of transnational cooperation, cross-border collaboration, and argues that the benefits of this activity are elusive and the problems encountered are slow to be overcome.

Hambleton (2000) suggests that cross-national exchange and dialogue involving local government are now so developed that an understanding of the changing nature of local democracy in the UK is only possible with some reference to local government management in other countries. In Europe a whole range of European Commission (EC) initiatives have further encouraged transnational exchange between local government within and outside the European Union (EU) (Williams 1996). In particular, considerable support has been provided for cooperative initiatives involving border regions, which are seen as having an important role in the process of European integration.

In recent guidelines the EC distinguished between two different types of transnational initiatives involving local government. The first of these is cross-border collaboration which itself has two forms – vicinity cooperation involving adjacent border regions and transnational cooperation between organisations that represent border regions. The second form of local government transnational initiative is interregional cooperation, which is subject-oriented often based on a specific theme and can involve local organisations at any location (CEC 1997). Examples of this second form include the many local government exchange networks established in Europe, such as the Car-free Cities network or the Medium-sized Cities Commission.

This distinction between cross-border collaboration and interregional cooperation has been slightly blurred by the recent EC-stimulated growth in transnational spatial planning, which perhaps represents a third type of local government cooperative initiative. These three strands of international cooperative activity are often collectively referred to as transboundary programmes. The recently adopted European Spatial Development Perspective (ESDP) seeks to encourage transnational spatial planning across large-scale cooperative zones, such as the Baltic Sea region which involves regions in 11 countries (CEC 1999). The ESDP is a non-statutory vision rather than a policy initiative and will probably require considerable integration between cross-border collaboration and interregional cooperation.

Cross-border collaboration, especially vicinity cooperation, has been a distinct element of local government cooperation in Europe for over a decade. Much of the funding has come from the EC INTERREG (international regions) I and II programme. This is a financially small programme. The INTERREG budget for 1989–93 was 1 billion ECUs. This had risen to 2.4 billion ECUs for 1994–99 which represented approximately 2 per cent of the Structural Operations budget. This is, however, significant politically, since it is the largest of the 13 Community initiatives which are the programmes allowing member states to address problems identified separately by the EC (Williams 1996). For 1994–99 INTERREG II accounted for just over 20 per cent of the total budget for Community Initiatives and 75 per cent of INTERREG II funds were spent in Objective 1 regions. Other sources of EC funds have supported cross-border initiatives in Eastern and central Europe. The EC's own evaluation of INTERREG between 1990 and 1996 suggests that expenditure was focused on transport and environment initiatives, with tourism and the promotion of small and medium-sized enterprises (SMEs) being other important areas of activity (Ernst and Young 2000).

Understanding cross-border collaboration

Numerous claims exist regarding the advantages and disadvantages for local government of transnational cooperative initiatives in Europe (see the contrasting conclusions of the chapters in Graute 1998). The central concern of this chapter, using the EC terminology, is with cross-border collaboration, particularly vicinity cooperation between authorities that share a border. Reference will also be made to other forms of transboundary cooperation, but there are two reasons for focusing on the cross-border initiatives. First, the EC has been supporting these initiatives through INTERREG for ten years and is planning to go on doing so until at least 2006–7 under INTERREG III. For the 2000–6 period between 5 and 6 billion euros may be available for INTERREG III (Brown and Nadin 2000). This scale of funding reflects the fact that in addition to supporting cross-border initiatives INTER-REG III will also fund interregional cooperation, especially among lagging regions and transnational spatial planning strategies linked to the ESDP. EC funding for cross-border vicinity collaboration has grown steadily and there is now over a decade of case study material and evidence to illustrate the benefits and problems that arise for local government.

The second reason for analysing cross-border vicinity cooperation is that in theory some of the border regions receiving INTERREG funds might be expected to provide good examples of well-developed transnational cooperation. Traditionally, the analysis of borders often emphasised their dividing role, which limited political and economic interaction. In the EU context of increased integration and declining border controls there are a number of reasons why cooperation between local authorities in certain border areas might be well developed. The need to liaise over customs, trade and border controls means that there will often be long-standing interaction between local authorities in EU border areas. Indeed, the Euregion Maas Rhine initiative involving local authorities in Belgium, Germany and the Netherlands, and cooperation in the Öresund region of Denmark and Sweden are collaborations that have both existed for over 25 years. Furthermore, a number of border regions in the EU are united by strong cross-border cultural and ethnic identities (Perkmann 1999).

As EU borders become more fluid then increased economic interaction may strengthen cross-border collaboration. Bennett (1997) has argued that successful new political spaces will often reflect restructuring economic spaces. In addition, local authorities in border areas will clearly have a shared interest in the frontier even if there are differences in economic and political structures. Barriers linked to different political systems, culture and language will confront all transnational local government initiatives. The changing history of economic, political and cultural exchange across many EU borders may make overcoming these barriers easier compared to local authorities who have a shared interest but are territorially distant. Furthermore, border regions have received considerable EC funds to promote transnational interaction, and political networks of these regions have been established in the form of LACE (Linkage Assistance and Co-operation for the European Border Regions) and AEBR (the Association of European Border Regions). Thus, there are a variety of factors that suggest that a decade of policy activity might have resulted in some well-developed cross-border collaborative initiatives that have started to overcome the barriers to transnational cooperation and generated useful outputs. The reality, as this chapter suggests, is somewhat different. Cross-border collaboration is a source of funds that local authorities have used to develop initiatives that are often of benefit to local communities. There are some clear gains, but often vicinity cooperation struggles to achieve its broader collaborative aims and faces a number of significant management problems.

This chapter uses a range of evidence to develop a critical appraisal of the politics and management of cross-border initiatives. In our previous writings on cross-border collaboration (Church and Reid 1996, 1999) we concentrated more on the theoretical implications of these new initiatives for the understanding of institutionalisation, regulation and urban politics. This earlier work was based on detailed semi-structured interviews with key actors in local authorities in northern France and southern England conducted in the mid and late 1990s. We again draw on some of the findings of these interviews, but in preparation for this chapter a limited number of further interviews were conducted in early 2000 with key actors in local government. Due to staff changes these were not always the same individuals as previously but were with those occupying similar positions. There has also been a recent expansion of research on cross-border initiatives in Europe produced by the EC, consultants and academic commentators (see for example the compilations in Scott et al. 1996, Westeren 1998, *Regional Studies* 1999).

This growing literature provides detailed findings on cross-border collaboration in many different parts of Europe. The aim of this chapter is
not to provide a review of the literature, but to use the key conclusions
of this research, combined with the past and recent findings from our
detailed case study, to provide a synthesised critical analysis of cross-
border collaboration.

Cross-border collaboration in the Transmanche region of France and England

The cross-border initiatives in our case study area in southern England
and northern France are outlined in detail elsewhere (Church and
Reid 1996, 1999). Our research has particularly focused on Kent
County Council and Nord–Pas de Calais Regional Council where
formal cross-border collaboration dates from 1987 when a joint accord
was signed to establish the Transmanche region (see Figure 12.1). This
initiative was partly motivated by the construction of the Channel
Tunnel but then provided a vehicle for obtaining INTERREG I funding
between 1992 and 1994. Accessing INTERREG funds represented a
major lobbying success since they were designated only for the land
borders of the EU, but the two authorities argued that the Tunnel
meant they shared a terrestrial border. Kent became the only British
authority to receive INTERREG I funds. In 1991 the cross-border collaboration expanded geographically with the signing of a joint declar-
ation to form the Transmanche Euroregion that involved Kent,
Nord–Pas de Calais and the regional governments of Flanders,
Wallonia and Brussels-Capital.

Other UK local government bodies have been extensively involved
in European networks but Kent was the first authority to be part of a
formal Euroregion. The Transmanche region, however, maintains its
own identity and separate INTERREG funding within the larger
Euroregion – see Figure 12.1 for a map of the areas. Kent and Nord–Pas
de Calais also obtained INTERREG II funding between 1995 and 1999.
Four other cooperative groupings in the UK gained INTERREG II
funding. Kent and their French partners were also involved in the
establishment of the Arc Manche cooperative network that included
five French regional authorities and nine English local government
bodies. These were from the littoral regions on either side of the
Channel and ranged from Brittany and Cornwall in the west to Kent
and Nord–Pas de Calais in the east. The Arc Manche initiative has
achieved only limited capacity and profile (Church and Reid 1999).

206

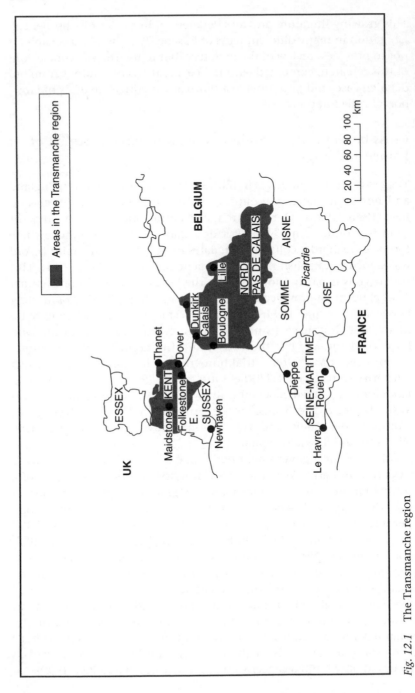

Fig. 12.1   The Transmanche region

The INTERREG programme, however, has been a significant initiative in Kent and Nord–Pas de Calais for a decade. The cost of the INTERREG II initiative in the Transmanche region between 1995 and 1999 was 95 million euros, with 45 million euros coming from the EC and the rest from mainly public sector match funding. The partners involved in the initiative now include not only Kent County Council and Regional Council of Nord–Pas de Calais, but also the more local district councils in Kent, general councils and *arrondissements* in Nord–Pas de Calais, educational bodies, and chambers of commerce. Central government is represented by the Préfecture in Nord–Pas de Calais and the Government Office for the South East in the UK. Central government plays a leading role in the Joint Monitoring Committee that is the key project approval body for INTERREG projects in the Transmanche region.

In the Transmanche region between 1992 and 1996 nearly two-thirds of INTERREG I funds went on land management, environmental projects and a tourism programme. Projects were varied and included harbour improvements, coastal cliff maintenance and joint tourism promotion. Under INTERREG II the Transmanche region initiative had four main objectives which were: to improve communication links; to improve the area's attractiveness for sustainable growth, technological and economic development; to alleviate the negative effects of changes in sea traffic; and to develop networks between organisations. Proposed projects are judged in relation to these objectives and in many senses these objectives are quite typical of other cross-border initiatives taking place elsewhere in Europe (AEBR 1996). For the INTERREG III programme it is possible that West-Vlaanderen in Belgium may also join the Transmanche region grouping. The long-term experience of the Transmanche region provides some detailed examples of the potential and problems of cross-border collaboration. The remainder of the chapter draws on the Transmanche region experience, but a more wide-ranging discussion is developed using the findings of research on cross-border collaboration and transboundary working elsewhere in Europe.

The motives and possible benefits of cross-border collaboration

Clearly the growing involvement of local government in cross-border collaboration has in part been motivated by the availability of EC funds. Indeed, it is tempting to interpret some cross-border initiatives as another example of the general growth of competitively motivated funding coalitions (Peck and Tickell 1994b). This would be rather unfair in the case of the Transmanche region, which was devised before funding was available. The recent consultation draft of the Kent European Strategy (Kent County Council 2000, p. 3) argues that: 'A key purpose of European activity is to secure resources, particularly from EU funds, where these help implement our strategic priorities. Therefore, whilst maximising funding is a prime objective, the European strategy should not be solely income-driven.' This quote clearly implies that income generation is a central goal of the European strategy, but the desire for funding is not indiscriminate and the strategy is linked to locally defined political imperatives. Elsewhere in Europe Perkmann (1999) argues that strong cross-border cultural and ethnic ties provide a significant motivation for collaboration beyond simply the desire to access funding. More generally, a wide range of processes lie behind the expansion of this form of local government activity. The increasing internationalisation of the economy encourages a collaborative approach to attracting increasingly mobile inward investment and this stimulates cross-border strategies (Church and Reid 1995). The integration aims of the EU and the associated Europeanisation of subnational government provide a further context promoting the growth of cooperative networks (John 2000). Within the UK, and many other states as well, the 'modernisation' of local government and competitive funding structures further encourage the development of new forms of partnership (Hambleton 2000).

Very different views exist regarding the potentialities of cross-border cooperation to promote European integration and stimulate policy innovation. Von Malchus (1998, p. 73) in a discussion of transfrontier spatial planning, claims that INTERREG-supported policies may in future contribute to enhancing democracy, human rights, equality and sustainable development. The specific successes of cross-border cooperation are claimed to be in the development of cross-border master plans and transport planning, and the expansion of spatial planning objectives (von Malchus 1998). Roch (1998), slightly less optimistically, claims to identify major advantages but also significant problems in the cross-border initiatives developed in Euregion Egrensis which includes parts of Saxony, Bavaria, Bohemia and a former 'Iron Curtain' border. In relation to environmental problems 'momentous decisions were made concerning what were to constitute priority measures' but, while important, these decisions have to be set against the finding that 'the efforts of the Euroregions to achieve interdepartmental and intercommunal co-operation are proving extremely laborious and given the absence of executive powers for transnational regional development, they are often in vain where they are not underpinned by national developments' (Roch 1998, pp. 80, 85).

In the same book as the writings by von Malchus (1998) and Roch (1998) there are far more negative conclusions on the existing and future contributions of cross-border initiatives and transfrontier planning. In a discussion of the Vienna/Bratislava region, Altzinger et al. (1998, p. 112) note that cross-border initiatives are limited in development so that: 'It could well be that Vienna and Bratislava have already squandered the opportunity to establish themselves as a potent hub in the European system of cities and regions.' Their analysis of regional economic and labour market data leads, however, to a more complex conclusion that due to uneven development in Slovakia the 'improved integration of the Vienna/Bratislava region may actually heighten internal stability in Slovakia, a factor which even now is often viewed as being set to jeopardise the economic development of central Europe as a whole' (Altzinger et al. 1998, p. 112). The discussion by Vartiainen (1998) of transfrontier cooperation in the Baltic Sea is more concerned with political issues. He notes that while there are institutional opportunities in such networking, 'Instead of truly interactive, horizontal co-operation, existing partnerships between local authorities seem to be very much tied in with the hierarchical structures of state administration and characterised by one-way communication and resource transformation' (Vartiainen 1998, p. 124).

The conclusions of these differing case studies partly serve to illustrate that the regional and national context is, not surprisingly, a significant influence on the nature of cross-border collaboration. Nevertheless, the findings from these and other comparative studies combined with our own research on the Transmanche region suggest it is possible to identify certain general political advantages and problems of cross-border initiatives.

The EC has ambitious aims for cross-border collaboration and transfrontier spatial planning to contribute to economic and social cohesion and a better territorial balance (van Ginneken 1998). Officials in Kent tended to argue that, in general, the economic and geographical integration of the EU had been beneficial despite short-term problems such as port jobs lost due to the removal of border controls. The draft Kent European strategy claims that over the last 30 years Kent has changed from being perceived as a relatively peripheral area in southern England to a region at the heart of the EU (Kent County Council

2000). Elected councillors, while admitting Kent had benefited from the changing nature of economic space in Europe, were increasingly questioning the benefits of EC initiatives designed to involve local government in the political integration process. In particular, there was a perceived danger of being overcommitted to policy networks in terms of resources and officer time. One elected councilor noted that 'the basic approach now is value for money. Financial pressures are greater and everything to do with Europe has to be examined.' Given the wide range of processes that contribute to European integration and patterns of territorial development, it is difficult to identify any clear impact of cross-border policies on these broad political and economic goals of the EC. Indeed, it is clearly intended that cross-border policies are merely one of a large number of policies promoting integration and cohesion (Williams 1996). Thus, to some degree, the advantages and problems of cross-border policies must be assessed within a wider political context.

A number of studies have noted that cross-border initiatives, often in combination with other EC-funded policies, can open up new institutional possibilities and support policy innovation (Newman and Paasi 1998). Effective cross-border collaboration could in theory contribute to the development of political and administrative capacity, which Stewart (1996a) argues is central to urban competitiveness. A recent consultancy report by the University of the West of England on behalf of the European Commission and Kent County Council compared 14 examples of cross-border collaboration and interregional cooperation including the Transmanche region. The report suggests that the management structures in some cases do facilitate policy innovation and that 'diversity is strength. The management of the programmes needs to be able to respond to the circumstances of particular transboundary regions ... the willingness of most participants to co-operate and make progress through establishing new ways of working is impressive' (Brown and Nadin 2000).

In an examination of the Baltic Sea region Vartiainen (1998) also notes the special opportunities that stem from transborder cooperation, but qualifies this by noting that these are very new initiatives even for the relatively internationalised Nordic cities and that the spatial reach is still very limited. Similarly, the comparative consultancy report argues that very few of the actual projects supported by cross-border collaboration can be properly evaluated since they have yet to make sufficient progress (Brown and Nadin 2000). Interviewees in the Transmanche region were keen to stress, however, that the opportunities for innovation through cross-border collaboration were linked to the broader development of other European initiatives. One officer claimed that 'the County see these border links and funding as a useful method of increasing trade and developing longer term networks as part of a major European programme'. It is hard to identify clearly the specific effects of cross-border collaboration on local government policy management and innovation given the influence of other European initiatives and the broader processes of change. Nevertheless, after a decade of policy activity it is noticeable that most commentators are still identifying potential opportunities rather than existing benefits.

Another potential advantage of cross-border collaboration stems from its contribution to broader spatial planning and vision making among the regions of Europe. The ESDP is an example of attempts to develop new spatial visions in Europe which promote the emergence of new political entities to reflect current and desired changes in economic and environmental space (Healey 1998). The ESDP is based on very large-scale spatial thinking and planning for macro regions. Selke (1998, p. 42) optimistically suggests that such 'transnational programmes may in the years ahead prove to be the decisive driving force along the road towards a more balanced development of the regions in a continent that is busy evolving into an organic whole'. Cross-border collaboration which itself encourages the development of new spatial thinking has the potential to underpin some of these broader transnational visions by clarifying spatial strategies and producing local political benefits (Brown and Nadin 2000). Indeed, Newman and Paasi (1998) suggest that imaginative new discourses and networks around borders can challenge the constraints and spatial structures of central states.

Again, however, optimism must be tempered with the reality of the actual performance of cross-border collaboration. A recent consultancy report specifically concerned with the Transmanche region argued that a new vision was needed for cross-border cooperation not because an earlier vision was outdated but because after 14 years of cooperation a clear vision had yet to emerge (Ernst and Young 2000). The report claims projects 'tended to be generated in a purely bottom-up fashion with organisations coming forward with their own proposals, there has been a lack of synergy between activities and little overall strategic direction' (Ernst and Young 2000). Similarly, a comparative study found that in many examples of cross-border collaboration the strategic framework was poorly developed due to concerns relating to maintaining the delivery of operational programmes (Brown and Nadin 2000). Our interviewees argued that this was the case within the Transmanche region and the response has been to develop an INTER-REG III programme that has fewer but larger projects than previously in an attempt to develop a strategic approach. Also local authority involvement in new transnational initiatives is often opportunistic and subject to rapid change. Elsewhere we have noted how the Arc Manche region was comprised of local authorities with very varied degrees of commitment, some of whom were involved just in case the initiative developed further but were prepared to withdraw rapidly if it did not progress (Church and Reid 1999). The cooperation and novel new spaces of cross-border collaboration might suggest visionary new spatial thinking. The reality is that strategic visions are often quite poorly developed, and cross-border initiatives are typified by a focus on the delivery of operational programmes loosely connected to some generalised objectives.

Even without clear strategic goals, cross-border collaboration can certainly bring short-term specific political gains for local government. In our earlier studies of the Transmanche region we noted that both French and English authorities had found INTERREG I a useful vehicle for developing their own operational programmes with only limited direction from central government. More generally, Hebbert (2000, p. 391), in a discussion of the Transpennine corridor in England and the wider North European axis, argues that these new transborder, politico-spatial imaginations serve a 'geo-political purpose . . . . The North European axis may have little basis in commercial geography but it engages participating elites in the European policy scenario. The Transpennine corridor bypasses London in every sense.' More recently, however, the role of cross-border collaboration in enhancing local political autonomy has been constrained as central government has become an increasingly stronger gatekeeper over local authority involvement in European initiatives (Martin and Pearce 1993). East Sussex County Council in southern England received funding under INTERREG II and felt that central government's Regional Office for South East England had strongly determined the direction of cross-border activities (Church and Reid 1999). Furthermore, some comparative evaluations of cross-border strategies suggest that strong and clear national involvement in these initiatives can be highly beneficial in terms of ensuring programmes are effectively devised and delivered (Brown and Nadin 2000).

While central government may have an increasing influence on the nature of cross-border collaborations, Hebbert's (2000) point about access to Brussels and the EC is still valid in a more general context. In Kent County Council cross-border collaboration is seen as one of a large number of European initiatives that have been used not only to generate funds but also to ensure that Kent has clear opportunities to communicate its own views to the EC (Kent County Council 2000). Thus, the opportunity for cross-border initiatives to stimulate local political autonomy are probably limited, but they do provide one important connection to the EC within the complex web of links many local authorities have established in order to access influential European institutions. In this sense cross-border initiatives generate an active politics for local government that goes beyond, but is heavily constrained by, the nation state.

In our past interviews it was often stressed that cross-border collaboration was significant in terms of knowledge, information and experience exchange (Church and Reid 1999). More generally, Hambleton (2000) emphasises the important role of international exchange in the redesign of political management arrangements in local government in the UK and other European countries. A number of recent interviewees suggested that these benefits of cross-border collaboration were growing in importance, with one senior officer claiming that 'the cross-border strategy and networks are about funding, but increasingly about intelligence and information gathering, best practice, added value and knowing what is going on'. Other interviewees also indicated that they were considering reorganising their involvement in European networks but that, currently, cross-border vicinity collaboration would remain their most important network.

In this context one of the key benefits of cross-border collaboration stems from proximity. For these initiatives not only provide an opportunity to compare best practice but also to gain directly relevant information on changes relating to the local economy and environment. One interviewee claimed that the intelligence gathered through cross-border initiatives was of significantly greater value than that obtained through theme networks. The available evidence suggests that the process of information exchange and the availability of funding will undoubtedly maintain the existing momentum of many cross-border initiatives, but other hoped-for benefits in the form of political autonomy, strategy and spatial vision are not yet clearly visible.

The problems of cross-border collaboration

The last decade of cross-border collaboration in the EU has also encountered some significant problems. Indeed, the previous discussion of the possible benefits has already highlighted certain difficulties in terms of strategy development and the harnessing of institutional possibilities. A number of studies have noted that one of the general problematic features of cross-border initiatives is that they contain internal contradictions since cooperative structures are imbued with competition (Anderson and O'Dowd 2000; Vartiainen 1994; Church and Reid 1996). The INTERREG bidding process has often involved intense competition between neighbouring local authorities at similar and different tiers of government who have chosen to join different cross-border groupings. Furthermore, interviewees in the Transmanche region admitted that Kent and Nord–Pas de Calais competed strongly for inward investment. They both are advantageously located for accessing north-western European markets, but offer contrasting locational characteristics in that northern France has more regional policy incentives whereas Kent stresses it has a more deregulated labour market. This is particularly true in the areas of eastern Kent that have above-average unemployment rates caused by the loss of jobs in traditional tourism, defence and coal-mining industries.

One officer responsible for regional policy claimed that the conditions of the local labour market in east Kent were often compared to those in northern France during discussions with inward investors and

> The high unemployment means that we have a workforce that is willing to work for what I consider low pay. I hate saying that because I don't want to set us up as a third world location and encourage firms to perpetuate the problem. But we have to start somewhere and getting outsiders in will encourage indigenous companies to pay more.

The competition within cross-border groupings and with neighbouring authorities may counteract the integrative and cohesive tendencies of cross-border collaboration that the EC is seeking to develop. As with some of the hoped-for benefits of cross-border collaboration, the potential difficulties stemming from these competitive tensions may take time to emerge. Their significance, however, needs to be acknowledged. The disadvantages of the general increase in competition for local authority funding have already been documented, and cross-border collaboration is no different from other partnerships in requiring regulatory mechanisms that limit the harmful effects of competitive funding environments (Stewart 1996a).

The competitive tendencies inherent in cross-border collaboration under INTERREG may partly explain the major management problem facing these initiatives, which is a lack of well-developed cooperation. Cooperative structures are established to bid for funds and to decide upon the projects that should receive financial support. In many examples of cross-border collaboration this has involved developing a secretariat, a monitoring/coordinating committee, a steering committee and then a series of thematic groups (Brown and Nadin 2000). These frameworks do not, however, guarantee cooperation either at the strategic or operational level. Often cross-border funding is used to support parallel programmes conducted on a unilateral rather than joint basis. In our earlier work in the Transmanche region interviewees suggested that tourism was a policy sphere where in-depth collaboration had been possible (Church and Reid 1999), and a recent consultancy study suggests that tourism along with culture provided good examples of joint cross-border working in the Transmanche region (Ernst and Young 2000). Nevertheless, in our recent interviews senior officers still considered that there 'was a need to ensure that cross-border projects are really cross-border and not contrived'. The consultancy study on the Transmanche region similarly concluded that under INTERREG III far more 'genuine' cross-border projects were required, and that past experience in certain supposed areas of cooperation, such as infrastructure, indicated it was hard to identify any genuinely cross-border projects (Ernst and Young 2000). The lack of real cooperative projects will reflect a range of processes including cultural differences and political asynchronicity, but this is clearly a significant problem if there are central policy fields where after ten years of cross-border collaboration little joint working has actually developed.

A further specific management problem relates to the issue of accountability and public awareness. In the Transmanche region key policy actors saw this as a problem in the mid-1990s (Church and Reid 1996) and in recent interviews were actually more explicit, claiming that 'the residents of areas where there are cross-border initiatives often know very little of them, this is certainly true in Kent and this needs to be addressed . . . the EC is very conscious of this'. The comparative study of 14 cross-border and transboundary EC programmes produced some particularly negative conclusions on the issue of accountability, arguing that 'There is considerable inconsistency in the extent to which the programmes meet basic principles such as transparency, efficiency and perceived impartiality in decision making' (Brown and Nadin 2000).

This comparative study also argued that a lack of accountability and awareness led to non-inclusive programmes, so that with only a few exceptions the key actors in transboundary initiatives were government representatives with very limited input from the private or voluntary sectors. Also only a few initiatives had made significant attempts to raise public awareness of cross-border activities (Brown and Nadin 2000). Detailed comparative studies identify some of the management processes that lie behind these general difficulties facing cross-border collaboration. The need for co-financing (match-funding) has often limited the involvement of certain types of organisation in particular EC programmes. Other specific problems include delays in programme establishment and funding provision, overburdened and sometimes inefficient committee structures, and management frameworks that were not compatible with operational programmes (Ernst and Young 2000, Brown and Nadin 2000). Overall, these are undoubtedly damning conclusions on the general nature and management structures of transboundary policies involving local and regional government. No doubt supporters of cross-border cooperation might dispute them by pointing to examples of good practice and suggesting a more inclusive approach will emerge once cross-border and other transboundary initiatives mature. Also the actual activities funded by programmes like INTERREG may be of significant value to communities in border areas. In a situation where resources are increasingly constrained, they can also be used to assist local authorities in their statutory duties to deliver certain services and maintain the environment. Nevertheless, these studies and our own findings suggest that key actors in cross-border collaboration recognise there is considerable scope to improve the nature and management of existing initiatives, and that this will require action from local authorities along with improved guidance and advice from national governments and the EC.

Conclusions

Some of the problems of cross-border collaboration will undoubtedly stem from the structural constraints on cross-boundary activities. Van Geenhuizen et al. (1996) identify a series of transport, technological, economic–institutional, sociocultural and political obstacles to transboundary working, ranging from political instability to physical barriers. The difficulties found in the Transmanche region may in part be accounted for by this being a relatively 'difficult' border within the EU since it is a maritime boundary with contrasting economies either side. Kent contains a poorly performing eastern area but is generally considered part of the relatively affluent south-east of England. Nord–Pas de Calais contains a clearly lagging European region with high unemployment and problems associated with industrial restructuring. Comparative and case studies in other locations suggest, however, that the problems facing cross-border collaboration are by no means confined to 'difficult' borders. The problems facing cross-border collaboration are fundamental, including underdeveloped strategic visions, limited management structures, a lack of 'genuine' joint working, and inadequate accountability and awareness-raising processes.

By way of qualification, it should be added that a number of INTER-REG evaluation studies have noted significant improvements in cross-border working between the first and second round of funding. A comparative evaluation of 31 INTERREG programmes in the early 1990s argued that 'value added' could also be identified in terms of new markets for SMEs, additional tourism, training and research and development collaboration between universities, improved communication and cross-border movement, and transnational partnership building (FERE 1996 quoted in Ernst and Young 2000). There are also examples of long-standing cross-border collaborations that predate INTERREG and which have developed a successful range of programmes (Scott 1996). Comparative studies suggest that long-standing links and experience of joint working have been a key factor in many of the more successful transboundary initiatives (Brown and Nadin 2000).

Clearly, any judgements on the merits of cross-border working will, in part, depend on what is expected of a programme such as INTER-REG, which has spread relatively small sums of money around a large number of EU border regions. In a discussion of urban networks Parkinson (1992) takes a rather pragmatic view, suggesting they have three main functions: to transfer best practice and policy innovation, to lobby for national and European resources, and to act as catalysts of economic cooperation. If INTERREG initiatives were judged against these three functions they might well be viewed quite favourably. Nevertheless, the benefits of cross-border cooperation remain somewhat elusive. An optimistic conclusion would be that the last decade has established a political acceptance of cross-border collaboration and the next decade will be used to overcome the management difficulties that stem from differences in political structures. More pessimistically, there is evidence to suggest that the considerable problems of existing cross-border initiatives may have complex structural roots that will not be easily overcome, and in some border regions these policies, while stimulating the political imagination, may provide little of long-term substance. Whatever the outcomes, the ten years of cross-border collaboration in the EU provide significant insights into the implications for democratic structures of the internationalisation of local government.

Bibliography

Advisory Commission on Intergovernmental Relations (1976) *Pragmatic Federalism: the Reassignment of Functional Responsibility*. Report M-105. Washington, DC: Government Printing Office

AEBR (Association of European Border Regions) (1996) *An Introduction to the Association of European Border Regions*. Berlin: Gronau

Agnew B. and Pascall G. (1997) '"Cooperate Regionally, Compete Globally" is Strategy for 21st Century', *News Tribune*, 26 August

Altzinger W., Maier G. and Fidrmuc J. (1998) 'Cross-Border Development in the Vienna/Bratislava Region: a Review', in Graute U. (ed.), *Sustainable Development for Central and Eastern Europe*. Berlin: Springer-Verlag

American Banker (1993) 'The Top 500 Banks in the World', *American Banker*, 29 July

Amin A. (1992) 'Big Firms versus the Regions in the Single European Market', in Dunford M. and Kafkalas G. (eds), *Cities and Regions in the New Europe: the Global–Local Interplay and Spatial Development Strategies*. London: Belhaven

Amin A. (1994) *Post-Fordism: a Reader*. Oxford; Cambridge, Mass.: Blackwell

Amin A. and Graham S. (1997) 'The Ordinary City', *Transactions of the Institute of British Geographers*, Vol. 22, pp. 411–29

Amin A. and Thrift N. (eds) (1994) 'Living in the Global', in *Globalisation, Institutions and Regional Development in Europe*. Oxford: Oxford University Press

Amin A. and Tomaney J. (1995) 'The Regional Dilemma in a Neo-Liberal Europe', *European Urban and Regional Studies*, Vol. 2, No. 2, pp. 171–88

Amsterdam, Rotterdam, Den Haag, Utrecht (1994) *Een deltaplan voor de grote steden. Werk, veiligheid, leefbaarheid. Memorandum grote steden aan de kabinetsformateur*, June

Anderson J. and O' Dowd L. (1999) 'Borders, Border Regions and Territoriality: Contradictory Meanings, Changing Significance', *Regional Studies*, Vol. 33, No. 7, pp. 593–604

Andrew C. and Goldsmith M. (1998) 'From Local Government to Local Governance – and Beyond?', *International Political Science Review*, Vol. 19, No. 2, pp. 101–17

Appadurai A. (1996) *Modernity at Large: Cultural Dimensions of Globalization*. Minneapolis: University of Minnesota Press

Artibise A.F.J. (1988) 'Canada as an Urban Nation', *Daedalus*, Vol. 114, pp. 237–64

Artibise A.F.J. (1995) 'Achieving Sustainability in Cascadia: an Emerging Model of Urban Growth Management in the Vancouver–Seattle–Portland Corridor', in Kresl P.K. and Gappert G. (eds), *North American Cities and the Global Economy*. Thousand Oaks, Calif.: Sage

Artibise A.F.J. (1997) 'Cascadian Adventures: Shared Visions, Strategic Alliances, and Ingrained Barriers in a Transborder Region'. Unpublished paper

Ascher F. (1995) *Métapolis, ou l'avenir des villes*. Paris: Editions Odile Jacob

Ascher F. (1998) *La République contre la ville. Essai sur l'avenir de la France urbaine.* La Tour d'Aigues: Editions de l'Aube

Ashkenasi A. (1988) 'Communal Policy, Conflict Management, and International Relations', *Jerusalem Journal of International Relations,* Vol. 10, No. 2, pp. 109–27

Atkinson R. and Larsen J.N. (2000) 'The Developing EU Urban Policy: Lessons from Kvarterloft and SRB'. Paper to the European Urban Research Association Workshop, 'Cities in the Region', Dublin, April

Audit Commission (1990) *We Can't Go on Meeting Like This. The Changing Role of Local Authority Members.* Management Paper 8, September. London: The Audit Commission

Audit Commission (1997) *Representing the People. The Role of Councillors.* Management Paper. London: The Audit Commission

Baade R. and Dye R. (1988) 'Sports Stadiums and Area Development: a Critical Review', *Economic Development Quarterly,* Vol. 2, pp. 265–75

Back H., Johannson F. and Larsen H.O. (2000) 'Local Government in Nordic Big Cities', in O.W. Gabriel, V. Hoffman-Martinot and H.V. Savitch (eds), *Urban Democracy.* Leverkusen: Verlag Leske and Budrich.

Backhaus-Maul H. (1993) 'Transformation kommunaler Sozialpolitik', in Pitschas R. (ed.), *Verwaltungsintegration in den neuen Bundesländern.* Berlin: Duncker and Humblot

Bagnasco A. and Le Galès, P. (eds) (1997) *Villes en Europe.* Paris: La Découverte

Bagnasco A. and Le Galès P. (1997) 'Les villes européennes comme société et comme acteur', in Bagnasco A. and Le Galès P. (eds), *Villes en Europe.* Paris: La Découverte

Baldersheim H. (1996) *Local Democracy in East-Central Europe.* Boulder, Colo.: Westview Press

Baldersheim H. et al. (eds) (1996) *Local Democracy and the Processes of Transformation in East-Central Europe.* Boulder, Colo.: Westview Press

Baldersheim H., Balme R., Clark T.N., Hoffman-Martinot V. and Magnusson H. (eds) (1989) *New Leaders, Parties, and Groups: Comparative Tendencies in Local Leadership.* Paris and Bordeaux: CERVEL

Balme R., Clark T.N., Becquart-Leclercq J., Hoffmann-Martinot V. and Nevers J. 'New Mayors: France and the United States', *The Tocqueville Review,* Vol. 8, (1986/87), pp. 263–78, University Press of Virginia, Charlottesville

Balme R. and Hoffmann-Martinot V. (eds) (1991) *Local and Regional Bureaucracies in Western Europe.* Bordeaux: Les Cahiers du CERVEL

Banner G. (1999) 'From Government to Governance: German Local Authorities between Regulation, Service Provision and Community Development', *The Annals of Public Administration Research,* No.17 (1999–2000). The Research Institute for Public Administration, Hanyang University, Seoul, Korea

Barber B.R. (1984) *Strong Democracy. Participatory Politics for a New Age.* Berkeley: University of California Press

Barnes W.R. and Ledebur L.C. (1998) *The New Regional Economies: the US Common Market and the Global Economy,* Newbury Park, Calif.: Sage

Barringer D. (1997) 'The New Urban Gamble', *The American Prospect,* September–October, pp. 28–34

Barron J., Crawley G. and Wood T. (1991) *Councillors in Crisis.* London: Macmillan – now Palgrave

Bartkowski J., Kowalczyk A. and Swianiewicz P. (1990) *Strategie wladz lokalnych.* University of Warsaw, Instytut Gospodarki Przestrzennej, Vol. 21

Bassand M. (1997) *Métropolisation et inégalités sociales.* Lausanne: Presses Polytechniques et Universitaires Romandes

Beauregard R.A. (1995) 'Theorizing the Global–Local Connection', in Knox P. and Taylor P. (eds), *World Cities in a World System.* Cambridge: Cambridge University Press

Beauregard R.A. and Body-Gendrot S. (eds) (1999) *The Urban Moment. Cosmopolitan Essays on the Late 20th Century City.* Thousand Oaks: Sage

Becquart-Leclerq J., Hoffman-Martinot V. and Nevers J.Y. (1987) *Austerité et Innovation Locale. Les Stratégies Politico-Financières des Municipalités Urbaines dans la Crise.* Vol. 1, 110 pp. Paris: Compte Rendu au Ministère de la Technologie

Bell D. (1973) *The Coming of Post Industrial Society.* New York: Basic Books

Benington J. and Harvey J. (1994) 'Spheres or Tiers? The Significance of Transnational Local Authority Networks', *Local Government Policy Making,* Vol. 20, No. 5, pp. 21–9

Benko G. and Strohmayer U. (eds) (1997) *Space and Social Theory.* London: Blackwell

Bennett R.J. (1997) 'Administrative Systems and Economic Spaces', *Regional Studies,* Vol. 31, No. 3, pp. 323–36

Benvenisti M.S. (1986) *Conflicts and Contradictions.* New York: Villard Books

Berry B.J.L. (1973) *The Human Consequences of Urbanisation.* New York: St Martin's Press – now Palgrave

Berry B.J.L. and Horton F.E. (1970) *Geographic Perspectives on Urban Systems.* Englewood Cliffs, NJ: Prentice Hall

Bevolkingsonderzoek (1994) *Regio Haaglanden, Onderdeel III Laak Escamp.* The Hague: Stafbureau Sociaal Wetenschappelijk Onderzoek Politie

Bianchini F. (1991) 'Urbanization and the Functions of Cities in the European Community. City case study: Naples'. Unpublished research report submitted to Centre for Urban Studies, University of Liverpool

Bilski R. and Galnoor I. (1980) 'Ideologies and Values in National Planning', in Bilski R., Galnoor I., Inbar D., Manor Y. and Sheffer G. *Can Planning Replace Politics? The Israeli Experience.* The Hague: Martinus Nijhoff

Bissinger B. (1997) *Prayer for the City.* New York: Vintage Books

Blank R. (1997) *It Takes a Nation: a New Agenda for Fighting Poverty.* New York: Russell Sage Foundation and Princeton University Press

Blazek J. and Kara J. (1992) 'Regional Policy in the Czech Republic in the Period of Transition', in Gorzelak G. and Kulinski A. (eds), *Dilemmas of Regional Policy in Eastern and Central Europe.* Warsaw: European Institute for Regional and Local Development

Blokland-Potters T. (1997) *Wat stadsbewoners bindt; Sociale relaties in een achterstadswijk.* Kampen: Kok Agora

Bobo L. and Gilliam F.D. (1990) 'Race, Socio-Economic Participation, and Black Empowerment', *American Political Science Review,* Vol. 84, pp. 344–93

Body-Gendrot S. (2000) *The Social Control of Cities? A Comparative Perspective.* Oxford: Blackwell

Bollens S.A. (1998a) 'Urban Planning amidst Ethnic Conflict: Jerusalem and Johannesburg', *Urban Studies,* Vol. 35, No. 4, pp. 729–50

Bollens S.A. (1998b) 'Ethnic Stability and Urban Reconstruction: Policy Dilemmas in Polarized Cities', *Comparative Political Studies*, Vol. 31, No. 6, pp. 683–713

Bollens S.A. (1999) *Urban Peace-Building in Divided Societies: Belfast and Johannesburg*. Boulder, Colo. and Oxford, UK: Westview Press

Bollens S.A. (2000) *On Narrow Ground: Urban Policy and Ethnic Conflict in Jerusalem and Belfast*. Albany: State University of New York Press

Boomkens R. (1999) 'Op zoek naar de andere burger', *Tijdschrift voor de Sociale Sector*, April

Borja J. and Castells M. (1997) *The Local and the Global: Cities in the Information Age*. London: Earthscan

Bowler S., Donovan T. and Tolbert C.J. (eds) (1998) *Citizens as Legislators: Direct Democracy in the United States*. Columbus: Ohio State University Press

Bowles S. and Gintis H. (1987) *Democracy and Capitalism*. New York: Basic Books

Broder D. (1998) 'Leaving Politics Aside', *Boulder Camera*, 20 July, 8A

Broussine M. (1998) *A Scheme for Continuous Learning for SOLACE Members*. Bristol: Bristol Business School, University of the West of England

Brown C. and Nadin V. (eds) (2000) *The Role and Operation of Transnational Management Structures in Achieving Effective Implementation of Transnational, Cross-border and Inter-regional Programmes*. Final report for Kent County Council and DG Regional Policy of the European Commission, Faculty of the Built Environment, University of the West of England, Bristol

Brown M.E. (1993) 'Causes and Implications of Ethnic Conflict', in Brown M.E. (ed.), *Ethnic Conflict and International Security*. Princeton: Princeton University Press

Brown M.E. (ed.) (1996) *The International Dimensions of Internal Conflict*. Cambridge, Mass.: Massachusetts Institute of Technology Press

Bruegmann R. (1995) 'Urban Aberration or Glimpse of the Future'. Unpublished manuscript

Buchanan P. (1998) *The Great Betrayed*. New York: Little Brown

Bureau of Economic Analysis (1991) *Census of City Population*. US Department of Commerce, Washington, DC

Burgers J. and Kloosterman R.C. (1996) 'Dutch Comfort; Postindustrial Transition and Social Exclusion in Spangen, Rotterdam', *Area*, Vol. 28, No. 4, December, pp. 433–45

Burns D. (2000) 'Can Local Democracy Survive Urban Governance?', *Urban Studies*, Vol. 37, No. 5–6, pp. 963–73

Burns D., Hambleton R. and Hoggett P. (1994) *The Politics of Decentralisation*. London: Macmillan – now Palgrave

Burton J.W. (ed.) (1990) *Conflict: Human Needs Theory*. New York: St Martin's Press – now Palgrave

Burton J.W. (1991) 'Conflict Resolution as a Political System', in Volkan V.D., Montville J.V. and Julius D.A. (eds), *The Psychodynamics of International Relationships*, Vol. II. Lexington, Mass.: D.C. Heath

Camagni R. and Gibelli M.C. (eds) (1997) *Développement urbain durable. Quatre métropoles européennes*. La Tour d'Aigues: Éditions de l'Aube

Carney E.N. (1998) 'Power Grab', *National Journal*, 11 April, pp. 798–801

Castells M. (1996) *The Information Age*. Vol. 1, *The Rise of the Network Society*. London: Blackwell

Castells M. (1997) *The Information Age*: Vol. 2, *The Power of Identity*. London: Blackwell

Castells M. and Hall P. (1994) *Technologies of the World*. London: Routledge

CEC (Commission of the European Communities) (1997) *Practical Handbook on Cross-border Collaboration*. Luxembourg: Office for Official Publications of the CEC

CEC (1999) *The European Spatial Development Perspective: Complete Draft*. Brussels: Committee on Spatial Development

Chandler J.A. and Clark T.N. (1995) 'Local Government (Around the World)', in Lipset S.M. (ed.), *The Encyclopedia of Democracy*. Washington, DC: Congressional Quarterly Books, Vol. 3, pp. 767–73.

Cheshire P., Carbonara G. and Hay D. (1986) 'Problems of Urban Decline and Growth in EEC Countries: or Measuring Degrees of Elephantness', *Urban Studies*, Vol. 23, No. 2, pp. 131–49

Church A. and Reid P. (1995) 'Transfrontier Co-operation, Spatial Development Strategies and the Emergence of a New Scale of Regulation: the Anglo-French Border', *Regional Studies*, Vol. 29, No. 3, pp. 297–316

Church A. and Reid P. (1996) 'Urban Power, International Networks and Competition: the Example of Cross-border Co-operation', *Urban Studies*, Vol. 33, No. 8, pp. 1297–1318

Church A. and Reid P. (1999) 'Cross-border Co-operation, Institutionalization and Political Space across the English Channel', *Regional Studies*, Vol. 33, No. 7, pp. 643–56

Cielecka A. and Gibson J. (1995) 'Local Government in Poland', in Coulson A. (ed.), *Local Government in Eastern Europe*. Aldershot: Edward Elgar

City of Speyer (1993) *Europäische Mittelstädte 2000 – European Medium Sized Towns 2000 – Villes Moyennes Européennes 2000*. Speyer: Stadtverwaltung

Clark T.N. (1974) 'Can You Cut a Budget Pie?', *Policy and Politics*, Vol. 3, pp. 3–32

Clark T.N. (ed.) (1976) *Citizen Preferences and Urban Public Policy: Models Measures, Uses*. Special issue of *Policy and Politics*, Vol. 4 (Also published as Vol. 34 in Sage Contemporary Social Science Issues Series, Sage Publications, Beverly Hills, Calif., 1976)

Clark T.N. (ed.) (1990) *Monitoring Local Governments: How Personal Computers Can Help Systematise Municipal Fiscal Analysis*. Dubuque, Iowa: Kendall/Hunt Publishing Co.

Clark T.N. (1993) 'Local Democracy and Innovation in Eastern Europe', *Government and Policy*, Vol. 11, pp. 171–98

Clark T.N. (1994a) *The International Mayor II*. Fiscal Austerity and Urban Innovation Project. The University of Chicago, Chicago

Clark T.N. (1994b) *The International Mayor II. Version 2.0*. Cross-national results from sample surveys of mayors conducted as part of the Fiscal Austerity and Urban Innovation Project

Clark T.N. (ed.) (1994c) *Urban Innovation. Creative Strategies for Turbulent Times*. London: Sage

Clark T.N. (1995) 'Les stratégies de l'innovation dan les collectivités territoriales: leçons internationales', *Politiques et Management Public*, Vol. 13, No. 3, pp. 29–64

Clark T.N. (ed.) (1998) *The International Mayor: Cross-National Results from Sample Surveys of Mayors Conducted as Part of the Fiscal Austerity and Urban Innovation Project*, Version 3

Clark T.N. (ed.) (1999) 'Trees and Real Violins: Building Post-Industrial Chicago'. Book draft manuscript

Clark T.N., Curtis K.L., Fox K. and Herhold S.H. (1986) *Business and Taxes in Chicago*. A Report to the City of Chicago, White Paper for Discussion, 130 pp. April

Clark T.N. and Ferguson L.C. (1983) *City Money: Political Processes, Fiscal Strain, and Retrenchment*. New York: Columbia University Press

Clark T.N. and Hoffmann-Martinot V. (eds) (1998) *The New Political Culture*. Boulder: Westview

Clark T.N. and Lipset S.M. (1991) 'Are Social Classes Dying?', *International Sociology*, Vol. 4, pp. 397–410

Clark T.N. and Lipset S.M. (2001) *The Breakdown of Class Politics: a Debate on Post-Industrial Stratification*. Baltimore: Johns Hopkins University Press

Clark T.N., Lipset S.M. and Rempel M. (1993) 'The Declining Political Significance of Social Class', *International Sociology*, Vol. 8, No. 3, September, pp. 293–316

Clark T.N. and Rempel M. (eds) (1997) *Citizen Politics in Post-Industrial Societies*. Boulder: Westview Press

Clarke M. and Stewart J. (1998) *Community Governance, Community Leadership and the New Local Government*. York: Joseph Rowntree Foundation

Clarke S.E. (ed.) (1989) *Urban Innovation and Autonomy: Political Implications of Policy Change*. Newbury Park: Sage Publications

Clarke S.E. (1998) 'Economic Development Roles in American Cities: a Contextual Analysis of Shifting Partnership Arrangements', in Walzer N. (ed.), *Public Private Partnerships in Local Economic Development*. New York: Greenwood Publications

Clarke S.E. and Gaile G.L. (1992) 'The Next Wave: Local Economic Development Strategies in the Post-Federal Era', *Economic Development Quarterly*, Vol. 6, pp. 189–98

Clarke S.E. and Gaile G.L. (1997) 'Local Politics in a Global Era: Thinking Locally, Acting Globally', *Annals: American Academy of Political and Social Sciences*, Vol. 551, March, pp. 27–42

Clarke S.E. and Gaile G.L. (1998) *The Work of Cities*. Minneapolis: University of Minneapolis Press

Clarke S.E., Staeheli L. and Brunell L. (1995) 'Women Redefining Local Politics', in Judge D. et al. (eds), *Theories of Urban Politics*. London: Sage

Coakley J. (1993) 'Introduction: the Territorial Management of Ethnic Conflict', in Coakley J. (ed.), *The Territorial Management of Ethnic Conflict*. London: Frank Cass

Cochrane A. (1986) 'Community Politics and Democracy', in D. Held and C. Pollitt (eds), *New Forms of Democracy*. London: Sage

Cochrane A. (1988) 'In and against the Market?', *Policy and Politics*, Vol. 16, No. 3, pp. 159–68

Cochrane A. (1993) *Whatever Happened to Local Government?* Buckingham, UK: Open University Press

Cockburn C. (1977) *The Local State*. London: Pluto

Collinge C. (1999) 'Self-organisation of Society by Scale: a Spatial Reworking of Regulation Theory', in *Environment and Planning D, Society and Space*, Vol. 17, No. 5, pp. 557–74

Collinge C. and Hall S. (1997) 'Hegemony and Regime in Urban Governance: towards a Theory of the Locally Networked State', in Jewson N. and McGregor S. (eds), *Transforming Cities*. London: Routledge

Commission Européenne (1995) *Vers une tarification équitable et efficace dans les transports*. Brussels

Commission Européenne (1996a) *Un réseau pour les citoyens. Comment tirer parti du potentiel des transports publics de passagers en Europe?* Brussels: Livre vert

Commission Européenne (1996b) *Villes durables en Europe. Rapport du groupe sur l'environnement urbain*. Brussels

Commission Européenne (1997) *L'Europe des villes. Actions communautaires dans les zones urbaines*. Brussels

Conférence Européenne des Ministres des Transports (1995) *Transports urbains et développement durable*. OECD

Cooke P. and Morgan K. (1993) 'The Network Paradigm: New Departures in Corporate and Regional Development', *Environment and Planning D: Society and Space*, Vol. 11, pp. 543–64

Cooke P. and Morgan K. (1998) *The Associated Economy: Firms, Regions, and Innovation*. Oxford: Oxford University Press

Coulson A. (ed.) (1995) *Local Government in Eastern Europe*. Aldershot: Edward Elgar

Cox K. (ed.) (1997) *Spaces of Globalisation. Reasserting the Power of the Local*. New York: Guilford Press

Coyle C. (ed.) (1994) *Local Administration in the Policy Process – an International Perspective. Research in Urban Policy*, Vol. 5. Greenwich, Conn. and London, England: JAI Press

Crevoisier O. (1996) 'The Innovation Milieu Approach: Integrating Territorial Dynamics in Innovation Theories', paper to the Nordic Innovation Network Conference, Oslo, 27–28 October 1995, updated December 1996

Dangschat J.S. and Ossenbrugge J. (1990) 'Hamburg: Crisis Management, Urban Regeneration and Social Democrats', in D. Judd and M. Parkinson (eds), *Political Leadership and Urban Regeneration*. London: Sage

Darden J., Hall R.C., Thomas J. and Thomas R. (1987) *Detroit: Race and Uneven Development*. Philadelphia: Temple University Press

Davidoff P. (1965) 'Advocacy and Pluralism in Planning', *Journal of the American Institute of Planners*, Vol. 31, pp. 596–615

De Boer N. (1999) 'De tien geboden van de wijkaanpak', *Tijdschrift voor de Sociale Sector*, June

De Coninck E. and Westerberg M. (1991) *Marktonderzoek Wijkbureau De Stede*. The Hague: Gemeentepolitie van 's-Gravenhage; Dienst Beleidszaken en Onderzoek

Delaney D. and Leitner H. (1997) 'The Political Construction of Scale', *Political Geography*, Vol. 16, pp. 93–7

DeLeon R.E. (1992) *Left Coast City: Progressive Politics in San Francisco*. Lawrence: University Press of Kansas

Di Gaetano A. and Klemanski J.S. (1999) *Power and City Governance. Comparative Perspectives on Urban Development*. Minneapolis: University of Minnesota Press

Donges J.B. (1991) *Deregulating the German Economy*. San Francisco: International Center for Economic Growth

226 *Bibliography*

Douglas J.N. and Boal F.W. (1982) 'The Northern Ireland Problem', in Boal F.W.
and Douglas J.N. (eds), *Integration and Division: Geographical Perspectives on the
Northern Ireland Problem.* London: Academic Press, pp. 1–18
Dubois-Taine G. and Chalas Y. (1997) (eds) *La ville émergente.* La Tour d'Aigues:
Éditions de l'Aube
Duncan S.S., Dickens P., Goodwin M. and Gray F. (1985) *Uses and Abuses of
Comparative Analysis.* International Sociological Association (ISA) Conference,
Sussex
Dunleavy P. and Hood C. (1994) 'From Old Public Administration to New
Public Management', *Public Money and Management*, Vol. 14, pp. 9–16
Duyvendak J.W. (1998) 'De gemengde wijk. Integratie door differentiatie',
Tijdschrift voor de Sociale Sector, March/April
Eichwede W. (1994) 'Widersprüche in der Rekonstruktion von Bürgerge-
sellschaften in Osteuropa', in Eichwede W. and Mandt H. (eds), *Die Zukunft
der Bürgergesellschaften in Europa.* Baden-Baden: Nomos Verlagsgesellschaft
Einhorn B. (1991) 'Where Have They All Gone? Women and the Women's
Movement in East Central Europe', *Feminist Review*, Vol. 39, pp. 16–36
Eisen A. (1996) 'Institutionenbildung und Institutioneller Wandel im Trans-
formationsprozess', in Eisen A. and Wollman H. (eds), *Institutionenbild-
ung in Ostdeutschland.* Opladen: Leske and Budrich
Eisinger P.K. (1988) *The Rise of the Entrepreneurial State: State and Local Economic
Development Policy in the United States.* Madison: The University of Wisconsin
Press
Eisinger P. (1998) 'City Politics in an Era of Federal Devolution', *Urban Affairs
Review*, Vol. 33, January, pp. 308–25
Elkin S. (1987) *City and Regime in the American Republic.* Chicago: University of
Chicago Press
Elkins D.R. (1995) 'The Structure and Context of the Urban Growth Coalition:
the View from the Chamber of Commerce', *Policy Studies Journal*, Vol. 23,
pp. 583–600
Ernst and Young (2000) *Final Report Cross Border Vision and Strategy –
Kent, Nord–Pas de Calais and West-Vlaanderen.* Report prepared for
Kent County Council by Ernst and Young Centre for Strategy and
Evaluation Services. Available from European Affairs, Kent County Council,
Maidstone
Esman M.J. (1973) 'The Management of Communal Conflict', *Public Policy*,
Vol. 21, No. 1, pp. 49–78
Esman M.J. (1985) 'Two Dimensions of Ethnic Politics: Defence of Homeland
and Immigrant Rights', *Ethnic and Racial Studies*, Vol. 8, pp. 438–41
Etzioni A. (1994) *The Spirit of Community. The Reinvention of American Society.*
New York: Touchstone
Euchner C.C. (1999) 'Tourism and Sports: the Serious Competition for Play', in
Judd D. and Fainstein S. (eds), *The Tourist City.* New Haven, Conn.: Yale
University Press
European Foundation for the Improvement of Living and Working Conditions
(1997) *Utopias and Realities of Sustainable Urban Development.* Dublin
Fabian K. and Straussman J.D. (1994) 'Post-communist Transition of Local
Government in Hungary: Managing Emergency Local Aid', *Public
Administration and Development*, Vol. 14, No. 3, pp. 271–80

Feagin J.R. (1988) 'Tallying the Social Costs of Urban Growth under Capitalism: the Case of Houston', in S. Cummings (ed.), *Business Elites and Urban Development: Case Studies and Critical Perspectives*. Albany: State University of New York Press

Ferge Z. (1996) 'Social Citizenship in the New Democracies: the Difficulties in Reviving Citizens' Rights in Hungary', *International Journal of Urban and Regional Research*, Vol. 20, No. 1, pp. 99–115

Ferman B. (1996) *Challenging the Growth Machine*. Lawrence: University Press of Kansas

Fisher P.S. and Peters A.H. (1998) *Industrial Incentives: Competition among American States and Cities*. Kalamazoo, Mich.: W.E. Upjohn Institute

Fishman R. (1990) 'Megalopolis Unbound', *Wilson Quarterly*, Winter, 25–48

Fitzmaurice J. (1996) *The Politics of Belgium: a Unique Federalism*. London: Hurst and Company

Forester J. (1989) *Planning in the Face of Power*. Berkeley: University of California Press

Forgie V., Cheyne C. and McDermott P. (1999) *Democracy in New Zealand Local Government: Purpose and Practice*. Occasional Paper 2. School of Resource and Environmental Planning. Palmerston North: Massey University

Forse M. and Langlois S. (eds) (1995) *Tendances comparées des sociétés post-industrielles*. Paris: PUF

Friedman S. (1991) 'An Unlikely Utopia: State and Civil Society in South Africa', *Politikon: South African Journal of Political Studies*, Vol. 19, No. 1, pp. 5–19

Frisken F. (ed.) (1994) *The Changing Canadian Metropolis: a Public Policy Perspective*. Berkeley: Institute of Governmental Studies Press and Toronto: Canadian Urban Institute

Frohlich N. and Oppenheimer J.A. (1997) 'Ethical Problems When Moving to Markets: Gaining Efficiency While Keeping an Eye on Distributive Justice', in Ullmann A.A. and Lewis A. (eds), *Privatization and Entrepreneurship*. New York: Haworth Press

Frydman R. and Rapaczynski A. (1994) *Privatization in Eastern Europe: Is the State Withering Away?* London: Central European University Press

Gabor P. (ed.) (1991) *Events and Changes: the First Steps of Local Transition in East-Central Europe*. Budapest: Local Democracy and Innovation Project

Gaffkin F. and Warf B. (1993) 'Urban Policy and the Post-Keynesian State in the United Kingdom and the United States', *International Journal of Urban and Regional Research*, Vol. 17, No. 1, pp. 67–84

Gallup J. and Sachs J. (1998) 'Geography and Economic Growth'. Paper delivered at the 1998 Annual World Bank Conference on Development Economics. http://www.worldbank.org/html/rad/abcde/html/sachs.htm.

Garber J. and Imbroscio D. (1996) 'The Myth of the North American City', *Urban Affairs Review*, Vol. 31, pp. 595–624

Garreau J. (1991) *Edge City: Life on the New Frontier*. New York: Doubleday

Garza G. (1999) 'Global Economy, Metropolitan Dynamics and Urban Polices in Mexico', *Cities*, Vol. 16, pp. 149–70

Gemeente Den Haag (1994) *Voortgangsrapportage Pilot-project Bouwlust/Vrederust*. January

Gemeente Den Haag (1998) *Omnibus-enquete Den Haag* 1998. The Hague: Centrum voor Onderzoek en Statistiek (COS)

Gemeente Den Haag (1999) *De kracht van den Haag: een stad die actief investeert in mensen, hun werk, wonen, cultuur en welzijn. (Haags plan grote stedenbeleid, periode 2000–2003/4)* October

Gibbs J. (1989) 'Conceptualization of Terrorism', *American Sociological Review*, Vol. 54, pp. 329–40

Giddens A. (1990) *The Consequences of Modernity*. Oxford: Polity Press

Giddens A. (1998) *The Third Way. The Renewal of Social Democracy*. Cambridge: Polity Press

Gittell M., Newman K., Bockmeyer J. and Lindsay R. (1998) 'Expanding Civic Opportunity: Urban Empowerment Zones', *Urban Affairs Review*, Vol. 33, pp. 530–58

Godard F. (ed.) (1997) *Le gouvernement des villes*. Éditions Descartes et Cie

Goetz E. (1990) 'Type II Policy and Mandated Benefits in Economic Development', *Urban Affairs Quarterly*, Vol. 26, pp. 170–90

Goetz E. (1993) *Shelter Burden*. Philadelphia: Temple University Press

Goetz E. (1994) 'Expanding Possibilities in Local Development Policy: an Examination of US Cities', *Political Research Quarterly*, Vol. 47, pp. 85–109

Goetz E.G. and Clarke S.E. (eds) (1993) *The New Localism: Comparative Urban Politics in a Global Era*. Newbury Park: Sage

Goldberg M.A. and Mercer J. (1986) *The Myth of the North American City: Continentalism Challenged*. Vancouver: University of British Columbia Press

Goldsmith M. (1993) 'The Europeanisation of Local Government', *Urban Studies*, Vol. 30, Nos 4/5, pp. 683–99

Goldsmith M.J.F. and Klausen K.K. (eds) (1997) *European Integration and Local Government*. Cheltenham: Edward Elgar

Goldsmith S. (1997) *The Twenty-first Century City. Resurrecting Urban America*. Washington: Regnery Publishing Inc.

Goozner M. (1998) 'The Porter Prescription', *The American Prospect*, Vol. 38, May–June, pp. 56–64

Gorzelak G. (1992) 'Dilemmas of Regional Policies during Transition', in Gorzelak G. and Kulinski A. (eds), *Dilemmas of Regional Policy in Eastern and Central Europe*. Warsaw: European Institute for Regional and Local Development

Gorzelak G. and Szul R. (1989) 'Spatial Order and Polish Disorder: Problems in the Polish Space Economy', *Geoforum*, Vol. 20, No. 2, pp. 175–85

Goss S. (ed.) (1999) *Managing Working with the Public*. London: Kogan Page

Graham S. (1997) 'Telecommunications and the Future of Cities: Debunking the Myths', *Cities*, Vol. 4, pp. 21–9

Graham S. and Marvin S. (1996) *Telecommunications and the City; Electronic Spaces, Urban Places*. London: Routledge

Granovetter M. (1985) 'Economic Action and Social Structure: the Problem of Embeddedness', *American Journal of Sociology*, Vol. 91, pp. 481–510

Graute U. (ed.) (1998) *Sustainable Development for Central and Eastern Europe*. Berlin: Springer-Verlag

Greer A. and Hoggett P. (1999) 'Public Policies, Private Strategies and Local Public Spending Bodies', *Public Administration*, Vol. 77, No. 2, pp. 235–56

Gurr T.R. (1993) 'Why Minorities Rebel: a Global Analysis of Communal Mobilization and Conflict since 1945', *International Political Science Review*, Vol. 14, No. 1, pp. 161–201

Gurr T.R. and Harff B. (1994) *Ethnic Conflict in World Politics*. Boulder: Westview

Gurr T.R. and Lichbach M. (1986) 'Forecasting Internal Conflict', *Comparative Political Studies*, Vol. 9, pp. 3–38

Hall P. (1988) *Cities of Tomorrow*. Oxford: Blackwell

Hall S., Mawson J. and Nicholson B. (1995) 'City Pride: the Birmingham Experience', *Local Economy*, Vol. 10, No. 2, pp. 108–16

Hambleton R. (1978) *Policy Planning and Local Government*. London: Hutchinson

Hambleton R. (1995) 'Cross-national Urban Policy Transfer – Insights from the USA', in Hambleton R. and Thomas H. (eds), *Urban Policy Evaluation*. London: Paul Chapman

Hambleton R. (1999) *Modernisation: Developing Managerial Leadership*. Merseyside: SOLACE

Hambleton R. (2000) 'Modernising Political Management in Local Government', *Urban Studies*, Vol. 37, Nos 5–6, pp. 931–50

Hambleton R., Hoggett P. and Razzaque K. (1996) *Freedom within Boundaries. Developing Effective Approaches to Decentralisation*. London: Local Government Management Board

Hambleton R. and Holder A. (1995) *Shaping Future Authorities. Achieving Successful Organisational Change*. Luton: Local Government Management Board

Hankiss E. (1990) *East European Alternatives*. Oxford: Clarendon Press

Hansen S. (1989) 'Industrial Policy and Corporatism in the American States', *Governance*, Vol. 2, pp. 172–97

Hanson R. (1993) 'Bidding for Business: a Second War between the States?', *Economic Development Quarterly*, Vol. 5, pp. 213–28

Harding A. (1994) 'Urban Regimes and Growth Machines: towards a Cross-national Research Agenda', *Urban Affairs Quarterly*, Vol. 29, No. 3, pp. 356–82

Harding A. (1995) 'Elite Theory and Growth Machines', in Judge D., Stoker G. and Wolman H. (eds), *Theories of Urban Politics*. London: Sage

Harding A., Wilks-Heeg S. and Hutchins M. (2000) 'Business, Government and the Business of Urban Governance', *Urban Studies*, Vol. 37, Nos 5–6, pp. 975–94

Harloe M., Pickvance C. and Urry J. (eds) (1990) *Place, Policy and Politics. Do Localities Matter?* London: Unwin Hyman

Harrington M. (1989) 'Toward a New Socialism', *Dissent*, Spring, pp. 3–13

Harvey D. (1985) *The Urbanisation of Capital*. Oxford: Blackwell

Harvey D. (1996) *Justice, Nature and the Geography of Difference*. Oxford: Blackwell

Haughton G. and While A. (1999) 'From Corporate City to Citizen's City?', *Urban Affairs Review*, Vol. 35, No. 1, pp. 3–23

Hawley A.H. (1951) 'Metropolitan Population and Municipal Government Expenditures', *Journal of Social Issues*, Vol. 7, pp. 100–8

Hawley A.H. and Zimmer B.G. (1970) *The Metropolitan Community*. Beverly Hills and London: Sage

Healey P. (1998) 'The Place of "Europe" in Contemporary Spatial Strategy Making', *European Urban and Regional Studies*, Vol. 5, No. 2, pp. 139–53

Hebbert M. (2000) 'Transpennine: Imaginative Geographies of an Interregional Corridor', *Transactions of the Institute of British Geographers*, Vol. 25, No. 3, pp. 379–92

Heilemann U. and Reinicke W.H. (1995) *Welcome to Hard Times*. Washington, DC: Brookings Institution and Johns Hopkins University

Heinelt H. (1998) 'Recent Debates on the Modernisation of Local Politics and Administration. An Attempt at a Systematic Overview'. Paper to the Third European Conference on Public Administration Modernisation, May, University of Lille

Held D. (1991) 'Democracy, the Nation-State and the Global System', *Economy and Society*, Vol. 20, pp. 138–72

Held D. and Pollitt C. (eds) (1986) *New Forms of Democracy*. London: Sage

Hiernaux-Nicholas D. (1999) 'Cancun Bliss', in Judd D. and Fainstein S. (eds), *The Tourist City*. New Haven, Conn.: Yale University Press

Hill D. (1994) *Citizens and Cities; Urban Policy in the 1990s*. New York/London: Harvester

Hill P.E. (1996) *Dallas. The Making of a Modern City*. Austin: University of Texas

Hirschman A.O. (1970) *Exit, Voice and Loyalty*. Cambridge, Mass.: Harvard University Press

Hirst P. and Thompson G. (1996) *Globalization in Question: the International Economy and the Possibilities of Governance*. Cambridge: Polity Press

Hobbs H.H. (1994) *City Hall Goes Abroad: the Foreign Policy of Local Politics*. Thousand Oaks, Calif.: Sage

Hoffman B. (1992) 'Current Research on Terrorism and Low-Intensity Conflict', *Studies in Conflict and Terrorism*, Vol. 15, pp. 25–37

Hoffman L. (1994) 'After the Fall: Crisis and Renewal in Urban Planning in the Czech Republic', *International Journal of Urban and Regional Research*, Vol. 18, No. 4, pp. 691–702

Hoggett P. (1991) 'A New Management in the Public Sector?', *Policy and Politics*, Vol. 19, No. 4, pp. 243–56

Hoggett P. (1997) *Contested Communities. Experiences, Struggles, Policies*. Bristol: The Policy Press

Hoggett P. and Hambleton R. (eds) (1987) *Decentralisation and Democracy. Localising Public Services*. Bristol: University of Bristol

Hood C. (1991) 'A Public Management for All Seasons', *Public Administration*, Vol. 69, pp. 3–19

Horan C. (1991) 'Beyond Governing Coalitions: Analyzing Urban Regimes in the 1990s', *Journal of Urban Affairs*, Vol. 13, pp. 119–35

Horowitz D.L. (1985) *Ethnic Groups in Conflict*. Berkeley: University of California Press. http://www.worldbank.org/abcde/stiglitz.pdf.

Human Rights Watch (1993) *World Report*

Humes S. (1991) *Local Governance and National Power*. Hemel Hempstead: Harvester Wheatsheaf

Hunter F. (1953) *Community Power Structure*. New York: Doubleday

Hutton W. and Giddens A. (2000) *On the Edge. Living with Global Capitalism*. London: Jonathan Cape

Ickes B.W. (1990) 'Obstacles to Economic Reform of Socialism: an Institutional-Choice Approach', *Annals of the American Academy of Political and Social Science*, Vol. 507, January, pp. 53–64

Imbroscio D.L. (1993) 'Overcoming the Economic Dependence of Urban America: a Review of Strategies', *Journal of Urban Affairs*, Vol. 15, pp. 173–90

Business Organisations

Bibliography 231

Imrie R., Thomas H. and Marshall T. (1995) 'Business Organisations, Local Dependence and the Politics of Urban Renewal in Britain', *Urban Studies*, Vol. 32, No. 1, pp. 31–47

INCORE (Initiative on Conflict Resolution and Ethnicity) (1995) *Programme Information*. University of Ulster at Coleraine (Northern Ireland) and The United Nations University

Inglehart R. (1990) *Culture Shift in Advanced Industrial Society*. Princeton, NJ: Princeton University Press

International Institute for Environment and Development (1976) *Human Settlements National Reports: Summaries and Reference Guide*. Prepared for Habitat: United Nations Conference on Human Settlements. Pergamon Press, Inc.

International Labour Office (1977) *Meeting Basic Needs: Strategies for Eradicating Mass Poverty and Unemployment*. Geneva: ILO

Jacobs J. (1961) *The Death and Life of Great American Cities*. New York: Vintage Books

Jacquier C. (1991) *Voyage dans dix quartiers Européens en crise*. Paris: l'Harmattan

Jeanrenaud C. and Clark T.N. (1989) 'Why Are (Most) Swiss Leaders Invisible? The Swiss Communal Ethic', in Baldersheim H. et al. (eds), *New Leaders, Parties and Groups: Comparative Tendencies in Local Leadership*. Paris and Bordeaux: CERVEL, pp. 113–32

Jessop B. (1993) 'Towards a Schumpeterian Workfare State? Preliminary Remarks on Post-Fordist Political Economy', *Studies in Political Economy*, Vol. 40, pp. 7–39

Jessop B. (1994) 'The Transition to Post-Fordism and the Schumpeterian Workfare State', in Burrows R. and Loader B. (eds), *Towards a Post-Fordist Welfare State*. London: Routledge

Jessop B. (1997) 'The Entrepreneurial City', in Jewson N. and MacGregor S. (eds), *Transforming Cities: Contested Governance and New Spatial Divisions*. London and New York: Routledge

John P. (1998) 'Urban Economic Policy Networks in Britain and France', *Environment and Planning C: Government and Policy*, Vol. 16, pp. 307–22

John P. (2000) 'The Europeanisation of Sub-national Governance', *Urban Studies*, Vol. 37, Nos 5–6, pp. 877–94

John P. (2001) *Local Governance in Europe*. London: Sage

John P. and Cole A. (1998) 'Urban Regimes and Local Governance in Britain and France', *Urban Affairs Review*, Vol. 33, pp. 382–404

Jones B. and Bachelor L. (1986) *The Sustaining Hand*. Lawrence: University of Kansas Press

Jouve B. and Lefèvre C. (eds) (2002) *Local Power, Territory and Institutions in European Metropolitan Regions*. London: Frank Cass

Judd D. (2000) 'Strong Leadership', *Urban Studies*, Vol. 37, Nos 5–6, pp. 951–61

Judd D. and Fainstein S. (1999) *The Tourist City*. New Haven, Conn.: Yale University Press

Judd D. and Parkinson M. (1990) *Leadership and Urban Regeneration*. London: Sage Publications

Judge D., Stoker G. and Wolman H. (eds) (1995) *Theories of Urban Politics*. Thousand Oaks, Calif.: Sage

Kamenitsa L. (1997) 'East German Feminists in the New German Democracy: Opportunities, Obstacles, and Adaptations', *Women and Politics*, Vol. 17, No. 3, pp. 41–67

Kaminski B. (1991) *The Collapse of State Socialism. The Case of Poland*. Princeton, NJ: Princeton University Press

Kantor P. and Savitch H.V. (1993) 'Can Politicians Bargain with Business? A Theoretical and Comparative Perspective on Urban Development', *Urban Affairs Quarterly*, Vol. 29, No. 2, pp. 230–55

Kaplan R.D. (1998) *An Empire Wilderness*. New York: Random House

Kasarda J.D. (1976) 'The Changing Occupational Structure of the American Metropolis', *Social Science Quarterly*, Vol. 61, December, pp. 369–400

Kasarda J.D. (1985) 'Urban Change and Minority Opportunities', in Peterson P.E. (ed.), *The New Urban Reality*. Washington, DC: Brookings, pp. 33–68

Katz B.J. (ed.) (1999) *Reflections on Regionalism*. Washington, DC: Brookings Institution Press

Katz J.L. (1996) 'After 60 Years, Most Control is Passing to States', *Congressional Quarterly*, 3 August, pp. 2190–6

Kearns A. and Paddison R. (2000) 'New Challenges for Urban Governance', *Urban Studies*, Vol. 37, Nos 5–6, pp. 845–50

Keating D. and Krumholz N. (1999) *Rebuilding Urban Neighbourhoods*. Thousand Oaks: Sage

Keating M. (1991) *Comparative Urban Politics*. Aldershot: Edward Elgar

Kemme D.M. (1991) *Economic Transition in Eastern Europe and the Soviet Union: Issues and Strategies*. New York: Institute for East–West Security Studies

Kent County Council (KCC) (2000) *European Strategy for Kent 2000–2006*. Maidstone: Kent County Council

Kiel L.D. (1993) 'Nonlinear Dynamical Analysis: Assessing Systems Concepts in a Governmental Agency', *Public Administration Review*, Vol. 53, No. 2, pp. 143–53

Kiernan M.J. (1983) 'Ideology, Politics, and Planning: Reflections on Theory and Practice of Urban Planning', *Environment and Planning B: Planning and Design*, Vol. 10, pp. 71–87

Kincaid J. (1984) 'The American Governors in International Affairs', *Publius: the Journal of Federalism*, Vol. 14, pp. 95–114

King D. (1990) 'Economic Activity and the Challenge to Local Government', in King D. and Pierre J. (eds), *Challenges to Local Government*. London: Sage

Klausen K.K. and Magnier A. (1998) *The Anonymous Leader. Appointed Chief Executive Officers in Western Local Government*. Odense: Odense University Press

Kleinman M. (1999) 'The Business Sector and the Governance of London'. Paper to the European Urban Research Association Conference, Paris, May

Kline J.M. (1984) 'The Expanding International Agenda for State Governments', *State Government*, Vol. 57, No. 1, p. 2

Kloosterman R.C. (1995) 'De cirkel leefomgeving', in *Interimverslag Sociale Vernieuwing in Bouwlust en Vrederust*. Utrecht: AWSB/ISOR

Kloosterman R.C. and van der Leun J.P. (1999) 'Just for Starters: Commercial Gentrification by Immigrant Entrepreneurs in Amsterdam and Rotterdam Neighbourhoods', *Housing Studies*, Vol. 14, No. 5, pp. 659–76

Knight R. and Gappert G. (eds) (1989) *Cities in a Global Society*. Newbury Park, Calif.: Sage Publications

Knox P. and Taylor P. (eds) (1995) *World Cities in a World System*. Cambridge: Cambridge University Press

König K. (1993) 'Transformation of Public Administration in Middle and Eastern Europe: the German Case'. Paper presented at the ASPA/CASU 54th National Training Conference, San Francisco, Calif.

Kooiman J. (1993) 'Social–political Governance: Introduction', in J. Kooiman (ed.), *Modern Governance*. London: Sage

Kovacic W. and Thorpe R. (1996) 'Antitrust and the Evolution of a Market Economy in Mongolia', in Slay B. (ed.), *De-monopolization and Competition Policy in Post-Communist Economies*. Boulder, Colo.: Westview

Kresl P.K. and Gappert G. (1995) *North American Cities and the Global Economy: Challenges and Opportunities*. Newbury Park, Calif.: Sage

Kretzmann J.P. and McKnight J.L. (1993) *Building Communities from the Inside Out: a Path toward Finding and Mobilizing a Community's Assets*. Chicago: ACTA Publications

Kruize P. and Kroes A. (1992) *Buurttypering en buurtproblemen werkeenheid Beresteinlaan: Resultaten van het bevolkingsonderzoek onder de wijkbewoners*. The Hague: SWO

Kudrin A. (1997) 'St. Petersburg's Progress towards the Market', *International Journal of Urban and Regional Research*, Vol. 21, No. 3, pp. 425–9

Ladanyi J. (1993) 'Patterns of Residential Segregation and the Gypsy Minority in Budapest', *International Journal of Urban and Regional Research*, Vol. 17, No. 1, pp. 30–41

Lake D. and Rothchild D. (1996) *Ethnic Fears and Global Engagement: the International Spread and Management of Ethnic Conflict*. Policy Paper No. 20. University of California, San Diego: Institute of Global Conflict and Co-operation

Lambooy J.G. and Moulaert F. (1996) 'The Economic Organization of Cities: an Institutional Perspective', *International Journal of Urban and Regional Research*, Vol. 20, No. 2, pp. 217–37

Larner A. (2000) 'Addressing Property Needs', *Public Finance*, 10–16 March, pp. 22–3

Lauria M. (ed.) (1997) *Reconstructing Urban Regime Theory*. Thousand Oaks: Sage

Leach S., Davis H., Game C. and Skelcher C. (1990) *After Abolition: the Operation of the Post-1986 Metropolitan Government System*. Birmingham: The University of Birmingham

Leach S. and Wilson D. (2000) *Local Political Leadership*. Bristol: The Policy Press

Lefèvre C. (1997) 'Metropolitan Government and Governance in Western Countries: a Critical Review', *International Journal of Urban and Regional Research*, Vol. 21, No. 4, pp. 9–25

Leimbrock H. (1997) 'Entwicklungs-, Planungs- und Partizipationsprozesse in ostdeutschen Mittelstädten', *Aus Politik und Zeitgeschichte*, Vol. 17, pp. 30–7

Lemon J.T. (1993) 'Social Planning and the Welfare-State', in Bourne L.S. and Ley D.F. (eds), *The Changing Social Geography of Canadian Cities*. Montreal and Kingston: McGill-Queen's University Press

Leo C. and Fenton R. (1990) 'Mediated Enforcement and the Evolution of the State: Development Corporations in Canadian City Centres', *International Journal of Urban and Regional Research*, Vol. 14, pp. 185–206

Leresche J.P., Joye D. and Bassand M. (1994) *Métropolisations. Interdépendances mondiales et implications lémaniques*. Geneva: Georg Éditeur, Institut Universitaire Kurt Bösch

Lever W.F. (1997) 'Delinking Urban Economies: the European Experience', *Journal of Urban Affairs*, Vol. 19, No. 2, pp. 227–38

Levine M.V. (1990) *The Reconquest of Montreal: Language Policy and Social Change in a Bilingual City*. Philadelphia: Temple University Press

Levine M.V. (1995) 'Globalisation and Wage Polarisation in US and Canadian Cities', in Kresl P.K. and Gappert G. (eds), *North American Cities and the Global Economy: Challenges and Opportunities*. Newbury Park, Calif.: Sage

Ley D.F. and Bourne L.S. (1993) 'Introduction: the Social Context and Diversity of Urban Canada', in Bourne L.S. and Ley D.F. (eds), *The Changing Social Geography of Canadian Cities*. Montreal and Kingston: McGill-Queen's University Press

Lijphart A. (1968) *The Politics of Accommodation: Pluralism and Democracy in the Netherlands*. Berkeley: Univ. of California Press

Lijphart A. (1977) *Democracy in Plural Societies: a Comparative Exploration*. New Haven: Yale University Press

Lipset S.M. and Raab E. (1978) 'The Message of Proposition 13', *Commentary*, Vol. 66, pp. 42–6

Logan J. R. and Molotch H. L. (1987) *Urban Fortunes. The Political Economy of Space*. Berkeley: University of California Press

Logan J.R., Whaley R.B. and Crowder K. (1997) 'The Character and Consequences of the Growth Regimes: an Assessment of 20 Years of Research', *Urban Affairs Review*, Vol. 32, May, pp. 603–30

Lowndes V., Stoker G., Pratchett L., Wilson D., Leach S. and Wingfield M. (1997) *Enhancing Public Participation in Local Government*. London: Department of the Environment, Transport and Regions

Lustick I. (1979) 'Stability in Deeply Divided Societies: Consociationalisation vs. Control', *World Politics*, Vol. 31, pp. 325–44

McAdam D., McCarthy J.D. and Zald M.N. (1996) 'Opportunities, Mobilizing Structures, and Framing Processes – toward a Synthetic, Comparative Perspective on Social Movements', in McAdam D., McCarthy J.D. and Zald Mn.N. (eds), *Comparative Perspectives on Social Movements*. Cambridge: Cambridge University Press

McMurrer D.P., Sawhill I.V. and Lerman R.I. (1997) *Welfare Reform and Opportunity in the Low Wage Labor Market*. Washington, DC: The Urban Institute

Mander J. and Goldsmith E. (eds) (1996) *The Case against the Global Economy*. San Francisco: Sierra Club Books

Markusen A., Yong-Sook L. and DiGiovanna S. (eds) (1999) *Second Tier Cities Rapid Growth Outside the Metropole in Brazil, South Korea, Japan, and the United States*. Minneapolis: University of Minnesota Press

Martens A. and Vervaeke M. (eds) (1997) *La polarisation sociale des villes européennes*. Paris: Éditions Anthropos

Martin S. and Pearce G. (1993) 'European Development Strategies: Strengthening Meso-Government in the UK?', *Regional Studies*, Vol. 27, No. 7, pp. 681–5

Massey D. and Denton N. (1993) *American Apartheid: Segregation and the Making of the Underclass*. Cambridge, Mass.: Harvard University Press

Mathesian C. (1998) 'The Stadium Trap', *Governing*, May, pp. 22–6

May N. et al. (eds) (1998) *La ville éclatée?* La Tour d'Aigues: Éditions de l'Aube

Means R. and Smith R. (1998) *Community Care. Policy and Practice*. London: Macmillan – now Palgrave

Meegan R. (1992) 'Liverpool – Sliding down the Urban Hierarchy: from Imperial Pre-eminence to Global and National Peripherality'. Paper presented at the conference 'A New Urban and Regional Hierarchy? Impacts of Modernization, Restructuring, and the End of Bipolarity', University of California, Los Angeles, 23–25 April

Meegan R. (1994) 'A "Europe of the Regions"? A View from Liverpool on the Atlantic Arc Periphery', *European Planning Studies*, Vol. 2, No. 1, pp. 59–80

Ministerie van Binnenlandse Zaken (1990) *Sociale vernieuwing; Opdracht en Handreiking*. The Hague: Ministerie van Binnenlandse Zaken

Miranda R. (1994) 'Contracting out: a Solution with Limits', in Clark T.N. (ed.), *Urban Innovation: Creative Strategies in Turbulent Times*. London: Sage

Miranda R. and Rosdil D. (1995) 'From Boosterism to Qualitative Growth', *Urban Affairs Review*, Vol. 30, pp. 868–79

Mollenkopf J.H. (1983) *The Contested City*. Princeton, NJ: Princeton University Press

Möller B. and Reissig R. (1996), 'Interaktionsbeziehungen lokaler Akteure im Politikfeld Wirtschaftsförderung', in Eisen A. and Wollmann H. (eds), *Institutionenbildung in Ostdeutschland*. Opladen: Leske and Budrich

Molotch H. (1976) 'The City as a Growth Machine', *American Journal of Sociology*, Vol. 82, pp. 483–99

Morgan B., Brooksbank D. and Connolly M. (2000) 'The Role of Networking in the New Political Economy of Regional Development', *European Planning Studies*, Vol. 8, No. 3, pp. 319–36

Mouritzen P.E. (ed.) (1992) *Managing Cities in Austerity: Urban Fiscal Stress in Ten Western Countries*. London: Sage Urban Innovation Series, Vol. 2

Mouritzen P.E. and Nielsen K.H. (1988) *Handbook of Comparative Urban Fiscal Data*. Odense: Danish Data Archives

Murdoch J. (1995) 'Actor-networks and the Evolution of Economic Forms: Combining Description and Explanation in Theories of Regulation, Flexible Specialization, and Networks', *Environment and Planning A*, Vol. 27, pp. 731–57

Murphy A.B. (1989) 'Territorial Policies in Multiethnic States', *Geographical Review*, Vol. 79, pp. 410–21

Murray R. (1991) *Local Space: Europe and the New Regionalism*. Manchester: Centre for Local Economic Strategies (CLES)

Mushkin S.J. (1979) *Proposition 13 and its Consequences for Public Management*. Cambridge, Mass.: Abt Books

Myant M. (1995) 'Transforming the Czech and Slovak Economies: Evidence at the District Level', *Regional Studies*, Vol. 29, No. 8, pp. 753–60

National League of Cities (NLC) (1997) *American Cities in the Global Economy*. Washington, DC: National League of Cities

Neenan W.B. (1972) *Political Economy of Urban Areas*. Chicago: Markham

Neithercut M. (1987) 'Detroit Twenty Years After: a Statistical Profile of the Detroit Area since 1967'. Unpublished research reports submitted to Center for Urban Studies, Wayne State University, Detroit

Newman D. and Paasi A. (1998) 'Fences and Neighbours in the Postmodern World: Boundary Narratives in Political Geography', *Progress in Human Geography*, Vol. 22, No. 2, pp. 186–207

Newman P. (1994) 'Urban Environmental Quality and Economic Competitiveness: an Australian Perspective'. Paper prepared for the conference on 'Cities in the New Global Economy' organised by the Government of Australia and the OECD, Melbourne, November

Noordanus P.G.A. (1999) 'Bouwen en de buurt. Over de ideologie van de stedelijke vernieuwing', *Socialisme & Democratie*, No. 10

Noponen H., Markusen A. and Driessen K. (1997) 'Trade and American Cities: Who has the Comparative Advantage?', *Economic Development Quarterly*, Vol. 11, pp. 67–87

Nordlinger E.A. (1972) *Conflict Regulation in Divided Societies*. Boston: Center for International Affairs, Harvard University

Norquist J.O. (1998) *The Wealth of Cities. Revitalising the Centres of American Life.* Reading, Mass.: Addison-Wesley

OECD (1992) *Urban Land Markets: Policies for the 1990s.* Paris: OECD Publication Service

OECD (1995) *Women in the City. Housing, Services and the Urban Environment.* Paris: OECD

OECD (Groupe des affaires urbaines) (1996) *Les politiques innovantes de développement urbain durable. La Cité écologique.* Paris

OECD (1998) *Integrating Distressed Urban Areas.* Paris: OECD

Oerlemans H. (1990) *Oude en Nieuwe Wijken; Een Terugblik op de Bouwexplosie van de Jaren Vijftig.* The Hague: Stichting Volkshuisvesting in de Kunst Bureau Aanpak Na-oorlogse Wijken

Ohmae K. (1990) *The Borderless World.* London: HarperCollins

O'Leary B. and McGarry J. (1995) 'Regulating Nations and Ethnic Communities', in Breton A., Galeotti G., Salmon P. and Wintrobe R. (eds), *Nationalism and Rationality.* Cambridge: Cambridge University Press

O'Regan F. and Conway M. (1993) *From the Bottom Up: Toward a Strategy for Income and Employment Generation among the Disadvantaged.* Washington, DC: The Aspen Institute

Osborne D. and Gaebler T. (1993) *Reinventing Government. How the Entrepreneurial Spirit is Transforming the Public Sector.* New York: Plume

Osborne D. and Plastrik P. (1997) *Banishing Bureaucracy.* Reading, Mass.: Addison-Wesley

Owen C.J. (1994) 'Local Government in Post-Communist Poland: a Study of Federalism and Executive Authority in Plock', *International Journal of Public Administration*, Vol. 17, No. 8, pp. 1437–58

Parkinson M. (1985) *Liverpool on the Brink.* Cambridge: Policy Journals

Parkinson M. (1992) 'City Links', *Town and Country Planning*, Vol. 61, No. 9, pp. 235–6

Parkinson M. and Russel H. (1994) 'Economic Attractiveness and Social Exclusion: the Case of Liverpool'. Paper prepared for the report *Europe 2000*, for the European Commission

Partrick N. (1994) 'Democracy under Limited Autonomy', *News from Within*, Vol. 10, No. 9, pp. 21–4. Jerusalem: Alternative Information Center

Peck J. (1995) 'Moving and Shaking : Business Elites, State Localism and Urban Privatism', *Progress in Human Geography*, Vol. 19, No. 1, pp. 16–46

Peck J. and Jones M. (1994) 'Training and Enterprise Councils: Schumpeterian Workfare State, or What?', *Environment and Planning A*, Vol. 27, pp. 1361–96

Peck J. and Tickell A. (1994a) 'Searching for a New Institutional Fix: the After-Fordist Crisis and the Global–Local Disorder', in Amin A. (ed.), *Post-Fordism: a Reader*. Oxford: Basil Blackwell

Peck J. and Tickell A. (1994b) 'Too Many Partners ... The Future for Regeneration Partnership', *Local Economy*, Vol. 9, pp. 251–65

Peirce N.R., Johnson V. and Hall J.S. (1993) *Citistates: How Urban America Can Prosper in a Competitive World*. Washington, DC: Seven Locks Press

Pensley D.S. (1995) 'City Planning and State Policy in the GDR: the Example of Neubaugebiet Hellersdorf', *International Journal of Urban and Regional Research*, Vol. 19, No. 4, pp. 549–75

Perkmann M. (1999) 'Building Governance Institutions across European Borders', *Regional Studies*, Vol. 33, No. 7, pp. 657–68

Peters B.G. (1996) *The Future of Governing: Four Emerging Models*. Lawrence: University of Kansas Press

Peters T. (1988) *Thriving on Chaos: Handbook for a Management Revolution*. New York: Alfred A. Knopf, Inc.

Peterson P.E. (1981) *City Limits*. Chicago: University of Chicago Press

Phillips A. (1994) *Local Democracy: the Terms of the Debate*. Research Report 2. Commission for Local Democracy. London: Municipal Journal

Pickvance C. and Preteceille E. (eds) (1991) *State Restructuring and Local Power: a Comparative Perspective*. London: Pinter

Pierre J. (ed.) (1998) *Partnerships in Urban Governance. European and American Experience*. London: Macmillan Press – now Palgrave

Pierre J. and Peters B.G. (2000) *Governance, Politics and the State*. London: Macmillan – now Palgrave

Piore M. and Sabel C. (1984) *The Second Industrial Divide*. New York: Basic Books

Polanyi K. (1944) *The Great Transformation*. New York: Holt, Rinehart

Pollitt C. (1990) *Managerialism in the Public Service*. Oxford: Blackwell

Pollitt C., Birchall J. and Putman K. (1998) *Decentralising Public Service Management*. London: Macmillan – now Palgrave

Porter M. (1995) 'The Competitive Advantage of the Inner City', *Harvard Business Review*, May–June, pp. 55–71

Porter M. (1997) 'New Strategies for Inner-city Economic Development', *Economic Development Quarterly*, Vol. 11, No. 1, pp. 11–27

Poznanski K. (1993) 'Restructuring of Property Rights in Poland: a Study in Evolutionary Economics', *East European Politics and Society*, Vol. 3, pp. 395–421

Priemus H., Kloosterman R.C., Lambregts B.W., Kruythoff H.M. and den Draak J. (1998) *De stedelijke investeringsopgave 1999–2010 gekwantificeerd. Naar economische vitaliteit, bereikbaarheid, sociale cohesie en duurzaamheid*. Stedelijke en regionale verkenningen, No.16, Delft: Delft University Press

Pröhl M. (ed.) (1997) *International Strategies and Techniques for Future Local Government. Practical Aspects towards Innovation and Reform*. Gütersloh: Bertelsmann Foundation Publishers

Prud'homme R. (1994) 'On the Economic Role of Cities'. Paper prepared for the conference on 'Cities in the New Global Economy' organised by the Government of Australia and the OECD, Melbourne, November
Prybyla J.S. (ed.) (1990) 'Privatizing and Marketizing Socialism', *Annals of the American Academy of Political and Social Science*, Vol. 507, pp. 9–141
Purdue D., Razzaque K., Hambleton R. and Stewart M. (2000) *Community Leadership in Area Regeneration*. Bristol: The Policy Press
Putnam R.D. (1993) *Making Democracy Work. Civic Traditions in Modern Italy*. Princeton, NJ: Princeton University Press
Putnam R.D. (2000) *Bowling Alone*. New York: Simon and Schuster
Raban J. (1974/1998) *Soft City*. London: The Harvill Press
Ranson S. and Stewart J. (1994) *Management for the Public Domain*. London: Macmillan – now Palgrave
Reese L.A. (1997) *Local Economic Development Policy: the United States and Canada*. New York: Garland
Reese L.A. (1998) 'Sharing the Benefits of Economic Development: What Cities Use Type II Policies?', *Urban Affairs Review*, Vol. 33, pp. 686–711
Reese L.A. and Fasenfast D. (1996) 'Local Economic Development Policy in Canada and the US: Similarities and Differences', *Canadian Journal of Urban Research*, Vol. 5, pp. 100–21
Regional Studies (1999) Special Issue Journal of the Regional Studies Association, Vol. 33, No. 7
Reich R. (1991) *The Work of Nations*. New York: Knopf
Reid M.F. (1994) 'Institutionalizing an Ethic of Change: Case Studies from East Germany and the United States', in Garcia-Zamor J. and Khator R. (eds), *Public Administration in the Global Village*. Westport, Conn.: Greenwood Press, pp. 155–69
Reid M.F. (1997) 'Institutional Preconditions of Privatization in Market-Based Political Economies', *Public Administration and Development*, Vol. 14, pp. 65–77
Reid M.F. (1999) 'Strategic Organizational Problems with Rapid Transitions to Market Economies: the Case of Eastern Germany', *International Journal of Public Administration*, Vol. 22, No. 6, pp. 879–916
Rhodes R.A.W. (1997) *Understanding Governance*. Buckingham: Open University Press
Rich M.J. (1993) *Federal Policymaking and the Poor: National Goals, Local Choices, and Distributional Outcomes*. Princeton, NJ: Princeton University Press
Ridley N. (1988) *The Local Right: Enabling not Providing*. Policy Study No. 92. London: Centre for Policy Studies
Riese J. (1995) 'Transformation als Oktroi von Abhängigkeit', in Wollmann H. and Wiesenthal H. (eds), *Transformation sozialistischer Gesellschaften: Am Ende des Anfangs*. Opladen: Westdeutscher Verlag
Rittel H. and Webber M. (1973) 'Dilemmas in a General Theory of Planning', *Policy Sciences*, Vol. 4, pp. 155–69
Robinson I.W. and Webster D.R. (1985) 'Regional Planning in Canada', *Journal of the American Planning Association*, Vol. 51, pp. 23–33
Roch I. (1998) 'Implementing Ecological Development Concepts in Border Regions', in Graute U. (ed.), *Sustainable Development for Central and Eastern Europe*. Berlin: Springer-Verlag

Romann M. and Weingrod A. (1991) *Living Together Separately: Arabs and Jews in Contemporary Jerusalem*. Princeton, NJ: Princeton University Press

Rondinelli D.A., Johnson J.H. and Kasarda J.D. (1998) 'The Changing Forces of Urban Economic Development: Globalization and City Competitiveness in the 21st Century', *Citiscape*, Vol. 3, No. 3, pp. 71–106

Rondinelli D.A. and Vastag G. (1997) 'Analyzing the International Competitiveness of Metropolitan Areas: the MICAM Model', *Economic Development Quarterly*, Vol. 1, pp. 347–66

Rose J. 'Foreign Relations at the State Level', *The Journal of State Government*

Rose R. and Seifert W. (1995) 'Materielle Lebensbedingungen und Einstellungen gegenüber der Marktwirtschaft und Demokratie im Transformationsprozess: Ostdeutschland und Osteuropa im Vergleich', in Wollmann H. and Wiesenthal H. (eds), *Transformation sozialistischer Gesellschaften: Am Ende des Anfangs*. Opladen: Westdeutscher Verlag

Rosenau J.N. (1990) *Turbulence in World Politics: a Theory of Change and Continuity*. Princeton, NJ: Princeton University Press

Rosentraub M., Swindell D., Przybylski M. and Mullins D. (1994) 'Sport and Downtown Development Strategy: If You Build It, Will Jobs Come?', *Journal of Urban Affairs*, Vol. 16, pp. 221–39

Rothblatt D.N. (1994) 'North American Metropolitan Planning: Canadian and US Perspectives', *Journal of the American Planning Association*, Vol. 60, pp. 501–20

Rothman J. (1992) *From Confrontation to Cooperation: Resolving Ethnic and Regional Conflict*. Newbury Park, Calif.: Sage

Rubin I. and Rubin H. (1987) 'Economic Development Incentives: the Poor (Cities) Pay More', *Urban Affairs Quarterly*, Vol. 23, pp. 37–62

Sabel P. (1989) 'Flexible Specialisation and the Re-Emergence of Regional Economies', in Hirst P. and Zeitlin J. (eds), *Reversing Industrial Decline: Industrial Structure and Policy in Britain and Her Competitors*. London: Berg

Sachs J. (1990) 'Eastern European Economies: What is to be Done?', *The Economist*, Vol. 13, 19 January, pp. 13–18

Sack R. (1981) 'Territorial Bases for Power', in Burnett A. and Taylor P. (eds), *Political Studies from Spatial Perspectives*. New York: John Wiley & Sons

Salamon L. (1991) 'Why Human Capital? Why Now?', in Hornbeck D.W. and Salamon L.S. (eds), *Human Capital and America's Future*. Baltimore, Md: Johns Hopkins University Press

Sandercock L. (1998) *Towards Cosmopolis: Planning for Multicultural Cities*. Chichester: John Wiley & Sons

Sassen S. (1991) *The Global City*. Princeton: Princeton University Press

Sassen S. (1994) *Cities in a World Economy*. Thousand Oaks: Pine Forge Press

Sassen S. (1996) *Losing Control? Sovereignty in an Age of Globalisation*. New York: Columbia University Press

Savitch H.V. (1988) *Post Industrial Cities: Politics and Planning in New York, Paris and London*. Princeton: Princeton University Press

Savitch H.V. (1998) 'Global Challenge and Institutional Capacity', *Administration and Society*, Vol. 30, pp. 248–73

Savitch H.V. and Ardashev G. (2001) 'Does Terror Have an Urban Future?', *Urban Studies*, Vol. 38, No. 13, pp. 2515–33

Savitch H.V. and Kantor P. (1995) 'City Business: an International Perspective on Marketplace Politics', *International Journal of Urban and Regional Planning*, Vol. 19, No. 4

Savitch H.V. and Vogel R. (1996) *Regional Politics: America in a Post City Age*. Newbury Park: Sage

Scherer R. and Blatter J. (1994) 'Preconditions for Successful Cross-border Cooperation on Environmental Issues. Research results and recommendations for a better practice', *EURES Discussion Paper 46*. Freiburg, Austria: EURES (http://www.unisg.ch/~siasr/people/bla.htm)

Schneider M. and Teske P. (1992) 'Toward a Theory of the Political Entrepreneur: Evidence from Local Government', *American Political Science Review*, Vol. 86, No. 3, pp. 737–46

Schultz R.H. (1991) 'The Low-Intensity Conflict Environment of the 1990s', *Annual American Academy of Political and Social Science*, Vol. 517, pp. 120–34

Scott A.J. (1992) 'The Collective Order of Flexible Production Agglomerations: Lessons for Local Economic Development Policy and Strategic Choice', *Economic Geography*, Vol. 68, pp. 219–33

Scott J. (1996) 'Dutch–German Euroregions: a Model for Transboundary Co-operation?', in Scott J., Sweedler A., Ganster P. and Eberwein W (eds), *Border Regions in Functional Transition: European and North American Perspectives*. Berlin: Institut für Regionalentwicklung und Strukturplanung Erkner

Scott J., Sweedler A., Ganster P. and Eberwein W. (eds) (1996) *Border Regions in Functional Transition: European and North American Perspectives*. Berlin: Institut für Regionalentwicklung und Strukturplanung Erkner

Selke W. (1998) 'Sustainable Development in Europe – a Challenge for Transnational Spatial Planning Policies', in Graute U. (ed.), *Sustainable Development for Central and Eastern Europe*. Berlin: Springer-Verlag

Setnikar-Cankar S. (1998) 'Reform of Public Services as Part of Public Administration Reform in Slovenia', *Public Enterprise*, Vol. 16, Nos 1–2, pp. 39–150

Sharp E. (ed.) (1999) *Culture Wars and Local Politics*. Lawrence: University Press of Kansas

Shuman M.H. (1986/87) 'Dateline Main Street: Local Foreign Policies', *Foreign Policy*, Winter, p. 10

Sik E. (1994) 'From the Multicoloured to the Black and White Economy: the Hungarian Second Economy and the Transformation', *International Journal of Urban and Regional Research*, Vol. 18, No. 1, pp. 46–70

Simmons J.W. (1986) 'The Impact of the Public Sector on the Canadian Urban System', in Stetler G.A. and Artibise A.F.J. (eds), *Power and Place: Canadian Urban Development in the North American Context*. Vancouver: University of British Columbia Press

Simonson W. (1994) 'Citizen Preferences'. Presented to Bristol, England urban conference, July 1994

Smith A. (1995) 'Regulation Theory, Strategies of Enterprise Integration and the Political Economy of Regional Economic Restructuring in Central and Eastern Europe: the Case of Slovakia', *Regional Studies*, Vol. 29, No. 8, pp. 761–72

Smith A.D. (1993) 'The Ethnic Sources of Nationalism', in Brown M.E. (ed.), *Ethnic Conflict and International Security*. Princeton: Princeton University Press

Smith M. (1969) 'Some Developments in the Analytic Framework of Pluralism', in Kuper L. and Smith M. (eds), *Pluralism in Africa*. Berkeley: University of California Press

Smith M.P. (1998) 'The Global City – Whose Social Construct Is It Anyway?', *Urban Affairs Review*, Vol. 33, pp. 482–8

Smith M.P. (2001) *Transnational Urbanism. Locating Globalisation*. Oxford: Blackwell

Snyder J. (1993) 'Nationalism and the Crisis of the Post-Soviet State', in Brown M.E. (ed.), *Ethnic Conflict and International Security*. Princeton: Princeton University Press

Sociaal-Economische Raad (1998) *Samen voor de stad. Advies Grotestedenbeleid*. The Hague: SER

Stanovcic V. (1992) 'Problems and Options in Institutionalizing Ethnic Relations', *International Political Science Review*, Vol. 13, No. 4, pp. 359–79

Stegman M. and Austin Turner M. (1996) 'The Future of Urban America in the Global Economy', *Journal of the American Planning Association*, Spring, pp. 157–64

Stempel J.D. (1991) 'The Decentralization of American Foreign Policy', *Journal of State Government*, Vol. 54, No. 1, pp. 122–4

Stewart J. (1971) *Management in Local Government: a Viewpoint*. London: Charles Knight

Stewart M. (1996a) 'Competition and Competitiveness in Urban Policy', *Public Policy and Management*, July–September, pp. 21–6

Stewart M. (1996b) 'Too Little, Too Late: the Politics of Local Complacency', *Journal of Urban Affairs*, Vol. 18, No. 2, pp. 119–37

Stewart M., Goss S., Gillanders G., Clarke R., Rowe J. and Shaftoe H. (1999) *Cross-cutting Issues Affecting Local Government*. London: Department of the Environment, Transport and Regions

Stiglitz J. (1998) 'Knowledge for Development: Economic Science, Economic Policy, and Economic Advice'. Paper delivered at the 1998 'Annual World Bank Conference on Development Economics'

Stoker G. (ed.) (2000) *The New Politics of British Local Governance*. Basingstoke: Macmillan – now Palgrave

Stoker G. and Mossberger K. (1994) 'Urban Regime Theory in Comparative Perspective', *Environment and Planning C*, Vol. 12, No. 2, pp. 195–212

Stoker G. and Young S. (1993) 'Networks: the New Driving Force', Chapter 8 in *Cities in the 1990s, Local Choice for a Balanced Strategy*. Harlow: Longman

Stone C. (1980) 'Systematic Power in Community Decision Making', *American Political Science Review*, Vol. 74, pp. 978–90

Stone C. (1989) *Regime Politics: Governing Atlanta 1946–1988*. Lawrence: University Press of Kansas

Storper M. (1997) *The Regional World: Territorial Development in a Global Economy*. New York: Guilford Press

Svara J.H. (1990) *Official Leadership in the City. Patterns of Conflict and Cooperation*. Oxford: Oxford University Press

Svara J.H. (ed.) (1994) *Facilitative Leadership in Local Government. Lessons from Successful Mayors and Chairpersons*. San Francisco: Jossey-Bass

Swanstrom T. (1996) 'Ideas Matter: Reflections on the New Regionalism', *Cityscape*, May, pp. 5–21

Swianiewicz P. (1996) 'The Policy Preferences and Ideologies of Candidates in the 1994 Polish Local Elections', *International Journal of Urban and Regional Research*, Vol. 20, No. 4, pp. 733–43

Szablowski G.J. and Derlien H.U. (1993) 'East European Transitions, Elites, Bureaucracies and the European Community', *Governance*, Vol. 6, No. 3, pp. 304–24

Szücs J. (1990) *Die drei historischen Regionen Europas*. Frankfurt: Verlag Neue Kritik

Tam H. (1998) *Communitarianism. A New Agenda for Politics and Citizenship*. London: Macmillan – now Palgrave

Tarrow S. (1994) *Power in Movement: Social Movements, Collective Action and Politics*. Cambridge: Cambridge University Press

Tatur M. (1995) 'Interessen und Norm: Politischer Kapitalismus und die Transformation des Staates in Polen und Russland', in *Transformation sozialistischer Gesellschaften: Am Ende des Anfangs*. Opladen: Westdeutscher Verlag

Taylor J.H. (1986) 'Urban Autonomy in Canada: Its Evolution and Decline', in Stetler G.A. and Artibise A.F.J. (eds), *Power and Place: Canadian Urban Development in the North American Context*. Vancouver: University of British Columbia Press

Taylor M. (2000) *Top Down Meets Bottom Up: Neighbourhood Management*. York: Joseph Rowntree Foundation

Terhorst P. and Drontmann I. (1991) *Sociale Vernieuwing: een Schijnbeweging*. Amsterdam: Centrum voor Grootstedelijk Onderzoek

Tilly C. (1978) *From Mobilization to Rebellion*. Reading, Mass.: Addison-Wesley

Tilly C. and Blockman W. (eds) (1994) *Cities and the Rise of the State in Europe*. Boulder: Westview Press

Tödtling F. (1999) 'Innovation Networks, Collective Learning, and Industrial Policy in Regions of Europe', *European Planning Studies*, Vol. 7, No. 6, pp. 693–7

Torgovnik E. (1990) *The Politics of Urban Planning Policy*. Lanham, Md: University Press of America

Török A. (1996) 'Competition Policy and De-monopolization in Hungary after 1990', in Slay B. (ed.), *De-monopolization and Competition Policy in Post-Communist Economies*. Boulder, Colo.: Westview

Trachte K. and Ross R. (1985) 'The Crisis of Detroit and the Emergence of Global Capitalism', *International Journal of Urban and Regional Research*, Vol. 9, pp. 186–217

Travers T., Jones G. and Burnham J. (1997) *The Role of the Local Authority Chief Executive in Local Governance*. York: Joseph Rowntree Foundation

Union Européenne (1997) *Schéma de développement de l'espace communautaire*. Noordwijk, June. Luxembourg: Office des Publications Officielles des Communautés Européennes

Urban Innovation in Illinois (1998) *Fourth Urban Innovation in Illiniois Awards Conference*. Chicago: Civic Federation

Urban Land Institute (1994) *ULI Market Profiles*. Washington, DC: ULI

US Department of Housing and Urban Development (1999) *The State of the Cities 1999*. (April) (www.huduser.org:80/publications/polleg/New_tsoc99/summ-04.html)

Van der Leun J.P., Snel E. and Engbersen G. (1998) 'Ongelijkheid en veiligheid', *Tijdschrift voor Criminologie*, Vol. 40, No. 4, pp. 370–84

Van Doorn J.J.A. (1955) 'Wijk en Stad: Reële Integratiekaders', in *Prae-adviezen voor het Congres over Social Samenhangen in Nieuwe Stadswijken*. Amsterdam: Instituut voor Sociaal Onderzoek van het Nederlandse Volk
Van Geenhuizen M., van der Knaap B. and Nijkamp P. (1996) 'Trans-border European Networking: Shifts in Corporate Strategy?', *European Planning Studies*, Vol. 4, No. 6, pp. 671–82
Van Ginneken K.M. (1998) 'Towards a European Spatial Development Perspective', in Graute U. (ed.), *Sustainable Development for Central and Eastern Europe*. Berlin: Springer-Verlag
Vartiainen P. (1994) 'Urban Region as a Geoeconomic and Geopolitical Unit: a Europe of Regions', in Braun G. O. (eds) *Managing and Marketing of Urban Development and Urban Life*. Berlin: Dietmar Reimer Verlag
Vartiainen P. (1998) 'Urban Networking as a Learning Process: an Exploratory Framework for Transborder Cooperation in the Baltic Sea Region', in Graute U. (ed.), *Sustainable Development for Central and Eastern Europe*. Berlin: Springer-Verlag
Veltz P. (1996) *Mondialisation, villes et territoires. L'économie archipel*. Paris: PUF
Vidal A. (1992) *Rebuilding Communities: a National Study of Urban Community Development Corporations*. New York: New School for Social Research
Visitatiecommissie Grote-Stedenbeleid (1998) *Groot onderhoud der steden. Samenwerking in samenhang*. The Hague: (B&A Groep), February
Von Malchus V.F. (1998) 'Transfrontier Cooperation in Spatial Planning at the External Border of the European Union', in Graute U. (ed.), *Sustainable Development for Central and Eastern Europe*. Berlin: Springer-Verlag
Wagner H. (1993) 'Reconstruction of the Financial System in East Germany: Description and Comparison with Eastern Europe', *Journal of Banking and Finance*, Vol. 17, pp. 1001–19
Walsh K. (1995) *Public Services and Market Mechanisms. Competition, Contracting and the New Public Management*. London: Macmillan – now Palgrave
Walzer N. and P'ng P. (1994) 'Economic Development Strategies'. Presented to International Sociological Association, Bielefeld, Germany, July
Weaver R.K. (1995) 'The Politics of Welfare Reform', in Weaver R.K. and Dickens W.T. (eds), *Looking before We Leap: Social Science and Welfare Reform*. Washington, DC: The Brookings Institution
Webber M. (1963) 'Order in Diversity: Community without Propinquity', in Wingo L. (ed.), *Cities and Space: the Future Use of Urban Land*. Baltimore, Md: Johns Hopkins University Press, pp. 23–54
Webber M. (1964) *The Urban Place and the Nonplace Urban Realm*. Philadelphia University of Pennsylvania Press
Weikart L.A. (1998) 'The New Public Management Agenda – How Successful is it?' Mimeo, School of Public Affairs, Baruch College, City University of New York, April
Weitzer R. (1990) *Transforming Settler States: Communal Conflict and Internal Security in Northern Ireland and Zimbabwe*. Berkeley: University of California Press
Westeren K.I. (ed.) (1998) *Cross Border Co-operation and Strategies for Development in Peripheral Regions*. Steinkjer: North Trondelag Research Institute
Wiatr J. (1980) 'The Civic Culture from a Marxist-sociological Perspective', in Almond G. and Verba S. (eds), *The Civic Culture Revisited*. Boston: Little Brown

Williams R.H. (1996) *European Union Spatial Policy and Planning*. London: Paul Chapman

Wills G. (1998) 'The War between the States ... and Washington', *New York Times Magazine*, 5 July, pp. 26–7

Wilson D. (1998) 'From Local Government to Local Governance: Recasting British Local Democracy', *Democratisation*, Vol. 5, No. 1, pp. 90–115

Wilson W.J. (1978) *The Declining Significance of Race*. Chicago: University of Chicago Press

Wilson W.J. (1987) *The Truly Disadvantaged*. Chicago: University of Chicago Press

Wollmann H. (1994) *Systemwandel und Städtebau in Mittel-und Osteuropa: Russland, Ukraine, Weissrussland, Baltische Länder, Polen, Ungarn, Tschechische und Slowakische Republik*. Basle: Birkhäuser Verlag

Wollmann H. (1997) 'Der Systemwechsel in Ostdeutschland, Ungarn, Polen und Russland', *Aus Politik und Zeitgeschichte*, Vol. 5, pp. 3–15

Wolman H. and Goldsmith M. (1992) *Urban Politics and Policy. A Comparative Approach*. Oxford: Blackwell

Wolman H. with Spitzley D. (1996) 'The Politics of Local Economic Development', *Economic Development Quarterly*, Vol. 10, May, pp. 115–50

Wyly E.K., Glickman N.J. and Lahr M.L. (1998) 'A Top Ten List of Things to Know about American Cities', *Cityscape*, Vol. 3, pp. 7–32

Yates D. (1973) *Neighbourhood Democracy*. Lexington, Mass.: Lexington Books

Yiftachel O. (1992) *Planning a Mixed Region in Israel: the Political Geography of Arab–Jewish Relations in the Galilee*. Aldershot: Avebury

Yiftachel O. (1995) 'The Dark Side of Modernism: Planning as Control of an Ethnic Minority', in Watson S. and Gibson K. (eds), *Postmodern Cities and Spaces*. Oxford: Blackwell

Young K. and Rao N. (1994) *Coming to Terms with Change? The Local Government Councillor in 1993*. York: Joseph Rowntree Foundation

Zijderveld A.C. (1998) *A Theory of Urbanity. The Economic and Civic Culture of Cities*. New Brunswick and London: Transaction Publishers

Index